APPROACHING
ZERO

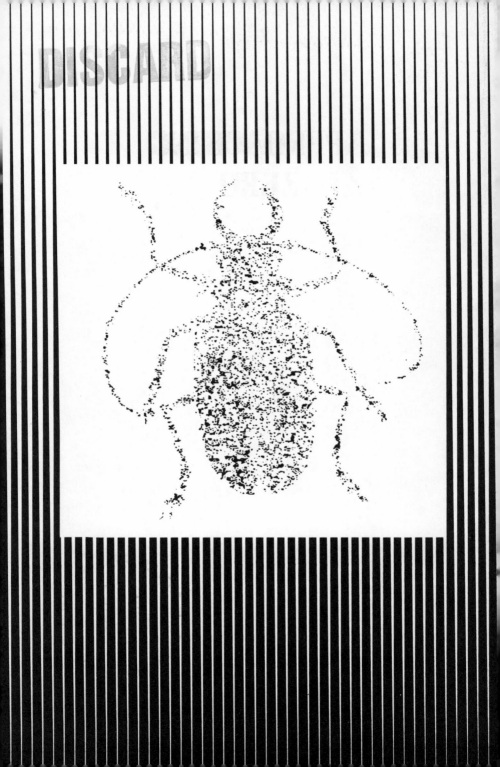

APPROACHING ZERO

■

THE EXTRAORDINARY UNDERWORLD OF HACKERS, PHREAKERS, VIRUS WRITERS, AND KEYBOARD CRIMINALS

■

PAUL MUNGO
AND
BRYAN CLOUGH

RANDOM HOUSE
NEW YORK

Library of Congress Cataloging-in-Publication Data
Mungo, Paul.
Approaching zero: the extraordinary underworld of hackers, phreakers, virus
writers, and keyboard criminals/by Paul Mungo and Bryan Clough.—
1st American ed.
p.   cm.
Includes bibliographical references.
ISBN 0-679-40938-6
1.–Computer crimes.—2.–Computer viruses.
I.–Clough, Bryan.—II.–Title.
HV6773.M86   1992   364.1'68—dc20   91-53159

Book design by Oksana Kushnir

7/93

ACKNOWLEDGMENTS

The authors would like to thank all those—often hackers, phreakers, and virus writers themselves—who contributed their time and confidences in the preparation of this book, particularly Erik Bloodaxe, Ralf Burger, John Draper, Fry Guy, Steve Gold, Rop Gonggrijp, Doc Holliday, Lubomir Mateev, Pat Riddle, Pengo, Robert Schifreen, Peter Sommer, Bill Squire, Todor Todorov, Mark Washburn, Steffen Wernery, and Nick Whiteley.

In addition, we would like to thank John Austen, Jim Bates, Noel Bonczoszek, Vesselin Bontchev, Owen Bowcott, Alan Dawson, Barry Donovan, Lee Felsenstein, Hans Gliss, Mike Godwin, Ross Greenberg, Bob Jones, Ian Leitch, Veni Markovski, Jamie Moles, Chris Pierce, Simon Royle, Fridrik Skulason, Andy Sharp, Alan Solomon, Bruce Sterling, Gail Thackeray, Peter Tippett, and Clive Warner for their invaluable help.

We would also like to express our gratitude to Michael Alexander of *Computerworld,* who gave freely of his time, advice, and files, and who waited patiently for months for the latter to be returned to him.

Special thanks are also due to our agent, Cat Ledger. Finally, we would like to acknowledge our debt to Ron Rosenbaum, whose article "Secrets of the Little Blue Box" (*Esquire,* October 1971) provided great insight into the early days of phreaking.

Some material in Chapter 5 originally appeared in a different form in an article, "Satanic Viruses" by Paul Mungo, published in the British edition of *GQ* (February 1991). Because of the sensitivity of much of the material in this book, the names of some individuals and companies and the order of certain events have been changed. Various details have also been deliberately altered in the descriptions of certain illegal acts, and some technical definitions have been simplified to aid comprehensibility. The substance and accuracy of the narrative have not been affected by these changes.

CONTENTS

Prologue   ix
1. Phreaking for Fun   3
2. Breaking and Entering   31
3. Data Crime   59
4. Viruses, Trojans, Worms, and Bombs   85
5. The Bulgarian Threat   107
6. Hacking for Profit   141
7. The Illuminati Conspiracy   170
8. Crackdown   198
9. The Future of Cyberspace   228
Notes   237
Select Bibliography   245

PROLOGUE

Fry Guy watched the computer screen as the cursor blinked. Beside him a small electronic box chattered through a call routine, the numbers clicking audibly as each of the eleven digits of the phone number was dialed. Then the box made a shrill, electronic whistle, which meant that the call had gone through; Fry Guy's computer had been connected to another system hundreds of miles away.

The cursor blinked again, and the screen suddenly changed. WELCOME TO CREDIT SYSTEMS OF AMERICA, it read, and below that, the cursor pulsed beside the prompt: ENTER ACCOUNT NUMBER.

Fry Guy smiled. He had just broken into one of the most secure computer systems in the United States, one which held the credit histories of millions of American citizens. And it had really been relatively simple. Two hours ago he had called an electronics store in Elmwood, Indiana, which—like thousands of other shops across the country—relied on Credit Systems of America to check its customers' credit cards.

"Hi, this is Joe Boyle from CSA . . . Credit Systems of America," he had said, dropping his voice two octaves to sound older—a lot older, he hoped—than his fifteen years. He also modulated his natural midwestern drawl, giving his voice an eastern twang: more big-city, more urgent.

"I need to speak to your credit manager . . . uh, what's the name? Yeah, Tom. Can you put me through?"

Tom answered.

"Tom, this is Joe Boyle from CSA. You've been having some trouble with your account?"

Tom hadn't heard of any trouble.

"No? That's really odd. . . . Look, I've got this report that says you've been having problems. Maybe there's a mistake somewhere down the line. Better give me your account number again."

And Tom did, obligingly reeling off the eight-character code that allowed his company to access the CSA files and confirm customer credit references. As Fry Guy continued his charade, running through a phony checklist, Tom, ever helpful, also supplied his store's confidential CSA password. Then Fry Guy keyed in the information on his home computer. "I don't know what's going on," he finally told Tom. "I'll check around and call you back."

But of course he never would. Fry Guy had all the information he needed: the account number and the password. They were the keys that would unlock the CSA computer for him. And if Tom ever phoned CSA and asked for Joe Boyle, he would find that no one at the credit bureau had ever heard of him. Joe Boyle was simply a name that Fry Guy had made up.

Fry Guy had discovered that by sounding authoritative and demonstrating his knowledge of computer systems, most of the time people believed he was who he said he was. And they gave him the information he asked for, everything from account codes and passwords to unlisted phone numbers. That was how he got the number for CSA; he just called the local telephone company's operations section.

"Hi, this is Bob Johnson, Indiana Bell tech support," he had said. "Listen, I need you to pull a file for me. Can you bring it up on your screen?"

The woman on the other end of the phone sounded uncertain. Fry Guy forged ahead, coaxing her through the routine: "Right, on your keyboard, type in K—P pulse. . . . Got that? Okay, now do one–two–one start, no M—A. . . . Okay?"

"Yeah? Can you read me the file? I need the number there. . . ."

It was simply a matter of confidence—and knowing the jargon. The directions he had given her controlled access to unlisted numbers, and because he knew the routine, she had read him the CSA number, a number that is confidential, or at least not generally available to fifteen-year-old kids like himself.

But on the phone Fry Guy found that he could be anyone he wanted to be: a CSA employee or a telephone engineer—merely by pretending to be an expert. He had also taught himself to exploit the psychology of the person on the other end of the line. If they seemed confident, he would appeal to their magnanimity: "I wonder if you can help me . . ." If they appeared passive, or unsure, he would be demanding: "Look, I haven't got all day to wait around. I need that number now." And if they didn't give him what he wanted, he could always hang up and try again.

Of course, you had to know a lot about the phone system to convince an Indiana Bell employee that you were an engineer. But exploring the telecommunications networks was Fry Guy's hobby: he knew *a lot* about the phone system.

Now he would put this knowledge to good use. From his little home computer he had dialed up CSA, the call going from his computer to the electronic box beside it, snaking through a cable to his telephone, and then passing through the phone lines to the unlisted number, which happened to be in Delaware.

The electronic box converted Fry Guy's own computer commands to signals that could be transmitted over the phone, while in Delaware, the CSA's computer converted those pulses back into computer commands. In essence, Fry Guy's home computer was talking to its big brother across the continent, and Fry Guy would be able to make it do whatever he wanted.

But first he needed to get inside. He typed in the account number Tom had given him earlier, pressed Return, and typed in the password. There was a momentary pause, then the screen filled with the CSA logo, followed by the directory of services—the "menu."

Fry Guy was completely on his own now, although he had a

good idea of what he was doing. He was going to delve deeply into the accounts section of the system, to the sector where CSA stored confidential information on individuals: their names, addresses, credit histories, bank loans, credit card numbers, and so on. But it was the credit card numbers that he really wanted. Fry Guy was short of cash, and like hundreds of other computer wizards, he had discovered how to pull off a high-tech robbery.

When Fry Guy was thirteen, in 1987, his parents had presented him with his first computer—a Commodore 64, one of the new, smaller machines designed for personal use. Fry Guy linked up the keyboard-sized system to an old television, which served as his video monitor.

On its own the Commodore didn't do much: it could play games or run short programs, but not a lot more. Even so, the machine fascinated him so much that he began to spend more and more time with it. Every day after school, he would hurry home to spend the rest of the evening and most of the night learning as much as possible about his new electronic plaything.

He didn't feel that he was missing out on anything. School bored him, and whenever he could get away with it, he skipped classes to spend more time working on the computer. He was a loner by nature; he had a lot of acquaintances at school, but no real friends, and while his peers were mostly into sports, he wasn't. He was tall and gawky and, at 140 pounds, not in the right shape to be much of an athlete. Instead he stayed at home.

About a year after he got the Commodore, he realized that he could link his computer to a larger world. With the aid of an electronic box, called a modem, and his own phone line, he could travel far beyond his home, school, and family.

He soon upgraded his system by selling off his unwanted possessions and bought a better computer, a color monitor, and various other external devices such as a printer and the electronic box that would give his computer access to the wider world. He also installed three telephone lines: one linked to the computer for data transmission, one for voice, and one that could be used for either.

Eventually he stumbled across the access number to an electronic message center called Atlantic Alliance, which was run by computer hackers. It provided him with the basic information on hacking; the rest he learned from telecommunications manuals.

Often he would work on the computer for hours on end, sometimes sitting up all night hunched over the keyboard. His room was a sixties time warp filled with psychedelic posters, strobes, black lights, lava lamps, those gift-shop relics with blobs of wax floating in oil, and a collection of science fiction books. But his computer terminal transported him to a completely different world that encompassed the whole nation and girdled the globe. With the electronic box and a phone line he could cover enormous distances, jumping through an endless array of communications links and telephone exchanges, dropping down into other computer systems almost anywhere on earth. Occasionally he accessed Altos, a business computer in Munich, Germany owned by a company that was tolerant of hackers. Inevitably, it became an international message center for computer freaks.

Hackers often use large systems like these to exchange information and have electronic chats with one another, but it is against hacker code to use one's real name. Instead, they use "handles," nicknames like The Tweaker, Doc Cypher and Knightmare. Fry Guy's handle came from a commercial for McDonald's that said "We are the fry guys."

Most of the other computer hackers he met were loners like he was, but some of them worked in gangs, such as the Legion of Doom, a U.S. group, or Chaos in Germany. Fry Guy didn't join a gang, because he preferred working in solitude. Besides, if he started blabbing to other hackers, he could get busted.

Fry Guy liked to explore the phone system. Phones were more than just a means to make a call: Indiana Bell led to an immense network of exchanges and connections, to phones, to other computers, and to an international array of interconnected phone systems and data transmission links. It was an electronic highway network that was unbelievably vast.

He learned how to dial into the nearest telephone exchange on his little Commodore and hack into the switch, the computer that controls all the phones in the area. He discovered that each phone is represented by a long code, the LEN (Line Equipment Number), which assigns functions and services to the phone, such as the chosen long-distance carrier, call forwarding, and so on. He knew how to manipulate the code to reroute calls, reassign numbers, and do dozens of other tricks, but best of all, he could manipulate the code so that all his calls would be free.

After a while Indiana Bell began to seem tame. It was a convenient launching pad, but technologically speaking it was a wasteland. So he moved on to BellSouth in Atlanta, which had all of the latest communications technology. There he became so familiar with the system that the other hackers recognized it as his SoI—sphere of influence—just as a New York hacker called Phiber Optik became the king of NYNEX (the New York–New England telephone system), and another hacker called Control C claimed the Michigan network. It didn't mean that BellSouth was his alone, only that the other members of the computer underworld identified him as its best hacker.

At the age of fifteen he started using chemicals as a way of staying awake. Working at his computer terminal up to twenty hours a day, sleeping only two or three hours a night, and sometimes not at all, the chemicals—uppers, speed—kept him alert, punching away at his keyboard, exploring his new world.

But outside this private world, life was getting more confusing. Problems with school and family were beginning to accumulate, and out of pure frustration, he thought of a plan to make some money.

In 1989 Fry Guy gathered all of the elements for his first hack of CSA. He had spent two years exploring computer systems and the phone company, and each new trick he learned added one more layer to his knowledge. He had become familiar with important computer operating systems, and he knew how the phone company worked. Since his plan involved hacking into CSA and then the phone system, it was essential to be expert in both.

The hack of CSA took longer than he thought it would. The account number and password he extracted from Tom only got him through the credit bureau's front door. But the codes gave him legitimacy; to CSA he looked like any one of thousands of subscribers. Still, he needed to get into the sector that listed individuals and their accounts—he couldn't just type in a person's name, like a real CSA subscriber; he would have to go into the sector through the back door, as CSA itself would do when it needed to update its own files.

Fry Guy had spent countless hours doing just this sort of thing: every time he accessed a new computer, wherever it was, he had to learn his way around, to make the machine yield privileges ordinarily reserved for the company that owned it. He was proficient at following the menus to new sectors and breaking through the security barriers that were placed in his way. This system would yield like all the others.

It took most of the afternoon, but by the end of the day he chanced on an area restricted to CSA staff that led the way to the account sector. He scrolled through name after name, reading personal credit histories, looking for an Indiana resident with a valid credit card.

He settled on a Visa card belonging to a Michael B. from Indianapolis; he took down his full name, account and telephone number. Exiting from the account sector, he accessed the main menu again. Now he had a name: he typed in Michael B. for a standard credit check.

Michael B., Fry Guy was pleased to see, was a financially responsible individual with a solid credit line.

Next came the easy part. Disengaging from CSA, Fry Guy directed his attention to the phone company. Hacking into a local switch in Indianapolis, he located the line equipment number for

Michael B. and rerouted his incoming calls to a phone booth in Paducah, Kentucky, about 250 miles from Elmwood. Then he manipulated the phone booth's setup to make it look like a residential number, and finally rerouted the calls to the phone box to one of the three numbers on his desk. That was a bit of extra security: if anything was ever traced, he wanted the authorities to think that the whole operation had been run from Paducah.

And that itself was a private joke. Fry Guy had picked Paducah precisely because it was not the sort of town that would be home to many hackers: technology in Paducah, he snickered, was still in the Stone Age.

Now he had to move quickly. He had rerouted all of Michael B.'s incoming calls to his own phone, but didn't want to have to deal with his personal messages. He called Western Union and instructed the company to wire $687 to its office in Paducah, to be picked up by—and here he gave the alias of a friend who happened to live there. The transfer would be charged to a certain Visa card belonging to Michael B.

Then he waited. A minute or so later Western Union called Michael B.'s number to confirm the transaction. But the call had been intercepted by the reprogrammed switch, rerouted to Paducah, and from there to a phone on Fry Guy's desk.

Fry Guy answered, his voice deeper and, he hoped, the sort that would belong to a man with a decent credit line. Yes, he was Michael B., and yes, he could confirm the transaction. But seconds later, he went back into the switches and quickly reprogrammed them. The pay phone in Paducah became a pay phone again, and Michael B., though he was unaware that anything had ever been amiss, could once again receive incoming calls. The whole transaction had taken less than ten minutes.

The next day, after his friend in Kentucky had picked up the $687, Fry Guy carried out a second successful transaction, this time worth $432. He would perform the trick again and again that summer, as often as he needed to buy more computer equipment and chemicals. He didn't steal huge amounts of money—indeed, the sums he took were almost insignificant, just enough for his own needs. But Fry Guy is only one of many, just one of a legion of adolescent computer wizards worldwide, whose ability to crash through high-tech security systems, to circumvent access controls, and to penetrate files holding sensitive information, is endangering our computer-dependent societies. These technology-obsessed electronic renegades form a distinct subculture. Some steal—though most don't; some look for information; some just like to play with computer systems. Together they probably represent the future of our computer-dependent society. Welcome to the computer underworld—a metaphysical place that exists only in the web of international data communications networks, peopled by electronics wizards who have made it their recreation center, meeting ground, and home. The members of the underworld are mostly adolescents like Fry Guy who prowl through computer systems looking for information, data, links to other webs, and credit card numbers. They are often extraordinarily clever, with an intuitive feel for electronics and telecommunications, and a shared antipathy for ordinary rules and regulations.

The electronics networks were designed to speed communications around the world, to link companies and research centers, and to transfer data from computer to computer. Because they must be accessible to a large number of users, they have been targeted by computer addicts like Fry Guy—sometimes for exploration, sometimes for theft.

Almost every computer system of note has been hacked: the Pentagon, NATO, NASA, universities, military and industrial research laboratories. The cost of the depradations attributed to computer fraud has been estimated at $4 billion each year in the United States alone. And an estimated 85 percent of computer crime is not even reported.

The computer underworld can also be vindictive. In the past five years the number of malicious programs—popularly known as viruses—has increased exponentially. Viruses usually serve no useful purpose: they simply cripple computer systems and destroy data. And yet the underworld that produces them continues to flourish. In a very short time it has become a major threat to the technology-dependent societies of the Western industrial world.

Computer viruses began to spread in 1987, though most of the early bugs were jokes with playful messages, or relatively harmless programs that caused computers to play tunes. They were essentially schoolboyish tricks. But eventually some of the jokes became malicious: later viruses could delete or modify information held on computers, simulate hardware faults, or even wipe data off machines completely.

The most publicized virus of all appeared in 1992. Its arrival was heralded by the FBI, by Britain's New Scotland Yard and by Japan's International Trade Ministry, all of which issued warnings about the bug's potential for damage. It had been programmed to wipe out all data on infected computers on March 6th—the anniversary of Michelangelo's birth. The virus became known, naturally, as Michelangelo.

It was thought that the bug may have infected as many as 5 million computers worldwide, and that data worth billions of dollars was at risk. This may have been true, but the warnings from police and government agencies, and the subsequent press coverage, caused most companies to take precautions. Computer systems were cleaned out; back-up copies of data were made; the cleverer (or perhaps lazier) users simply reprogrammed their machines so that their internal calendars jumped from March 5th to March 7th, missing the dreaded 6th completely. (It was a perfectly reasonable precaution: Michelangelo will normally only strike when the computer's own calendar registers March 6.)

Still, Michelangelo hasn't been eradicated. There are certainly copies of the virus still at large, probably being passed on innocently from computer user to computer user. And of course March 6th still comes once a year.

The rise of the computer underworld to the point at which a single malicious program like Michelangelo can cause law enforcement agencies, government ministries, and corporations to take special precautions, when credit bureau information can be stolen and individuals' credit card accounts can be easily plundered, began thirty years ago. Its impetus, curiously enough, was a simple decision by Bell Telephone to replace its human operators with computers.

APPROACHING ZERO

1
■
PHREAKING FOR FUN

The culture of the technological underworld was formed in the early sixties, at a time when computers were vast pieces of complex machinery used only by big corporations and big government. It grew out of the social revolution that the term *the sixties* has come to represent, and it remains an antiestablishment, anarchic, and sometimes "New Age" technological movement organized against a background of music, drugs, and the remains of the counterculture.

The goal of the underground was to liberate technology from the controls of state and industry, a feat that was accomplished more by accident than by design. The process began not with computers but with a fad that later became known as phreaking—a play on the words *freak, phone,* and *free.* In the beginning phreaking was a simple pastime: its purpose was nothing more than the manipulation of the Bell Telephone system in the United States, where most phreakers lived, for free long-distance phone calls.

Most of the earliest phreakers happened to be blind children, in part because it was a natural hobby for unsighted lonely youngsters. Phreaking was something they could excel at: you didn't need sight to phreak, just hearing and a talent for electronics.

Phreaking exploited the holes in Bell's long-distance, direct-dial system. "Ma Bell" was the company the counterculture both loved and loathed: it allowed communication, but at a price. Thus, ripping off the phone company was liberating technology, and not really criminal.

Phreakers had been carrying on their activities for almost a decade, forming an underground community of electronic pirates long before the American public had heard about them. In October 1971 *Esquire* magazine heralded the phreaker craze in an article by Ron Rosenbaum entitled "The Secrets of the Little Blue Box," the first account of phreaking in a mass-circulation publication, and still the only article to trace its beginnings. It was also undoubtedly the principal popularizer of the movement. But of course Rosenbaum was only the messenger; the subculture existed before he wrote about it and would have continued to grow even if the article had never been published. Nonetheless, his piece had an extraordinary impact: until then most Americans had thought of the phone, if they thought of it at all, as an unattractive lump of metal and plastic that sat on a desk and could be used to make and receive calls. That it was also the gateway to an Alice-in-Wonderland world where the user controlled the phone company and not vice versa was a revelation. Rosenbaum himself acknowledges that the revelations contained in his story had far more impact than he had expected at the time.

The inspiration for the first generation of phreakers was said to be a man known as Mark Bernay (though that wasn't his real name). Bernay was identified in Rosenbaum's article as a sort of electronic Pied Piper who traveled up and down the West Coast of the United States, pasting stickers in phone booths, inviting everyone to share his discovery of the mysteries of "loop-around-pairs," a mechanism that allowed users to make toll-free calls.

Bernay himself found out about loop-around-pairs from a friendly telephone company engineer, who explained that within the millions of connections and interlinked local exchanges of what in those days made up the Bell network there were test numbers used by engineers to check connections between the exchanges. These numbers often occurred in consecutive pairs,

say (213)– – – 9001 and (213)– – – 9002, and were wired together
so that a caller to one number was automatically looped around
to the other. Hence the name, loop-around-pairs. Bernay publicized the fact that if two people anywhere in the country dialed
any set of consecutive test numbers, they could talk together for
free. He introduced a whole generation of people to the idea that
the phone company wasn't an impregnable fortress: Ma Bell had
a very exploitable gap in its defenses that anyone could use, just
by knowing the secret. Bernay, steeped in the ethos of the sixties,
was a visionary motivated by altruism—as well as by the commonly held belief that the phone system had been magically created to be used by anyone who needed it. The seeds he planted
grew, over the next years, into a full-blown social phenomenon.

Legend has it that one of the early users of Bernay's system was
a young man in Seattle, who told a blind friend about it, who in
turn brought the idea to a winter camp for blind kids in Los
Angeles. They dispersed back to their own hometowns and told
their friends, who spread the secret so rapidly that within a year
blind children throughout the country were linked together by the
electronic strands of the Bell system. They had created a sort of
community, an electronic clubhouse, and the web they spun
across the country had a single purpose: communication. The
early phreakers simply wanted to talk to each other without
running up huge long-distance bills.

It wasn't long, though, before the means displaced the end, and
some of the early phreakers found that the technology of the
phone system could provide a lot more fun than could be had by
merely calling someone. In a few years phreakers would learn
other skills and begin to look deeper. They found a labyrinth of
electronic passages and hidden sections within the Bell network
and began charting it. Then they realized they were really looking
at the inside of a computer, that the Bell system was simply a giant
network of terminals—known as telephones—with a vast series of
switches, wires, and loops stretching all across the country. It was
an actual place, though it only existed at the end of a phone

receiver, a nearly limitless electronic universe accessible by dialing numbers on a phone. And what made this space open to phreakers was the spread of electronic gadgets that would completely overwhelm the Bell system.

According to Bell Telephone, the first known instance of theft of long-distance telephone service by an electronic device was discovered in 1961, after a local office manager in the company's Pacific Northwest division noticed some inordinately lengthy calls to an out-of-area directory-information number. The calls were from a studio at Washington State College, and when Bell's engineers went to investigate, they found what they described as "a strange-looking device on a blue metal chassis" attached to the phone, which they immediately nicknamed a "blue box."

The color of the device was incidental, but the name stuck. Its purpose was to enable users to make free long-distance calls, and it was a huge advancement on simple loop-around-pairs: not only could the blue box set up calls to any number anywhere, it would also allow the user to roam through areas of the Bell system that were off-limits to ordinary subscribers.

The blue box was a direct result of Bell's decision in the mid-1950s to build its new direct-dial system around multifrequency tones—musical notes generated by dialing that instruct the local exchange to route the call to a specific number. The tones weren't the same as the notes heard when pressing the numbers on a push-button phone: they were based on twelve electronically generated combinations of six master tones. These tones controlled the whole system: hence they were secret.

Or almost. In 1954 an article entitled "In-band Signal Frequency Signaling," appeared in the *Bell System Technical System Journal,* which described the electronic signals used for routing long-distance calls around the country, for "call completion" (hanging up), and for billing. The phone company then released the rest of its secrets when the November 1960 issue of the same journal described the frequencies of the tones used to dial the numbers.

The journal was intended only for Bell's own technical staff, but the company had apparently forgotten that most engineering colleges subscribed to it as well. The articles proved to be the combination to Bell's safe. Belatedly realizing its error, Bell tried to recall the two issues. But they had already become collectors' items, endlessly photocopied and passed around among engineering students all over the country.

Once Bell's tone system was known, it was relatively simple for engineering students to reproduce the tones, and then—by knowing the signaling methods—to employ them to get around the billing system. The early blue boxes used vacuum tubes (the forerunners of transistors) and were just slightly larger than the telephones they were connected to. They were really nothing more than a device that reproduced Bell's multifrequency tones, and for that reason hard-core phreakers called them MF-ers—for multifrequency transmitters. (The acronym was also understood to stand for "motherfuckers," because they were used to fuck around with Ma Bell.)

Engineering students have always been notorious for attempting to rip off the phone company. In the late 1950s Bell was making strenuous efforts to stamp out a device that much later was nicknamed the red box—presumably to distinguish it from the blue box. The red box was a primitive gizmo, often no more than an army-surplus field telephone or a modified standard phone linked to an operating Bell set. Legend has it that engineering students would wire up a red box for Mom and Dad before they left for college so that they could call home for free. Technically very simple, red boxes employed a switch that would send a signal to the local telephone office to indicate that the phone had been picked up. But the signal was momentary, just long enough to alert the local office and cause the ringing to stop, but not long enough to send the signal to the telephone office in the city where the call was originated. That was the trick: the billing was set up in the originating office, and to the originating office it would seem as though the phone was still ringing. When Pop took his finger off the switch on the box, he and Junior could talk free of charge.

The red boxes had one serious drawback: the phone company could become suspicious if it found that Junior had ostensibly spent a half an hour listening to the phone ring back at the family homestead. A more obvious problem was that Mom and Pop—if one believes the legend that red boxes were used by college kids to call home—would quickly tire of their role in ripping off the phone company only to make it easier for Junior to call and ask for more money.

Inevitably there were other boxes, too, all exploiting other holes in the Bell system. A later variation of the red box, sometimes called a black box, was popular with bookies. It caused the ringing to cease prior to the phone being picked up, thereby preventing the originating office from billing the call. There was also another sort of red box that imitated the sound of coins being dropped into the slot on pay phones. It was used to convince operators that a call was being paid for.[1]

The blue box, however, was the most sophisticated of all. It put users directly in control of long-distance switching equipment. To avoid toll-call charges, users of blue boxes would dial free numbers—out-of-area directory enquiries or commercial 1-800 numbers—then reroute the call by using the tones in the MF-er.

This is how it worked: long-distance calls are first routed through a subscriber's own local telephone office. The first digits tell the office that the call is long-distance, and it is switched to an idle long-distance line. An idle line emits a constant 2600-cycle whistling tone, the signal that it is ready to receive a call. As the caller finishes dialing the desired number—called the address digits—the call is completed—all of which takes place in the time it takes to punch in the number.

At the local office, billing begins when the long-distance call is answered and ends when the caller puts his receiver down. The act of hanging up is the signal to the local office that the call is completed. The local office then tells the line that it can process any other call by sending it the same 2600-cycle tone, and the line begins emitting the tone again.

A phreaker made his free call by first accessing, say, the 1-800 number for Holiday Inn. His local office noted that it was processing a long-distance call, found an idly whistling line, and marked the call down as routed to a free number. At that point, before Holiday Inn answered, the phreaker pressed a button on his MF-er, which reproduced Bell's 2600-cycle whistle. This signified that the Holiday Inn call had been completed—or that the caller had hung up prior to getting an answer—and it stood by to accept another call.

But at the local office no hanging-up signal had been received; hence the local office presumed the Holiday Inn call was still going through. The phreaker, still connected to a patiently whistling long-distance line, then punched in the address digits of any number he wanted to be connected to, while his local office assumed that he was really making a free call.

Blue boxes could also link into forbidden areas in the Bell system. Users of MF-ers soon discovered that having a merrily whistling trunk line at their disposal could open many more possibilities than just free phone calls: they could dial into phone-company test switches, to long-distance route operators, and into conference lines—which meant they could set up their own phreaker conference calls. Quite simply, possession of a blue box gave the user the same control and access as a Bell operator. When operator-controlled dialing to Europe was introduced in 1963, phreakers with MF-ers found they could direct-dial across the Atlantic, something ordinary subscribers couldn't do until 1970.

The only real flaw with blue boxes was that Bell Telephone's accounts department might become suspicious of subscribers who seemed to spend a lot of time connected to the 1-800 numbers of, say, Holiday Inn or the army recruiting office and might begin monitoring the line. Phreaking, after all, was technically theft of service, and phreakers could be prosecuted under various state and federal laws.

To get around this, canny phreakers began to use public phone booths, preferably isolated ones. The phone company could hardly monitor every public telephone in the United States, and even when the accounts department realized that a particular pay phone had been used suspiciously, the phreaker would have long since disappeared.

By the late 1960s blue boxes had become smaller and more portable. The bulky vacuum tubes mounted on a metal chassis had been replaced by transistors in slim boxes only as large as their keypads. Some were built to look like cigarette packs or transistor radios. Cleverer ones—probably used by drug dealers or bookies—were actually working transistor radios that concealed the components of an operational blue box within their wiring.

What made Bell's technology particularly vulnerable was that almost anything musical could be used to reproduce the tone frequencies. Musical instruments such as flutes, horns, or organs could be made to re-create Bell's notes, which could then be taped, and a simple cassette player could serve as a primitive MF device. One of the easiest ways to make a free call was to record the tones for a desired number in the correct sequence onto a cassette tape, go to a phone, and play the tape back into the mouthpiece. To Bell's exasperation, some people could even make free phone calls just by whistling.

Joe Engressia, the original whistling phreaker, was blind, and was said to have been born with perfect pitch. As a child he became fascinated by phones: he liked to dial nonworking numbers around the country just to listen to the recording say, "This number is not in service." When he was eight, he was accidentally introduced to the theory of multifrequency tones, though he didn't realize it at the time. While listening to an out-of-service tape in Los Angeles, he began whistling and the phone went dead.

He tried it again, and the same thing happened. Then he phoned his local office and reportedly said, "I'm Joe. I'm eight years old and I want to know why when I whistle this tune, the line clicks off."

The engineer told Joe about what was sometimes known as talk-off, a phenomenon that happened occasionally when one party to a conversation began whistling and accidentally hit a 2600-cycle tone. That could make the line think that the caller had hung up, and cause it to go dead. Joe didn't understand the explanation then, but within a few years he would probably know more about it than the engineer.

Joe became famous in 1971 when Ron Rosenbaum catalogued his phreaking skills in the *Esquire* article. But he had first come to public attention two years earlier, when he was discovered whistling into a pay phone at the University of South Florida. Joe, by this time a twenty-year-old university student, had mastered the science of multifrequency tones and, with perfect pitch, could simply whistle the 2600-cycle note down the line, and then whistle up any phone number he wanted to call. The local telephone company, determined to stamp out phreaking, had publicized the case, and Joe's college had disciplined him. Later, realizing that he was too well known to the authorities to continue phreaking in Florida, he moved on to Memphis, which was where Rosenbaum found him.

In 1970 Joe was living in a small room surrounded by the paraphernalia of phreaking. Even more than phreaking, however, Joe's real obsession was the phone system itself. His ambition, he told Rosenbaum, was to work for Ma Bell. He was in love with the phone system, and his hobby, he claimed, was something he called phone tripping: he liked to visit telephone switching stations and quiz the company engineers about the workings of the system. Often he knew more than they did. Being blind, he couldn't see anything, but he would run his hands down the masses of wiring coiled around the banks of circuitry. He could learn how the links were made just by feeling his way through the connections in the wiring, and in this way, probably gained more knowledge than most sighted visitors.

Joe had moved to Tennessee because that state had some interesting independent phone districts. Like many phreakers, Joe was fascinated by the independents—small, private phone companies not controlled by Bell—because of their idiosyncrasies. Though all of the independents were linked to Bell as part of the larger North American phone network, they often used different equipment (some of it older), or had oddities within the system that phreakers liked to explore.

By that time the really topflight phreakers were more interested in exploring than making free calls. They had discovered that the system, with all of its links, connections, and switches, was like a giant electronic playground, with tunnels from one section to another, pathways that could take calls from North America to Europe and back again, and links that could reach satellites capable of beaming calls anywhere in the world.

One of the early celebrated figures was a New York–based phreaker who used his blue box to call his girlfriend in Boston on weekends—but never directly. First he would call a 1-800 number somewhere in the country, skip out of it onto the international operator's circuit, and surface in Rome, where he would redirect the call to an operator in Hamburg. The Hamburg operator would assume the call originated in Rome and accept the instructions to patch it to Boston. Then the phreaker would speak to his girlfriend, his voice bouncing across the Atlantic to a switch in Rome, up to Hamburg, and then back to Boston via satellite. The delay would have made conversation difficult, but, of course, conversation was never the point.

Few phreakers ever reached that level of expertise. The community was never huge—there were probably never more than a few hundred real, diehard phone phreaks—but it suddenly began to grow in the late 1960s as the techniques became more widely known. Part of the impetus for this growth was the increased access to conference lines, which allowed skills and lore to be more widely disseminated.

Conference lines—or conference bridges—are simply special switches that allow several callers to participate in a conversation at the same time. The service, in those days, was generally promoted to businesses, but bridges were also used by the telephone company for testing and training. For instance, the 1121 conference lines were used to train Bell operators: they could dial the number to hear a recording of calls being made from a pay phone, including the pings of the coins as they dropped, so that they could become familiar with the system. If two phreakers rang any one of the 1121 training numbers, they could converse, though the constant pinging as the coins dropped on the recording was distracting.

Far better were lines like 2111, the internal company code for Telex testing. For six months in the late 1960s phreakers congregated on a disused 2111 test line located somewhere in a telephone office in Vancouver. It became an enormous clubhouse, attracting both neophyte and experienced MF-ers in a continuing conference call. To participate, phreakers needed only to MF their way through a 1-800 number onto the Vancouver exchange and then punch out 2111. The clubhouse may have existed only in the electronic ether around a test number in a switching office somewhere in Canada, but it was a meeting place nonetheless.

Joe Engressia's life in Memphis revolved around phreaker conference lines, but when Rosenbaum talked to him, he was getting worried about being discovered.

> "I want to work for Ma Bell. I don't hate Ma Bell the way some phone phreaks do. I don't want to screw Ma Bell. With me it's the pleasure of pure knowledge. There's something beautiful about the system when you know it intimately the way I do. But I don't know how much they know about me here. I have a very intuitive feel for the condition of the line I'm on, and I think they're monitoring me off and on lately, but I haven't been doing much illegal. . . . Once I took an acid trip and was having these auditory hallucinations . . . and all of a

sudden I had to phone phreak out of there. For some
reason I had to call Kansas City, but that's all."

Joe's intuition was correct: he was indeed being monitored.
Shortly after that interview, agents from the phone company's
security department, accompanied by local police, broke into his
room and confiscated every bit of telecommunications equipment. Joe was arrested and spent the night in jail.

The charges against him were eventually reduced from possession of a blue box and theft of service to malicious mischief. His
jail sentence was suspended. But in return he had to promise never
to phreak again—and to make sure he kept his promise, the local
phone company refused to restore his telephone line.[2]

One of Joe's friends at that time was a man called John Draper,
better known as Captain Crunch. Like Joe, Draper was interested
in the system: he liked to play on it, to chart out the links and
connections between phone switching offices, overseas lines, and
satellites. His alias came from the Quaker Oats breakfast cereal
Cap'n Crunch, which once, in the late 1960s, had included a tiny
plastic whistle in each box as a children's toy. Unknown to the
company, it could be used to phreak calls.

The potential of the little whistle was said to have been discovered by accident. The toy was tuned to a high-A note that closely
reproduced the 2600-cycle tone used by Bell in its long-distance
lines. Kids demonstrating their new toy over the phone to Granny
in another city would sometimes find that the phone went dead,
which caused Bell to spend a perplexing few weeks looking for the
source of the problem.

Draper first became involved with phreaking in 1969, when he
was twenty-six and living in San Jose. One day he received what
he later described as a "very strange call" from a man who
introduced himself as Denny and said he wanted to show him
something to do with musical notes and phones. Intrigued, Draper visited Denny, who demonstrated how tones played on a

Hammond organ could be recorded and sent down the line to produce free long-distance calls. The problem was that a recording had to be made for each number required, unless Draper, who was an electronics engineer, could build a device that could combine the abilities of the organ and the recorder. The man explained that such a device would be very useful to a certain group of blind kids, and he wanted to know if Draper could help.

After the meeting Draper went home and immediately wired up a primitive multifrequency transmitter—a blue box. The device was about the size of a telephone. Ironically it wouldn't work in San Jose (where long-distance calls were still routed through an operator), so Draper had to drive back to San Francisco to demonstrate it. To his surprise it worked perfectly. "Stay low," he told the youngsters. "This thing's illegal."

But the blind kids were already into phreaking in a big way. They had already discovered the potential of the Cap'n Crunch plastic whistle, and had even found that to make it hit the 2600-cycle tone every time, all it needed was a drop of glue on the outlet hole.

Draper began to supply blue boxes to clients—generally unsighted youngsters—in the Bay Area and beyond. He was also fascinated by the little whistle, and early the next year, when he took a month's vacation in England, he took one with him. When a friend rang him from the States, Draper blew the little toy into the phone, sending the 2600-cycle "on-hook" (hanging-up) signal to the caller's local office in America. The "on-hook" tone signified that the call had been terminated, and the U.S. office—where billing was originated—stopped racking up toll charges. But because the British phone system didn't respond to the 2600-cycle whistle, the connection was maintained, and Draper could continue the conversation for free. He only used the whistle once in England, but the incident became part of phreaker legend and gave Draper his alias.

While in Britain, Draper received a stream of transatlantic calls from his blind friends. One of them, who lived in New York, had discovered that Bell engineers had a special code to dial England to check the new international direct-dial system, which was just coming on-line. The access code was 182, followed by a number in Britain. All of the calls placed in this way were free. The discovery spread rapidly among the phreaker community; everyone wanted to try direct-dialing to England, but since no one knew anyone there, Draper was the recipient of most of the calls.

This was, of course, long before the days when people would routinely make international calls. Even in America, where the phone culture was at its most developed, no one would casually pick up a telephone and call a friend halfway across the world. An international call, particularly a transatlantic call, was an event, and if families had relatives abroad, they would probably phone them only once a year, usually at Christmas. The call could easily take half a day to get through, the whole family would take turns talking, and everyone would shout—in those days, perhaps in awe of the great distance their voices were being carried, international callers always shouted. It would take another two decades before transatlantic calls became as commonplace as ringing across the country.

Naturally the British GPO (General Post Office), who ran the U.K. telephone system in those days, became somewhat suspicious of a vacationer who routinely received five or six calls a day from the United States. They began monitoring Draper's line; then investigators were sent to interview him. They wanted to know why he had been receiving so many calls from across the Atlantic. He replied that he was on holiday and that he supposed he was popular, but the investigators were unimpressed. Draper immediately contacted his friends in America and said, "No more."

At about this time, Draper had become the king of phreakers. He had rigged up a VW van with a switchboard and a high-tech MF-er and roamed the highways in California looking for isolated telephone booths. He would often spend hours at these telephones, sending calls around the world, bouncing them off communications satellites, leapfrogging them from the West Coast to London to Moscow to Sydney and then back again.

The Captain also liked to stack up tandems, which are the instruments that send the whistling tone from one switching office to another. What the Captain would do is shoot from one tandem right across the country to another, then back again to a third tandem, stacking them up as he went back and forth, once reportedly shooting across America twenty times. Then he might bounce the call over to a more exotic place, such as a phone box in London's Victoria Station, or to the American embassy in Moscow. He didn't have anything to say to the startled commuter who happened to pick up the phone at Victoria, or to the receptionist at the embassy in Moscow—that wasn't the point. Sometimes he simply asked about the weather.

The unit he carried in the back of the van was computer-operated, and Draper was proud of the fact that it was more powerful and faster than the phone company's own equipment. It could, he claimed, "do extraordinary things," and the vagueness of the statement only added to the mystique.

Once, making a call around the world, he sent a call to Tokyo, which connected him to India, then Greece, then South Africa, South America, and London, which put him through to New York, which connected him to an L.A. operator—who dialed the number of the phone booth next to the one he was using. He had to shout to hear himself but, he claimed, the echo was "far out." Another time, using two phone booths located side by side, Draper sent his voice one way around the world from one of the telephones to the other, and simultaneously from the second phone booth he placed a call via satellite in the other direction back to the first phone. The trick had absolutely no practical value, but the Captain was much more interested in the mechanics of telecommunications than in actually calling anyone. "I'm learning about a system," he once said. "The phone company is a system, a computer is a system. Computers and systems—that's my bag."

But by this time the Captain was only stating the obvious. To advanced phreakers the system linking the millions of phones around the world—that spider's web of lines, loops, and tandems—was infinitely more interesting than anything they would ever hope to see. Most of the phreakers were technology junkies anyway, the sort of kids who took apart radios to see how they worked, who played with electronics when they were older, and who naturally progressed to exploring the phone system, if only because it was the biggest and best piece of technology they could lay their hands on. And the growing awareness that they were liberating computer technology from Ma Bell made their hobby even more exciting.

In time even Mark Bernay, who had helped spread phone phreaking across America, found that his interests were changing. By 1969, he had settled in the Pacific Northwest and was working as a computer programmer in a company with access to a large time-share mainframe—a central computer accessed by telephone that was shared among hundreds of smaller companies. Following normal practice, each user had his own log-in—identification code, or ID—and password, which he would need to type in before being allowed access to the computer's files. Even then, to prevent companies from seeing each other's data, users were confined to their own sectors of the computer.

But Bernay quickly tired of this arrangement. He wrote a program that allowed him to read everyone else's ID and password, which he then used to enter the other sectors, and he began leaving messages for users in their files, signing them "The Midnight Skulker." He didn't particularly want to get caught, but he did want to impress others with what he could do; he wanted some sort of reaction. When the computer operators changed the passwords, Bernay quickly found another way to access them. He left clues about his identity in certain files, and even wrote a program that, if activated, would destroy his own password-catching program. He wanted to play, to have his original program destroyed so that he could write another one to undo what he had, in effect, done to himself, and then reappear. But the management refused to play. So he left more clues, all signed by "The Midnight Skulker."

Eventually the management reacted: they interrogated everyone who had access to the mainframe, and inevitably, one of Bernay's colleagues fingered him. Bernay was fired.[3]

When Rosenbaum wrote his article in 1971 the practice of breaking into computers was so new and so bizarre, it didn't even have a name. Rosenbaum called it computer freaking—the *f* used to distinguish it from ordinary phone phreaking. But what was being described was the birth of hacking.

It was Draper, alias Captain Crunch, who, while serving a jail sentence, unintentionally spread the techniques of phreaking and hacking to the underworld—the real underworld of criminals and drug dealers. Part of the reason Draper went to jail, he now says, was because of the *Esquire* article: "I knew I was in trouble as soon as I read it." As a direct result of the article, five states set up grand juries to investigate phone phreaking and, incidentally, Captain Crunch's part in it. The authorities also began to monitor Draper's movements and the phones he used. He was first arrested in 1972, about a year after the article appeared, while phreaking a call to Sydney, Australia. Typically, he wasn't actually speaking to anyone; he had called up a number that played a recording of the Australian Top Ten.

Four years later he was convicted and sent to Lompoc Federal Prison in California for two months, which was where the criminal classes first learned the details of his techniques. It was, he says, a matter of life or death. As soon as he was inside, he was asked to cooperate and was badly beaten up when he refused. He realized that in order to survive, he would have to share his knowledge. In jail, he figured, it was too easy to get killed. "It happens all the time. There are just too many members of the 'Five Hundred Club,' guys who spend most of their time pumping iron and lifting five-hundred-pound weights," he says.

So he picked out the top dog, the biggest, meanest, and strongest inmate, as his protector. But in return Draper had to tell what he knew. Every day he gave his protector a tutorial about phreaking: how to set up secure loops, or eavesdrop on other telephone conversations. Every day the information was passed on to people who could put it to use on the outside. Draper remains convinced that the techniques that are still used by drug runners for computer surveillance of federal agents can be traced back to his tutorials.

But criminals were far from the only group to whom Draper's skills appealed. Rosenbaum's 1971 article introduced Americans for the first time to a new high-tech counterculture that had grown up in their midst, a group of technology junkies that epitomized the ethos of the new decade. As the sixties ended, and the seventies began, youth culture—that odd mix of music, fashion, and adolescent posturing—had become hardened and more radical. Woodstock had succumbed to Altamont; Haight-Ashbury to political activism; the Berkeley Free Speech Movement to the Weathermen and the Students for a Democratic Society.

Playing with Ma Bell's phone system was too intriguing to be dismissed as just a simple technological game. It was seen as an attack on corporate America—or "Amerika," as it was often spelt then to suggest an incipient Nazism within the state—and phreaking, a mostly apolitical pastime, was adopted by the radical movement. It was an odd mix, the high-tech junkies alongside the theatrical revolutionaries of the far left, but they were all part of the counterculture.

Draper himself was adopted by the guru of the whole revolutionary movement. Shortly after his arrest, he was contacted by Abbie Hoffman, the cofounder of the Youth International Party Line (YIPL). Hoffman invited Draper to attend the group's 1972 national convention in Miami and offered to organize a campaign fund for his defense.

At the time Hoffman was the best-known political activist in America. An anti–Vietnam war campaigner, a defendant in the

Chicago Seven trial, he had floated YIPL in 1971 as the technical offshoot of his radical Yippie party. Hoffman had decided that communications would be an important factor in his revolution and had committed the party to the "liberation" of Ma Bell, inevitably portrayed as a fascist organization whose influence needed to be stemmed.

YIPL produced the first underground phreaker newsletter, initially under its own name. In September 1973 it became *TAP,* an acronym that stood for Technological Assistance Program. The newsletter provided its readers with information on telephone tapping and phreaking techniques and agitated against the profits being made by Ma Bell.

Draper went to the YIPL convention, at his own expense, but came back empty-handed. It was, according to Draper, "a total waste of time," and the defense fund was never organized. But ironically, while the political posturing of the radicals had little discernible effect on the world, the new dimensions of technology—represented, if imperfectly, by the phreakers—would undeniably engender a revolution.

Before he went to jail, Draper was an habitué of the People's Computer Company (PCC), which met in Menlo Park, California. Started in 1972 with the aim of demystifying computers, it was a highly informal association, with no members as such; the twenty-five or so enthusiasts who gathered at PCC meetings would simply be taught the mysteries of computing, using an old DEC machine. They also hosted pot-luck dinners and Greek dances; it was as much a social club as a computer group.

But there was a new buzz in the air: personal computers, small, compact machines that could be used by anyone. A few of the PCC-ites gathered together to form a new society, one that would "brew" their own home computers, which would be called the Homebrew Computer Club. Thirty-two people turned up for the inaugural meeting of the society on March 5, 1975, held in a garage in Menlo Park.

The club grew exponentially, from sixty members in April to one hundred and fifty in May. The Homebrewers outgrew the Menlo Park garage and, within four months, moved to an auditorium on the Stanford campus. Eventually, Homebrew boasted five or six hundred members. With Haight-Ashbury down the road and Berkeley across the bay, the club members shared the countercultural attitudes of the San Francisco area. The club decried the "commercialization" of computers and espoused the notion of giving computer power to the people.

In those days the now-ubiquitous personal computer was making its first, tentative appearance. Before the early 1970s, computers were massive machines, called mainframes because the electronic equipment had to be mounted on a fixed frame. They were kept in purpose-built, climate-controlled blocks and were operated by punch card or paper tape; access was limited—few knew enough about the machines to make use of them anyway—and their functions were limited. The idea of a small, lightweight computer that was cheap enough to be bought by any member of the public was revolutionary, and it was wholeheartedly endorsed by the technological radicals as their contribution to the counterculture. They assumed that moving computing power away from the government and large corporations and bringing it to the public could only be a good thing.

The birthplace of personal computing is widely believed to be a shop sandwiched between a Laundromat and a massage parlor in a run-down suburban shopping center in Albuquerque, New Mexico. It was there, in the early 1970s, that a small team of self-proclaimed rebels and misfits designed the first personal computer, the Altair 8800, which was supposedly named after one of the brightest stars in the universe. Formally launched in January 1975, it was heralded by *Popular Electronics* as "the first mini-computer kit to rival commercial models," and it cost $395.

The proclaimed mission of the Altair design team was to liberate technology, to "make computing available to millions of people and do it so fast that the US Stupid Government [*sic*] couldn't do anything about it." They believed that Congress was about to pass a law requiring operators to have a license before programming a computer. "We figured we had to have several hundred machines in people's hands before this dangerous idea emerged from committee. Otherwise, 1984 would really have been 1984," said David Bunnell, a member of the original design team.

The group looked upon the personal computer, in Bunnell's words, as "just as important to New Age people as the six-shooter was to the original pioneers. It was our six-shooter. A tool to fight back with. The PC gave the little guy a fighting chance when it came to starting a business, organizing a revolution, or just feeling powerful."

In common with other early PCs,[4] the Altair was sold in kit form, limiting its appeal to hobbyists and computer buffs whose enthusiasm for computing would see them through the laborious and difficult process of putting the machines together. Once assembled, the kit actually did very little. It was a piece of hardware; the software—the programs that can make a PC actually do something, such as word processing or accounting—didn't exist. By present-day standards it also looked forbidding, a gray box with a metallic cover housing a multitude of LED lights and switches. The concept of "user-friendliness" had not yet emerged.

The launch of the Altair was the catalyst for the founding of the Homebrew Computer Club. Motivated by the success of the little machine, the members began working on their own designs, using borrowed parts and operating systems cadged from other computers. Two members of the club, however, were well ahead of the others. Inspired by Rosenbaum's article in *Esquire,* these two young men had decided to build their own blue boxes and sell them around the neighboring Stanford and Berkeley campuses. Though Rosenbaum had deliberately left out much of the technical detail, including the multifrequency tone cycles, the pair scratched together the missing data from local research libraries and were able to start manufacturing blue boxes in sizeable quantities. To keep their identities secret, they adopted aliases: Steve

Jobs, the effusive, glib salesman of the two, became Berkeley Blue; Steve Wozniak, or Woz, the consummate technician, became—as far as he can remember—Oak Toebark. The company they founded in Jobs's parents' garage was to become Apple Computer.

The duo's primitive blue-box factory began to manufacture MF-ers on nearly an assembly-line basis. Jobs, whose sales ability was apparent even then, managed to find buyers who would purchase up to ten at a time. In interviews given since, they estimated that they probably sold a couple hundred of the devices. Under California law at the time, selling blue boxes was perfectly legal, although using them was an offense. They got close to getting caught only once, when they were approached by the highway patrol while using one of their own blue boxes at a telephone booth. They weren't arrested—but only because the patrolman didn't recognize the strange device they had with them.

The two Steves had grown up in the area around Los Altos, part of that stretch of Santa Clara County between San Francisco and San Jose that would later become known as Silicon Valley. They had both been brought up surrounded by the ideas and technology that were to transform the area: Wozniak's father was an electronics engineer at Lockheed Missiles and Space Company and helped his son learn to design logic circuits. When the two boys first met, Jobs was particularly impressed that Wozniak had already built a computer that had won the top prize at the Bay Area science fair.

It has been said that Jobs and Wozniak were the perfect team, and that without Jobs, the entrepreneur, Woz would never have outgrown Homebrew. Wozniak was, at heart, a hacker and a phreaker; at the club he liked to swap stories with Draper, and he once tried to phreak a call to the pope by pretending to be Henry Kissinger. Before a Vatican official caught on, he had almost succeeded in getting through. Jobs, on the other hand, was first and foremost a businessman. He needed Wozniak to design the products—the blue boxes, the computers—for him to sell.

The Apple computer happened almost by accident. Had he had enough money, Woz would have been happy to go out and buy a model from one of the established manufacturers. But he was broke, so he sat down and began designing his own homemade model.

He had set out to build something comparable to the desktop computer he used at Hewlett-Packard, where he worked at the time. That computer was called the 9830 and sold for $10,000 a unit. Its biggest advantage was that it used BASIC, a computer language that closely resembles normal English. BASIC alleviated a lot of complications: a user could sit down, turn on the machine, and begin typing, which wasn't always possible with other computer languages.

BASIC—an acronym for Beginner's All-purpose Symbolic Instruction Code—had already been adapted by software pioneers Bill Gates and Paul Allen for use on the Altair. (Gates—soon to become America's youngest billionaire—and Allen went on to found Microsoft, probably the world's most powerful software company.) The language was compact, in that it required very little computer memory to run, an essential requirement for microcomputers. Woz began work on his new computer by adapting BASIC to run with a microprocessor—a sort of mini computer brain, invented earlier in the decade, which packed all the functions of the central processing unit (CPU) of a large computer onto a tiny semiconductor chip. The invention allowed the manufacture of smaller computers, but attracted little attention from traditional computer companies, who foresaw no market at all for PCs. All the action in those days was with mainframes.

Woz's prototype was first demonstrated to the self-proclaimed radicals at the Homebrew Club, who liked it enough to place a few orders. Even more encouraging, the local computer store, the Byte Shop, placed a single order for $50,000 worth of the kits.

The Byte Shop was one of the first retail computer stores in the world, and its manager knew that a fully assembled, inexpensive home computer would sell very well. The idea was suggested to Jobs, who began looking for the financial backing necessary to turn the garage assembly operation he and Woz now ran into a real manufacturing concern.

How the two Steves raised the money for Apple has been told before. Traditional manufacturers turned them down, and venture capitalists had difficulty seeing beyond appearance and philosophy. It was a clash of cultures. Jobs and Woz didn't look like serious computer manufacturers; with their long hair and standard uniform of sandals and jeans, they looked like student radicals. One venture capitalist, sent out to meet Jobs at the garage, described him as an unusual business prospect, but eventually they did find a backer.

The first public showing of what was called the Apple II was at the West Coast Computer Fair in San Francisco in April 1977. The tiny company's dozen or so employees had worked through the night to prepare the five functioning models that were to be demonstrated. They were sleek little computers: fully assembled, light, wrapped in smart gray cases with the six-color Apple logo discreetly positioned over the keyboard. What would set them apart in particular, though, was their floppy-disk capability, which became available on the machines in 1979.

The floppy disk—or diskette—is a data-storage system developed for larger computers. The diskette itself is a thin piece of plastic, protected by a card cover, that looks a little like a 45-rpm record, and is used to load programs or to store data. Prior to the launch of the Apple II, all microcomputers used cassette tapes and ordinary cassette recorders for data storage, a time-consuming and inefficient process. The inclusion of the floppy-disk system gave the Apple II a competitive edge: users would no longer need to fiddle about with tapes and recorders, and the use of diskettes, as well as the simple operating system that Woz had built into the computer, encouraged other companies to write software for the new machines.

This last development more than anything else boosted the

Apple II out of the hobbyist ghetto. The new Apple spawned a plethora of software: word-processing packages, graphics and arts programs, accounting systems, and computer games. The launch two years later of the VisiCalc spread sheet, a business forecasting program, made the Apple particularly attractive to corporate users.

Even Captain Crunch wrote software for the Apple II. At the time, in 1979, he was incarcerated in Northampton State Prison in Pennsylvania for a second phreaking offense. While on a rehabilitation course that allowed him access to a computer he developed a program called EasyWriter, one of the first word-processing packages, which for a short time became the second-best-selling program in America. Draper went on to write other applications, marketed under the "Captain Software" label.

The Apple II filled a niche in the market, one that traditional computer manufacturers hadn't realized was there. The Apple was small and light, it was easy to use and could perform useful functions. A new purchaser could go home, take the components out of their boxes, plug them in, load the software, then sit down and write a book, plot a company's cash flow, or play a game.

By any standards Apple's subsequent growth was phenomenal. In its first year of operation, 1977, it sold $2.5 million worth of computers. The next year sales grew to $15 million, then in 1979 to $70 million. In 1980 the company broke through the $100 million mark, with sales of $117 million. The figures continued to rise, bounding to $335 million in 1981 and $583 million in 1982. Along the way the founders of Apple became millionaires, and in 1980, when the company went public, Jobs became worth $165 million and Wozniak $88 million.

The story of Apple, though, isn't just the story of two young men who made an enviable amount of money. What Jobs and Wozniak began with their invention was a revolution. Bigger than Berkeley's Free Speech Movement and "the summer of love" in Haight-Asbury, the technological revolution represented by the personal computer has brought a real change to society. It gave people access to data, programs, and computing power they had never had before. In an early promotional video for Apple, an earnest employee says, "We build a device that gives people the same power over information that large corporations and the government have over people."

The statement deliberately echoes the "power to the people" anthem of the sixties, but while much of the political radicals' time was spent merely posturing, the technological revolutionaries were delivering a product that brought the power of information to the masses. That the technological pioneers became rich and that the funky little companies they founded turned into massive corporations is perhaps testament to capitalism's capacity to direct change, or to coopt a revolution.

Apple was joined in the PC market by hundreds of other companies, including "Big Blue" itself—IBM. When the giant computer manufacturer launched its own PC in 1981, it expected to sell 250,000 units over five years. Again, the popular hunger for computing power was underestimated. In a short while, IBM was selling 250,000 units a month. Penetration of personal computers has now reached between 15 and 35 percent of all homes in the major industrialized countries. There are said to be 50 to 90 million PCs in use in homes and offices throughout the world, and the number is still rising.

And though the PC revolution would probably have happened without Wozniak and Jobs, it may not have happened as quickly. It's worth remembering that the catalyst for all this was a magazine article about phreaking.

Computers are more than just boxes that sit on desks. Within the machines and the programs that run them is a sort of mathematical precision that is breathtaking in the simplicity of its basic premise. Computers work, essentially, by routing commands, represented by electrical impulses, through a series of gates that can only be open or closed—nothing else. Open or closed; on or off. The two functions are represented symbolically as 1 (open/

on) or 0 (closed/off). The route the pulse takes through the gates determines the function. It is technology at its purest: utter simplicity generating infinite complexity.

The revolution that occurred was over the control of the power represented by this mathematical precision. And the argument is still going on, although it is now concerned not with the control of computers but with the control of information. Computers need not be isolated: with a modem—the boxlike machine that converts computer commands to tones that can be carried over the phone lines—they can be hooked up to vast networks of mainframe computers run by industry, government, universities, and research centers. These networks, all linked by telephone lines, form a part of a cohesive international web that has been nicknamed Worldnet. Worldnet is not a real organization: it is the name given to the international agglomeration of computers, workstations, and networks, a mix sometimes called information technology. Access to Worldnet is limited to those who work for the appropriate organizations, who have the correct passwords, and who are cleared to receive the material available on the network.

For quite obvious reasons, the companies and organizations that control the data on these networks want to restrict access, to limit the number of people wandering through their systems and rifling through their electronic filing cabinets. But there is a counterargument: the power of information, the idealists say, should be made available to as many people as possible, and the revolution wrought by PCs won't be complete until the data and research available on computer networks can be accessed by all.

This argument has become the philosophical justification for hacking—although in practice, hacking usually operates on a much more mundane level. Hacking, like phreaking, is inspired by simple curiosity about what makes the system tick. But hackers are often much more interested in accessing a computer just to see if it can be done than in actually reading the information they might find, just as phreakers became more interested in the phone company than in making free calls. The curiosity that impelled phreakers is the same one that fuels hackers; the two groups merged neatly into one high-tech subculture.

Hacking, these days, means the unauthorized access of computers or computer systems. Back in the sixties it meant writing the best, fastest, and cleverest computer programs. The original hackers were a bunch of technological wizards at MIT, all considered among the brightest in their field, who worked together writing programs for the new computer systems then being developed. Their habits were eccentric: they often worked all night or for thirty-six hours straight, then disappeared for two days. Dress codes and ordinary standards were overlooked: they were a disheveled, anarchic bunch. But they were there to push back the frontiers of computing, to explore areas of the new technology that no one had seen before, to test the limits of computer science.

2
■
BREAKING AND
ENTERING

In the early eighties, the computer underground, like the computer industry itself, was centered in the United States. But technology flows quickly across boundaries, as do fads and trends, and the ethos of the technological counterculture became another slice of Americana that, like Hollywood movies and Coca-Cola, was embraced internationally.

Although the United States nurtured the computer underground, the conditions that spawned it existed in other countries as well. There were plenty of young men all over the world who would become obsessed with PC technology and the vistas it offered, and many who would be attracted to the new society, with its special jargon and rituals. The renegade spirit that created the computer underground in the first place exists worldwide.

In 1984, the British branch of the technological counterculture probably began with a small group that used to meet on an ad hoc basis in a Chinese restaurant in North London. The group had a floating membership, but usually numbered about a dozen; its meetings were an excuse to eat and drink, and to exchange hacker lore and gossip.

Steve Gold, then a junior accountant with the Regional Health Authority in Sheffield and a part-time computer journalist, was twenty-five, and as one of the oldest of the group, had been active when phone phreaking first came to England. Gold liked to tell stories about Captain Crunch, the legendary emissary from America who had carried the fad across the Atlantic.

The Captain can take most of the credit for exporting his hobby to Great Britain during his holiday there in 1970. Because the U.S. and British telephone systems were entirely different, MF-ers were of no use in England—except, of course, to reduce charges on calls originating in America. The British telephone network didn't use the same multifrequency tones (it used 2280 cycles), so the equipment had to be modified or new ways had to be devised to fool the British system. Naturally the Captain had risen to the challenge and carried out the most audacious phreak in England. The British telephone system was hierarchical, with three tiers: local switching offices, zone exchanges comprised of a number of local offices, and group offices linking various zones.[1] Much of the equipment in the local exchanges in those days dated back to the 1920s; in the zone and group offices the electronics had been put in during the 1950s, when Britain introduced national long-distance dialing, or STD (Standard Trunk Dialing), as it was then known. The Captain quickly discovered that users could avoid expensive long-distance charges by routing their calls from the local exchange to one nearby. The mechanism was simple: all a caller needed to do was dial the area code—known in Britain as the STD code—for the nearest out-of-area local exchange and then add a 9. The 9 would give the caller another dial tone, and he could then dial through to any other number in the country. He would only be charged, however, for the call to the nearby local exchange. The process was known as chaining, or sometimes bunny hopping.

With his usual enthusiasm for exploring phone networks, Captain Crunch decided to test the limits of the system. He notified a friend in Edinburgh to wait for his call from London while the Captain began a long, slow crawl up through local exchanges, dialing from one to the other, through England and then into Scotland. He is reputed to have chained six local exchanges; he could hear the call slowly clicking its way through exchange after exchange (the call was being routed through 1920s equipment) on its snaillike progression northward. Thirty minutes later the Captain's call finally rang at his friend's house. The connection, it is said, was terrible.

Steve Gold, like many others, had become an enthusiastic phreaker after learning the Captain's techniques. But like everyone else around the table at the restaurant, his interest had eventually turned to hacking as soon as personal computers became generally available. The group was part of the first generation to take advantage of the technological revolution that took place in the 1960s and 1970s: they had all learned about computers in school, having benefited from a sudden awareness that computer literacy was important, not merely an arcane specialty reserved for hobbyists and engineers. The science fiction of the 1960s had become a reality, and though it had been less than eight years since Jobs and Wozniak began assembling Apples in a California garage, and less than a decade since the Altair had been introduced, computers were no longer frightening or mysterious to the new generation. Mainframes had been supplanted by small, compact PCs that were increasingly user-friendly, thus allowing even the least technically-minded access to computing power.

Also among the group in the Chinese restaurant that night was a twenty-year-old hacker known as Triludan the Warrior, a close friend of Steve Gold's. Triludan had discovered Prestel, a data and information service established by British Telecom (the successor to the GPO) in the early 1980s that contained thousands of pages of news on finance, business, travel, and sport as well as company reports. The information, updated regularly, was often supplied by outside contractors including publishing houses and newspapers. The pages were read like an electronic news bulletin on the subscriber's computer screen and were accessed with the help of the system's first page, which indexed the information available. Prestel was also supposed to provide other services, such as on-line telephone directories and home shopping, but there was never sufficient demand.

A Prestel subscriber dialed into the service via a normal phone line connected to his PC by a modem. At Prestel, another modem linked the PC to the system's own computer. This arrangement allowed the user to manipulate Prestel's computer from his home.

Like all public-access computer systems, Prestel required users to key in their ID (sometimes called a log-in or a user-name) and their password. These are personal and known only to the individual subscribers. On Prestel, the ID was a ten-character string of letters and numbers, and the password was a four-character string. Prestel also provided subscribers with their own "electronic mailboxes," or MBXs, in which messages from other subscribers could be received. The system also included an index of all subscribers and their MBX addresses, so users could communicate with each other.

Triludan's penetration of the Prestel system was a lucky fluke. In February 1984 he had dialed up Prestel from his home computer at 2:30 A.M. For no obvious reason, he entered ten 2's. To his surprise, a message came back saying, CORRECT. He assumed that if the ID was that simple, then the four-character password must be equally obvious. He tried 1234, and WELCOME TO THE PRESTEL TEST came up on the screen. *So this is hacking,* he thought to himself.

The service Triludan had accessed was only the test system, set up for Prestel engineers to verify that their computers were operating correctly. Prestel subscribers dialed into any one of ten mainframes scattered around the country; the test system was confined to four other computers that simply monitored the mainframes, and because they were isolated from the actual Prestel service, it afforded few opportunities for exploration. Nonetheless, Triludan continued to access the test system once a week to see if he could make any progress. One day in October 1984 he dialed up as usual and found an ID and password on the front page, just below the WELCOME TO THE PRESTEL TEST message. He then redialed the test service and entered the new ID. It turned out to be that of the system manager.

Hacking, Triludan decided, was stumbling across other people's mistakes.

The ID and password had been listed on the front page for the convenience of Prestel's engineers, who would need to know them to roam through the system. The test service, after all, was itself supposedly secured by a ten-digit ID and a four-digit password. Prestel had no idea that the test service's security had already been blown. Now it was doubly blown, because the system manager's codes would allow Triludan to explore anywhere he wanted throughout the entire Prestel network.

The system manager, or "sysman," is the person in control of a computer installation. Like the manager of a large building who has keys to all the offices and knows the combinations to all of the secure areas, he has the keys—IDs and passwords—to all areas of his system: he controls and changes on-line data, updates indexes, assigns mailboxes, and oversees security. With his system-manager status, Triludan the Warrior had become king of Prestel. He could do anything: he could run up bills for any of the 50,000 subscribers, tamper with information, delete files, and read anything in the mailboxes.

When Triludan told the rest of the group at the meeting that he had captured sysman status on Prestel, they were amazed. In 1984 British hacking was still in its infancy; though American techniques were slowly spreading across the ocean, English hackers, unlike their American counterparts, had never managed to pull off any of the spectacular stunts that attracted press and publicity. Their access to Prestel seemed like the ideal opportunity to put British hacking on the map. They discussed plans and schemes: they knew well that with sysman status they could easily cripple the system. But none of them was malicious. Pranks were harder to pull, and they seemed more fun.

Accordingly they broke into the mailbox of His Royal Highness, Prince Philip, and were rewarded by seeing the message GOOD EVENING. HRH DUKE OF EDINBURGH come up on the computer screen. They left a message for the real sysman, in his mailbox, saying, I DO SO ENJOY PUZZLES AND GAMES. TA. TA. PIP! PIP! HRH ROYAL HACKER. Then they modified the foreign-exchange page on Prestel, provided by the *Financial Times,* so that for a few hours on the second of November the pound-to-dollar exchange rate was a glorious fifty dollars to the pound.

Triludan himself capped all the tricks: when subscribers dial into Prestel, they immediately see page one, which indexes all other services. Only the system manager can alter or update listings on this page, but Triludan, exploiting his sysman status, made a modest change and altered the word *Index* to read *Idnex.* Though it was perfectly harmless, the change was enough to signal to Prestel that its security had been breached. The other pranks had been worrisome, but altering the first page was tantamount to telling Prestel that its entire system was insecure. The company reacted quickly. It notified all its customers to change their passwords immediately, and then altered the sysman codes, thus stopping Triludan and his friends from tampering with the system again.

Six months later Triludan was arrested. Though he had lost sysman status, he had continued hacking the system, using other four-digit combinations. He even continued to leave messages for the system manager, just to prove that he could still gain access, and his games had badly embarrassed Prestel and its owner, British Telecom. The revelation that hackers had penetrated the Prestel system and broken into Prince Philip's mailbox had proved irresistible to the British press, which had cheerfully hyped the story into page-one news. The royal connection ensured that the item got international coverage, most of it implying that hackers had breached royal security systems and read Prince Philip's private and confidential electronic mail.[2]

To catch their hacker, Prestel put monitors on the incoming lines. These filtered all calls to the system, looking for unusual activity such as users trying different passwords or repeatedly failing to key in correct IDs. After watching the lines for a month, the authorities were convinced that they had two intruders, not one. The first was calling from London; the second appeared to be dialing in from Sheffield. British Telecom traced the two callers and put supplementary monitors on their home lines.

Despite the fact that the company had evidence from the messages to the system manager that Triludan was still breaking into the system, they needed hard evidence, so they continued monitoring the lines in London and Sheffield, carefully noting the times the two callers dialed into Prestel. Finally they decided to mount simultaneous raids.

On April 10, 1985, a posse of three British Telecom investigators and four policemen raided the north London address. Just after ten P.M. the police knocked on the door, which was opened by a young man who was six feet four inches tall with thick black hair. His name was Robert Schifreen, and yes, he was Triludan the Warrior—as well as Hex and Hexmaniac, two other hacker aliases that had appeared on Prestel. He was arrested and his equipment confiscated. The police were civil and polite, and they allowed the suspect to bring his bottle of antihistamine tablets with him. Its brand name was Triludan.

Schifreen was taken to Holborn police station to spend the night in the cells. He was charged and released on bail the next day.

At the same time Schifreen was arrested, another raid was taking place in Sheffield at the home of Schifreen's friend and companion, Steve Gold. Gold had also continued to hack Prestel. Along with Schifreen, he had been the most excited by the chance to play with the system. Gold remembers the knock on his door as coming at eight minutes past ten P.M. When he answered, he found three policemen and three British Telecom investigators, who read him his rights and promptly took him down to the local police station, where he spent an uncomfortable night. At nine the next morning he was driven down to London to be charged.

Because there were no laws in Britain addressing computer hacking at the time, the two were charged with forgery—specifically, forging passwords. Five specimen charges were listed in the warrant for Schifreen, four for Gold. The charges involved a total loss of about $20 to the Prestel users whose IDs had been hacked. What became known as the Gold and Schifreen case was Britain's first attempt to prosecute for computer hacking.

The case was tried before a jury some twelve months later. At the beginning of the trial the judge told counsel: "This isn't murder, but it's a very important case. It will set a very important precedent." After nine days the two were found guilty. Schifreen was fined about $1,500, Gold about $1,200; they had to pay the court almost $2,000 each for costs.

The duo appealed the verdict, and after another twelve months the case was heard in Britain's highest court of appeal by the Lord Chief Justice, Lord Lane, who ruled that copying an electronic password was not covered by the Forgery Act, and overturned the jury's verdict. The prosecution appealed that decision, and after another twelve-month delay, the House of Lords—which carries out many of the functions of America's Supreme Court—upheld Lord Lane's decision. Gold and Schifreen were acquitted.

Since then, Gold and Schifreen have both gone on to respectable careers in computer journalism. And from time to time they still meet in Chinese restaurants, though neither continues to hack.

But their case, which cost the British taxpayers about $3.5 million, gave a misleading signal to the country's hackers and phreakers. Because Gold and Schifreen had admitted hacking while denying forgery, it was assumed that the courts had decided that hacking itself was not against the law.

That's certainly what Nick Whiteley believed.

Briefly, in 1990, Nick Whiteley was the most famous hacker in Britain. A quiet, unremarkable young man with a pedestrian job at a chemical supplies company, by night he became the Mad Hacker and roamed through computer systems nationwide. To the alarm of the authorities, he was believed to have broken into computers at the Ministry of Defense and MI5, Britain's counterintelligence security service. More troublesome still, there were messages sent by the Mad Hacker that strongly suggested he had evidence that some type of "surveillance" had been carried out against the opposition Labor party, the Campaign for Nuclear Disarmament (CND), and even the British Cabinet. It was unclear who was supposed to be carrying out the surveillance, but it was presumed to be MI5.

When Nick was arrested in 1988, he was interviewed for up to six hours by agents he believes were from the Ministry of Defense and MI5. They were accompanied by an expert from International Computers Limited (ICL), at the time Britain's only independent mainframe computer manufacturer (the company is now controlled by Fujitsu of Japan). Nick was passionate in his admiration for ICL computers; he never hacked anything else, and both the MoD and MI5 use them.

Whiteley's ambition was to buy his own ICL: he especially coveted the 3980, their top-of-the-line mainframe. In his daytime job, he worked on an ICL 2966, a smaller model, but still a formidable mainframe. Whenever Nick felt his fellow workers were making fun of him—which he believed they did because he was only an operator, rather than a real programmer—he would fantasize about the 3980. It was twenty times faster than the 2966 and could support far more individual users. But he had to admit that on his salary it would take a long time to earn the down payment on the almost $2 million purchase price.

Nick had originally wanted to be a computer programmer or to work in technical support. But without a university degree his chances of becoming a programmer were limited: he would need to go back to college to get the qualifications. So instead he became an operator, or "tape monkey," employed to ensure that there was enough computer tape in the drive and enough paper in the printer to keep the machinery running. Though he had been offered a promotion to senior operator, he had turned it down against a vague promise of a job in technical support sometime in the future.

Then nineteen years old, Nick lived with his parents in their home in Enfield in north London. He was affable, intelligent, and articulate, was generally casually dressed—sweatshirt, jeans, sneakers—and had nicotine-stained fingers.

Nick's life became consumed by his passion for the ICL. He was fascinated by its operating system and by the language— called SCL (System Control Language)—used to write its programs. Of course he had to admit that his ambition to buy an ICL 3980 was pretty unrealistic. Even if he had enough money to buy one, he would certainly have no use for a computer that was designed for large businesses. But then he would begin to worry about what would happen if he lost his job or had to leave the company. Where would he go to work on an ICL then?

In his bedroom in his parents' house Nick had a personal computer, a Commodore Amiga 1000, equipped with a modem. He had intended to use the modem to dial in to electronic bulletin boards—specialist data and information services, like Prestel but generally run by private individuals. It was never his intention to start hacking, he says; he thought it would be boring. Nonetheless, he started reading a guide called *The Hacker's Handbook.* The *Handbook* had been written by a British hacker known as "Hugo Cornwall" and achieved instant notoriety when it was first published in March 1985. Guided by the *Handbook,* he began dialing into more bulletin boards. (He found that about 20 percent of them had hacker sections.) With the information he obtained from the *Handbook* and the bulletin boards he learned how to find the access phone numbers for other computers, and how to deal with IDs and passwords. The *Handbook* was especially useful: it contained a list of phone numbers that gave access to JANET.

JANET is the earnestly friendly acronym for the Joint Academic Network, a system that links computers in eighty to ninety universities, polytechnics, and research centers throughout the United Kingdom. Because it is designed to be used by students and researchers, the network needs to be relatively open, and tries to present a friendly face to users: hence the feminine acronym and the useful tutorial and guide provided by the system when a user types HELP. The network's various data banks also contain a wealth of information on subjects as dissimilar as military research and theoretical physics. For Nick, however, the chief appeal of JANET was that it linked a number of ICLs on different sites around the country. By accessing JANET he could play around on his favorite computers from his home, just by using his little Commodore.

Nick attempted his first hack in January 1988. He first dialed up a number for the computer center at Queen Mary College, where he knew there was an ICL 2988. Because Queen Mary is not far from Nick's home, the telephone charges would be lower; also, most colleges are easy targets because they generally have weak security. He got the dial-up from *The Hacker's Handbook*— but that, as he knew, would only get him to the front door. Access to the QMC computer would be like gaining entry to the Prestel system. To get inside, Nick would need both a user-name—a log-in or ID—and a password. The user-name at QMC is an individual seven-character ID; the password is a one-way encrypted code. (*One way* means the code can only be encrypted once and is entirely random; if the user forgets the password, a new one needs to be created.)

That was the theory, anyway. But Nick knew that some software supplied by ICL includes a standard, or default, "low-security" user-name, one that doesn't require a password. Nick had learned the default user-name from his job and his constant reading of ICL promotional material, manuals, and security information. And because Queen Mary College had never changed its default user-name, it had left its back door wide open, making it easy for Nick to walk right in to the college's mainframe ICL on his first try.

The sole drawback from Nick's point of view was that the low-security user-name gave him only restricted access to the computer. The QMC computer had a strict hierarchy of user status, and the environment of low-security users—the areas on the computer they could enter—was severely limited. Most ordinary users had higher status, though their environment was usually restricted by the nature of their tasks. At the apex of the hierarchy, as with Prestel, was the systems manager, who had access to everything. At QMC the sysman is in complete control of the computer, assigning status to other users, overseeing the functioning of the system, and managing the programs and data.

Nick's objective was to capture sysman status. Without it his options were too limited, his environment too restricted. He began searching through the files, using his knowledge of the minutiae of ICL operating systems to find his way through the electronic pathways of the QMC computer. He ran into walls or traps designed to keep him out of restricted areas, but he kept trying.

Nick's hobby, his only one, was collecting unlisted commands for ICL computers. These are keyboard operations that the company doesn't document, which can be discovered by experimentation. Sometimes these got him around the traps and farther into the system. Slowly he moved through the back alleys of the QMC systems until finally he was able to access the operator libraries, the collection of programs that manage the computer. He knew that the keys to raising his status lay among the programs. He had been hacking for hours by then, but he didn't notice the time or his own tiredness. He played with commands, his little PC sending signals from his bedroom in Enfield through the telephone lines to the mainframe at QMC. He went through the programs systematically, coaxing the ICL, trying to outsmart the security systems that had been put in place precisely to stop someone like him. Eventually the machine yielded. On his first hack Nick had managed to capture system-manager status.

He decided not to play with the QMC computer too much—the capture of sysman status was too valuable to lose by leaving obvious evidence; also, he needed QMC as a jumping-off point for other computers on JANET. He roamed about the QMC computer for a bit, looking at electronic mailboxes and assessing different files. Then he used his sysman status to create four new user-names, OLAD011, OLAD024, OLAD028, and OLAD059, which would allow him continual entry to the QMC machine. He assigned the four user-names to Alan Dolby.

The best part of the JANET network, from Nick's point of view, was that it was a freeway: entry into one point on the system gave a direct route to other points. That meant that he could dial into QMC and then link into other ICLs at other sites. Conveniently, the ever-friendly network listed the sites on the system by computer manufacturer, so he knew just where to go to find more ICLs.

One of Nick's targets was an ICL at Glasgow University in Scotland. Eventually he linked into Glasgow by logging in as a guest user. He used the same technique to break into the ICL at Hull University and others in Nottingham, Belfast, and Bath.

Nick saw hacking as simply a means to play on ICLs. He wasn't interested in stealing information from the network, and in fact, he had no real purpose at all. He was hooked on ICLs and wanted only to be able to work on them, to play around on the operating system, to explore the complexities of the network. He told his parents there wasn't anything illegal in what he was doing, and technically he was correct: at the time there were no laws in the U.K. that specifically addressed hacking, and the Gold-Schifreen case had seemed to make the practice beyond the law.

Once Nick had started hacking the Whiteley family phone bills soared from around $100 a quarter to over $1,600. But Nick always paid his share. He could afford to do so because he had no other social life: no expensive habits, no girlfriends. He went to work, came home, and started hacking. He hacked at night because it fit into his schedule, and also because the phone rates were cheaper, there was less line noise, and the target computers would be unmanned. The trick was, he said later, to stay awake; sometimes he hacked all through the night and then had to go to work the next morning. His "day" could stretch to twenty-eight hours: first eight hours at work, then a night spent hacking, then another eight hours at work trying to stay awake while keeping the printer stuffed with paper and the tape running in the drive. After a marathon stretch like that he would take the next night off and go to bed early.

"It was obsessive," Nick later explained. "Five or six hours can seem like five minutes." He drank coffee and Coke and ingested caffeine tablets to keep going. "When you get into a system, you must keep going. It might take four or five hours to penetrate the defenses and another four or five hours to protect the position that has been established. If protection isn't put into place, then the earlier work could be wasted." The challenge was in beating the system; success came from staying awake. It gave him a feeling of power: he enjoyed knowing that while the designated sysman thought he controlled the computer, in fact it was himself, Nick, who had manipulated system-manager status and was really in control.

Nick compared hacking to a game of chess, a battle of wits between himself and the system, nothing criminal, just a game:

> The excitement comes from knowing that a computer in the bedroom at home can be used to break into multimillion-dollar installations. There's the thrill of exploration, of going around the world electronically. The objective is to try to gain the highest status within the system, that of system manager, and once there, to begin making the rules instead of following them. If the system manager blocks one way in, then you find another. It becomes a game with the systems manager; the hacker's goal is simply to try to persuade the computer that he should have increased privileges.

One person who didn't see it as a game was Bob Jones, the chief programmer at Queen Mary College. A tall, well-built man with beard and glasses and an academic uniform that sometimes runs to jeans and T-shirts, he had been at the college since 1968, first as a physics student, then staying on to work full-time at the QMC computer center after earning his degree in 1971.

He worked out of a large office on the top floor of the computer science block, a nondescript concrete shell of a building in east London. His office was near the computer center, a cramped room packed with mainframes, some of them ICLs. In the room's center were eight consoles set up on adjoining desks, which allowed the activities of the mainframes to be monitored but were usually unmanned, particularly at night.

Jones first realized that the QMC system had been breached by a hacker on February 19, 1988. He had heard reports from colleagues at the Universities of Glasgow and Hull that their own systems had been hacked by someone calling himself Alan Dolby. What he saw on his computer was a series of files that had been incorrectly stored in the memory, one of which had been labeled AD. He began searching for signs of further tampering, and he soon found it: the four OLAD user files Nick had created to give himself a smooth path into the QMC computer. The files appeared to have been created a month previously.

Jones immediately reported the intrusion to his superior, Jeremy Brandon, the director of the computer center, although it was clear that their options were limited. They could attempt to lock their hacker out by closing all of the OLAD files, but that might force the hacker to try more devious back-door methods to regain access. If he entered the system through such a method, they might not be able to find him again—and he might do some real damage. Instead, they decided to leave the files as they were and watch him, although they did remove the Mad Hacker's sysman status.

When Jones came into the office on the morning of March 30th, he found that there had been no work processed on the computer since about two A.M., when the scheduler (the program listing the priority of jobs) had failed. Its failure coincided with a successful hack of the system made by OLAD028.

Jones and Brandon decided to record future intrusions on a

dedicated journal within the computer. They also decided to wipe out three of the user-names, leaving only OLAD028, the one the hacker had consistently employed. It would be easier to track him this way.

By this time the hacking incidents had been reported to QMC's head of security, who passed on the information to Scotland Yard's Computer Crime Unit. Although established in 1971, the CCU had until 1985 consisted of only one officer. Then, as computer crime escalated and the government became concerned about the vulnerability of its own systems, it was eventually enlarged to four officers—still not a big force, given that Scotland Yard can be called in on cases anywhere in Great Britain. The unit is headed by John Austen, who was the officer assigned to investigate the Mad Hacker affair.

Austen knew that the only way to catch the hacker was to monitor the lines, the same time-consuming process used to track down Triludan the Warrior. That meant involving British Telecom, which needed to assign an engineer to trace calls. And because the Mad Hacker worked at night, that would involve overtime. For the first few days the investigation was bogged down over the overtime question: neither British Telecom nor QMC nor Scotland Yard were willing to pay. Eventually the phone company gave in and set up a twenty-four-hour trace, to be activated whenever the hacker was detected on the QMC system.

As the Mad Hacker gained confidence and experience, his activities took on a new twist. To Bob Jones it seemed malicious, as if the hacker had declared war on the system. One night the Mad Hacker ordered the QMC computer to print, I THINK YOU SHOULD KNOW I AM MAD . . . I AM ALSO DEPRESSED, over and over. To Hull University he sent a message saying, I AM TAKING UP THE CHALLENGE, then loaded a "rabbit" onto the system. A rabbit is a piece of software that orders a computer to perform useless tasks endlessly, multiplying ever more work orders until they finally overwhelm the computer and it can cope with nothing else. The Hull computer was down for ten hours after this particular rabbit began breeding. THAT WILL FILL UP YOUR SODDING SYSTEM, another message said.

He then dropped a rabbit into the Glasgow computer. But this time, it didn't work. As he was on-line, the computer operator discovered him and sent him a message demanding that he call the operations department. ALAN DOLBY DOESN'T MAKE CALLS, he wrote back.

Glasgow was where Dolby had first been rumbled, three months previously, when a file he had created as a back door had been discovered. It was Glasgow that had alerted the rest of the system operators on JANET that there was a hacker. So there may have been an element of revenge when, one night, the Glasgow system manager, Dr. Roger MacKenzie, tried to access the mainframe from his home PC and found that he had been "locked out"—barred from his own computer. It was later discovered that the Mad Hacker had captured sysman status that night and instructed the mainframe to kick out MacKenzie.

At QMC an increasingly irritated Bob Jones was watching as intrusion after intrusion was recorded in the computer journal. At first these were just messages left for the sysman, schoolboyish nonsense such as WILL ET PLEASE PHONE HOME and WILL NORMAN BATES PLEASE REPORT TO THE SHOWER ROOM. But then things became more serious: the Mad Hacker instructed the QMC computer to generate copies of reports from its memory, which prevented it from processing necessary work, and on more than one occasion his intrusions caused the computer to crash. It seemed as if the Mad Hacker had become vindictive and malicious.

Once, he left a message asking, WHY DON'T YOU LOCK ME OUT? It was obvious to Jones that his hacker wanted to play, but he ignored the messages.

Monitoring the lines was slowly getting results. When the Mad Hacker was spotted making an unusual daytime appearance, Bob Jones called the twenty-four-hour emergency number at British

Telecom—which rang and rang. In frustration he gave the receiver to someone else to hold while he called a contact at British Telecom direct.

"There's no one answering my emergency call," he shouted.

"Well, yes," the Telecom man said patiently. "The service doesn't start until five P.M." As they spoke, an assistant passed him a note saying that the hacker had left the system. Jones, still steaming, explained the precise meaning of "twenty-four-hour service."

The monitoring intensified. In early July the engineers at the telephone office nearest QMC finally traced the hacker back to a telephone in Enfield. Another monitor was placed on the suspect number to record all future activity.

On July 5th Jones came in to work to find that the computer journal recording the Mad Hacker's intrusions had been wiped out. That could only have happened if the hacker had captured sysman status again. He also found this message:

THIS INSTALLATION HAS BEEN HACKED BY ALAN DOLBY.

ALAN DOLBY IS A REGISTERED MEMBER OF HACKING INC. (ICL DIVISION), WHICH IS A SUBSIDIARY OF HACKING INTER-NATIONAL.

THIS HACK IS © 1988 BY ALAN DOLBY (THE MAD HACKER).

The announcement was followed by a message for Marlyn, a computer operator previously employed by QMC and mistakenly believed by the Mad Hacker to be the sysman:

NOW MARLYN IS PROBABLY THINKING, !@£?$ (SH*T) HOW THE HELL DID HE GET IN THIS TIME? . . . I BETTER HAVE A LOOK AT WHERE I KEEP HIS JOURNALS. OH SHIT, SHE SAYS, THEY ARE NOT THERE ANYMORE. !@£?$

NOW, MARLYN, IT'S GETTING PRETTY BORING HAVING TO KEEP ON TEACHING YOU MANNERS. I'D RATHER BE AT MY

OTHER SYSMAN HACK SITES. SO I HOPE YOU HAVE LEARNED (EXCEPT HOW I DID IT) FROM THIS, MARLYN, AND REPLY TO MY MESSAGES; OTHERWISE YOU WILL MAKE ME VERY VERY ANGRY, AND ROGER WILL TELL YOU ONE THING, YOU WON'T LIKE IT WHEN I'M ANGRY.

The reference was to the Mad Hacker's successful lockout of Roger MacKenzie from his own system. The message continued:

STILL, DON'T GET TOO DESPONDENT MARLYN, I MEAN WHAT DID YOU EXPECT? IF I CAN HACK ROGER'S PLACE TWICE, THEN ANYTHING ELSE IS JUST A PIECE OF CAKE, AND I MEAN YOU'RE NO GURU, MARLYN. ROGER IS THE GURU, HE WRITES PROGRAMS, HE DOESN'T PHONE UP SAYING, OH, ROGER, HELP ME, ROGER.

HAVE I WOUND YOU UP ENOUGH, MARLYN?

YOU WON'T BELIEVE HOW I GOT IN, MARLYN . . . HAHAHAHAHAHAHAHAHAHAHHAAAA

YOURS HACKINGLY, ALAN DOLBY . . . THE MAD HACKER!!!

THE MAD HACKER THE MAD HACKER ALAN DOLBY ALAN DOLBY . . .

Though the Mad Hacker had destroyed the journal when he hacked in to QMC that night, he didn't destroy the evidence. Like most computer users, QMC keeps backup copies of files, so the record of the Mad Hacker's intrusions still existed. But it was becoming evident that eventually real damage to the system could be caused if the hacking continued. It had already become very frustrating to Jones, who was spending more and more time cleaning up after the Mad Hacker and less time doing his real work. But even worse, Scotland Yard had become concerned about hints that were contained in some of his computer messages that Alan Dolby was hacking into the Ministry of Defense computer, also an ICL. The break-ins might still be a game to the Mad Hacker, but it was becoming deadly serious to everyone else.

They decided to go for a bust that very evening.

An arrest for computer hacking is not a straightforward affair. To make the charge stick, the police would have to arrest the Mad Hacker while he was actually in the middle of a hack, with the unauthorized dial-up on his computer screen and his fingers on the keyboard. Evidence that the hacking had been committed from his phone number was not sufficient: it could, after all, have been done by his mother.

The team assembled for the bust was enormous. There were four policemen from the Computer Crime Unit, two technical-support specialists, two experts from ICL, a police photographer, two British Telecom engineers, and a phalanx of uniformed policemen. In addition Jones had to monitor the QMC computer to alert the team when the Mad Hacker broke in. He was joined in his vigil by the managers at other ICL sites on the JANET network, as well as by internal British Telecom staff to monitor the phone lines. In total the team numbered forty people.

As luck would have it, however, on that evening nothing happened; the Mad Hacker simply went to bed early. But the next night, he decided to dial in to QMC once more to see if anyone had replied to his message. According to the computer record, he logged on at 7:48 P.M.

Just a few minutes before 8:00 P.M. the Whiteley family heard a knock on the door. The police later described it as a gentle tap; to Nick, upstairs in his bedroom, it sounded like loud banging. He thought it odd: why didn't they use the doorbell? Then he walked to his window and saw four men approaching the door. He said later that he could tell from their appearance that they weren't Jehovah's Witnesses, and for one awful second he thought they might be Mafia.

Downstairs Nick's father was at the door bewilderedly reading a warrant presented to him by the policemen. Nick sat down on his bed. He thought that perhaps they were after a spy or a murderer. They couldn't be after him: he was nineteen years old and liked to play games with computers, that was all.

The police moved upstairs to arrest Nick. By this time, there were twelve members of the team in the tiny house, communicating by portable phone to their colleagues outside. John Austen from the CCU told Nick he was being arrested for "criminal damage." Nick looked at him incredulously, then burst out laughing. He thought it must be a mistake.

Though hacking wasn't illegal at that time, the case against Whiteley had been put together around the concept of criminal damage, which boiled down to loss of data and denial of computer service as a result of his hacks. QMC alone had valued the downtime to fix its computers at $48,000.

Police photographers moved in to record the computer screen, keyboard, and modem. Every inch of the room was photographed: Nick's files, the books on his bookshelf, the posters on the wall. The police stayed until midnight: they confiscated Nick's Commodore and all the other equipment, loading the evidence into bags; they removed from Nick's room books, blank paper, empty folders, even the posters; and they interviewed Nick's older brother, Christopher. Nick's mother, who was out when the raid began, came home to find the team searching Nick's car.

Nick was still stunned: he was convinced it was all a mistake and that soon the police would apologize and go away. He presumed that he had never been locked out of the QMC mainframe because the systems manager wanted him to test the security, that he was playing the game too. Nick was the stereotypical hacker: a kid who wanted to play a big-time computer game to demonstrate how clever he was. He didn't want to damage anything, although he did enjoy playing a few malicious pranks from time to time. When he was busted, Nick had only been hacking for six months.

Two days after the raid, he was taken to Bow Street magistrate's court and charged with having caused a total of $115,000 damage to computer hardware and disks. But what concerned the authorities the most were the suggestions that Nick had been hacking into MoD and MI5; in his room they found a little red notebook with dial-ups for ICLs operated by government agencies. They also wanted to know about the messages that had been left by Nick on the QMC computer alleging that he had knowledge of "surveillance" of the Labor party, CND (the Campaign for Nuclear Disarmament) and the Cabinet.

Nick told the police, and later two agents he presumed to be from the MoD and MI5, that he had never used the numbers in his book; they were for future reference. As for the messages about surveillance, they were fantasy, part of the games he was playing with the sysman at QMC.[3]

The police were unimpressed. Nick was released on bail, but only after promising not to continue hacking. In May 1990, almost two years after the incidents took place, he was tried for criminal damage at London's Southwark crown court. The defense accepted the prosecution's charges, but argued that there had been no real criminal damage. Nick's lawyers were confident of getting him off, but it's said that he made a bad impression as a witness in his own defense: he was too sure of himself, too clever. Bob Jones later described him as "flippant and sneering." Nick himself thinks he was destined for a harsh sentence from the start.

"They wanted to make an example of me," he said. "They'd have sent me to jail for a parking ticket."

In the end, amid a flurry of national publicity, he was cleared of causing criminal damage to computer hardware, but convicted on four counts of damaging disks. After the verdict, defense counsel asked for but were refused bail. Whiteley was sentenced to a year's imprisonment, but eight months were suspended, and with good behavior in jail, he was paroled after serving only two months. He was released in March 1991.

Nick was the first person in Britain to be convicted of offenses relating to hacking. The overtones in his case—and the allegations of MI5 snooping and break-ins at the MoD—were enough to bring pressure on Parliament to propose a new computer crime law. The Computer Misuse Act came into effect in 1990: it made any attempt, successful or otherwise, to alter computer data with criminal intent an offense punishable by up to five years in jail. It could be called Nick Whiteley's legacy.

The contrast between Nick—generally polite, easygoing, and articulate—and his alter ego, the Mad Hacker, impressed everyone who met him. Nick Whiteley would never leave messages redolent with sexual aggression for Marlyn: that was the Mad Hacker, or Alan Dolby. Nick Whiteley wouldn't cause damage to an ICL: again, that was the Mad Hacker. Like so many hackers, Nick played out his fantasies on the computer keyboard. He was no longer Nick Whiteley from Enfield when he was hacking, he was the Mad Hacker, the Mr. Hyde of QMC, Hull, Glasgow, and JANET. With a computer he could become anyone he wanted to be; without it he was just Nick Whiteley.

Even when the computer underground was in its infancy, in the United States back in the early sixties, the use of aliases was symbolic of the growing subculture. Early phreakers had names such as Cheshire Catalyst, Dr. No, Midnight Skulker, and of course Captain Crunch. Hackers continued to use aliases to hide their identities—and more often than not to disguise their real selves behind a fearsome mask. Later, aliases became known as handles, after CB slang.

A handle with high-tech allusions (Fiber Cables, Apple Maniac, Byte Ripper) or suggesting personal instability (Perfect Asshole, the Prisoner, Right Wing Fool) is considered perfectly acceptable. Some hackers opt for fiercer handles (Knight Stalker, Scorpion) or just co-opt the names of celebrities (there are hackers called Pink Floyd and Robin Williams). Behind these sometimes demonic handles often lurks a fourteen- or fifteen-year-old boy who is hooked on technology and spends hours alone in his bedroom, hacking into remote computers. Armchair psychology suggests that the fiercer the handle, the meeker the kid behind it. There is a huge element of role-playing in hacking, a need to be accepted among the community, not as the person one really is but as the person suggested by the handle. Hacking brings out the Mr. Hyde in all the little technological Dr. Jekylls.

Adopting a handle is essential for a novice to be accepted on pirate hacker boards, where he can access information about his hobby and pass on messages to other hackers. The computer underground is amorphous; any structure it does have is provided through communication within the community via the boards and a variety of other technical modes—electronic and voice mailboxes, conference bridges, and even loop-around-pairs, the old phreaker technology. A handle is a hacker's badge of belonging, his calling card; the pirate boards serve as electronic meeting places, the high-tech equivalent of hanging out at the mall.

Boards are simply computers loaded with some specialist software and linked to a modem. They are generally owned and operated by a single person, who becomes the system operator and controls access. There may be hundreds in existence—the majority are in North America—and they come and go, as does their status within the hacker community. At any given time there may be only two or three "hot boards" that attract the top hackers. Getting access to one of these boards is a sign of having arrived in the computer underground, a mark of respect. Belonging to a particular board means belonging to the group that uses the board: it means becoming part of what one U.S. attorney called a high-tech street gang.

Hacker boards are never publicized. Obtaining the dial-up number is itself a sign that a potential member has some credibility within the community, but that alone is not enough; no self-respecting pirate systems operator wants his board cluttered up with "lamers," kids who pretend to be hackers but don't really have what it takes.

The registration procedure on pirate boards is a careful process. First-time callers are met with a request for their user-name and their phone number. Lamers who enter their real name and real phone number have already blown it. The correct procedure is to enter a handle and a fake phone number—a healthy dose of paranoia is a good sign that a caller is a real hacker. The next step is to provide personal references, which will determine the level of access to the pirate board. Hacker boards often have several grades of users, and only the most trusted callers are able to access the "good stuff." The reference query is designed to elicit the names of other pirate boards the caller has access to, his level of access on those boards, and the handles of any other trusted hackers he may know. If the references prove satisfactory, the caller will be granted leave to use the board.

Some boards go a step farther: they ask the caller to write a short statement explaining his reasons for wanting access, or to complete a questionnaire, to test his technical expertise. Some operators, particularly on "cracker" boards (those used by software pirates to swap "cracked"—illegally copied—programs) demand that a caller prove himself by supplying what is called *warez*—for wares, or pirated software.

Complementing the boards is a sporadically functioning electronic underground press—newsletters, most distributed electronically, that contain articles about busts, tips on hacking and phreaking, and technical descriptions of computer operating systems. The oldest is *PHRACK Inc.* (the name is an amalgamation of *phreak* and *hack*), which was available off and on from 1985 until 1990. Others that have appeared from time to time include the *Legion of Doom: Hackers Technical Journal, Phreakers/ Hackers Underground Network,* and the *Activist Times.* A traditional, printed, publication, *2600 The Hacker Quarterly,* has been published since 1987, and is available on some newsstands. The *2600* in its title is a bow to the infamous frequency tone used by phreakers to make toll-free long-distance calls.

Membership in the computer underground simply means belonging to a self-selected group of high-tech junkies. Some individual hackers—generally members of a particular bulletin board—work as a group and acquire a gang handle. In 1982 the Inner Circle was the first group to claim credit for breaking into the U.S. military computer network. The 414 gang, named after its local Wisconsin area code, specialized in cracking telephone-company systems.

The telephone company, or "telco," as it is called, is still a favorite target for many hackers. Those who specialize in exploring the telco system are sometimes called phreakers like their predecessors Captain Crunch and Joe Engressia. In words that echo Joe Engressia, one telco phreak wrote, "The phone system is the most interesting, fascinating thing I know of. There is so much to know. I myself would like to work for the telco, doing something interesting, like programming a switch—something that isn't slave labor bullshit. Exploring the system is something that you enjoy, but have to take risks in order to participate in, unless you are lucky enough to work for the telco. To have access to telco things, manuals, etc., would be great."

If there is a credo that unites all members of the computer underground, it is probably the one first expounded by Steven Levy in his 1984 book, *Hackers:* "Access to computers, and anything that might teach you something about the way the world works, should be unlimited and total." This belief implies a code of ethics that, put simply, boils down to "Look, but don't touch." Hackers, according to this code, may break into computers or computer networks with impunity, but should not tamper with files or programs.

In the real world it rarely works like that. Though hackers see themselves as a useful part of the system, discovering design flaws and security deficiencies, the urge to demonstrate that a particular computer has been cracked tempts hackers to leave evidence, which involves tampering with the computer. The ethical code is easy to overlook, and sometimes tampering can become malicious and damaging.

For the authorities, the whole thing is a giant can of worms. Patrolling the access points and communications webs that make up Worldnet is an impossible task; in the end, policing in the information age is necessarily reactive. Adding to the problems of the authorities is the increasing internationalization of the computer underground. Laws are formed to cover local conditions, in which the crime, the victim, and the perpetrator share a common territory. International crime, in which the victim is in America, say, and the perpetrator in Europe, while the scene of the crime—the computer that was violated—may be located in a third country, makes enforcement all the more difficult. Police agencies only rarely cooperate internationally, language differences create artificial barriers, and the laws and legal systems are never the same.

Still, the authorities are bound to try. The argument that began as the information age dawned, encapsulated in Stephen Levy's uncompromising view that access to data should be "unlimited and total," has never ended. The government, corporations, and state agencies will never allow unlimited access for very obvious reasons: state security, the privacy of individuals, the intellectual property conventions . . . the list goes on and on. In all western countries, hacking is now illegal; the theft of information from computers, and in some cases even unauthorized access, is punishable by fines and jail sentences. The position is rigid and clear: the computer underground is a renegade movement, in conflict with the authority of the state.

But there are still good hackers and bad hackers. And it is even true that sometimes hackers can be helpful to the authorities—or at least, it's happened once. A hacker named Michael Synergy (he has legally changed his name to his handle) once broke into the computer system at a giant credit agency that holds financial information on 80 million Americans, to have a look at then-president Ronald Reagan's files. He located the files easily and discovered sixty-three other requests for the president's credit records, all logged that day from enquirers with unlikely names. Synergy also found something even odder—a group of about seven hundred people who all appeared to hold one specific credit card. Their credit histories were bizarre, and to Synergy they all seemed to have appeared out of nowhere, as if "they had no previous experience." It then occurred to him that he was almost certainly looking at the credit history—and names and addresses—of people who were in the U.S. government's Witness Protection Program.[4]

Synergy, a good citizen, notified the FBI about the potential breach of the Witness Program's security. That was hacker ethics. But not every hacker is as good a citizen.

3
■
DATA CRIME

Pat Riddle has never claimed to be a good citizen. He is proud of being the first hacker in America to be prosecuted. Even now, as a thirty-four-year-old computer security consultant, he is fond of describing cases he has worked on in which the law, if not actually broken, is overlooked. "I've never been entirely straight," he says.

As a child growing up in a suburb of Philadelphia, he, like most hackers, was fascinated by technology. He built model rockets, played with electronics, and he liked to watch space launches. When he became a little older, his interests turned to telecommunications and computers.

Pat and his friends used to rummage through the garbage left outside the back doors of phone company offices for discarded manuals or internal memos that would tell them more about the telephone system—a practice known as dumpster diving. He learned how to make a "butt set," a portable phone carried by phone repairmen to check the lines, and first started "line tapping"—literally, listening in on telephone calls—in the early 1970s, when he was fourteen or fifteen.

The butt set he had built was a simple hand-held instrument with a dial on the back and two alligator clips dangling from one end. All the materials he used were purchased from hardware and electronics stores. To line-tap, he would search out a neighborhood telephone box where the lines for all the local phones come together. Every three-block area, roughly, has one, either attached to a telephone pole or freestanding. Opening the box with a special wrench—also available from most good hardware stores—he would attach the clips to two terminals and listen in on conversations.

Sometimes, if the telephone box was in a public area, he would run two long wires from the clips so that he could sit behind the bushes and listen in on conversations without getting caught. To find out whose phone he was listening to, he would simply use his butt set to call the operator and pretend to be a lineman. He would give the correct code, which he had learned from his hours of dumpster diving, and then ask, "What's this number?" Despite being fourteen, he was never refused. "So long as you know the lingo, you can get people to do anything," Pat says.

The area where he grew up was a dull place, however, and he never heard anything more interesting than a girl talking to her date. "It was basically boring and mundane," he says, "but at that age any tittle-tattle seemed exciting."

Pat learned about hacking from a guy he met while shoplifting electronic parts at Radio Shack. Doctor Diode, as his new friend was called, didn't really know much more about hacking than Pat, but the two of them discovered the procedures together. They began playing with the school's computer, and then found that with a modem they could actually call into a maintenance port—a dial-up—at the phone company's switching office. The phone company was the preferred target for phreakers-turned-hackers: it was huge, it was secretive, and it was a lot of fun to play on.

Breaking into a switch through a maintenance port shouldn't have been easy, but in those days security was light. "For years and years the phone company never had any problems because they were so secret," Pat says. "They never expected anyone to try to break into their systems." The switch used an operating system called UNIX, designed by the phone company, that was relatively simple to use. "It had lots of menus," recalls Pat with satisfaction.

Menus are the lists of functions and services available to the computer user, or in this case, the computer hacker. Used skillfully, menus are like a map of the computer.

As Pat learned his way around the switch, he began to play little jokes, such as resetting the time. This, he says, was absurdly simple: the command for the clock was Time. Pat would reset the clock from a peak time—when telephone charges were highest—to an off-peak time. The clock controlled the telephone company's charges, so until the billing department noticed it was out of kilter, local telephone users enjoyed a period of relatively inexpensive calls. He also learned how to disconnect subscriber's phones and to manipulate the accounts files. The latter facility enabled him to "pay" bills, at first at the phone company and later, he claims, at the electric company and at credit card offices. He would perform this service for a fee of 10 percent of the bill, which became a useful source of extra income.

He also started to play on the Defense Department's Advanced Research Projects Agency (ARPA) computer network. ARPANET was the oldest and the largest of the many computer nets—webs of interconnected mainframes and workstations—that facilitated the Defense Department's transfer of data. ARPANET was conceived in the 1950s—largely to protect the ability of the U.S. military to communicate after a nuclear strike—and finally established in the late 1960s. It eventually linked about sixty thousand computers, or nodes, and interacted with other networks, both in the United States and elsewhere in the world, making it an integral part of Worldnet. Most universities, research centers, defense contractors, military installations, and government departments were connected through ARPANET. Because there was no "center" to the system, it functioned like a highway network, connecting each node to every other; accessing it at one point meant accessing the whole system.

Pat used to commune regularly with other hackers on pirate bulletin boards, where he exchanged information on hacking sites, known computer dial-ups, and sometimes even stolen IDs and passwords. From one of these pirate boards he obtained the dial-up numbers for several ARPANET nodes.

He began his hack of ARPANET by first breaking into Sprint, the long-distance phone carrier. He was looking for long-distance access codes, the five-digit numbers that would get him onto the long-distance lines for free. In the old days he could have used a blue box, but since then the phone system had become more sophisticated. Blue boxes were said to have been killed off once and for all in 1983 when Bell completed the upgrading of its system to what is called Common Channel Interoffice Signaling (CCIS). Very simply, CCIS separates the signaling—the transmission of the multifrequency tones—from the voice lines.[1]

To get the codes he wanted, Pat employed a technique known as war-dialing, in which a program instructs the computer to systematically call various combinations of digits until it finds a "good" one, a valid access code. The system is crude but effective; a few hours spent war-dialing can usually garner a few good codes.

These long-distance codes are necessary because of the time-consuming nature of hacking. It takes patience and persistence to break into a target computer, but once inside, there is a myriad of menus and routes to explore, to say nothing of other linked computers to jump to. Hackers can be on the phone for hours, and whenever possible, they make certain their calls are free.

Pat's target was an ARPANET-linked computer at MIT, a favorite for hackers because at that time security was light. In common with many other universities, MIT practiced a sort of open access, believing that its computers were there to be used. The difficulty for MIT, and other computer operators, is that if security is light, the computers are abused, but if security is tight, they become more difficult for even authorized users to access.

Authorized users are given a personal ID and a password, which hackers spend a considerable amount of time collecting through pirate bulletin boards, peering over someone's shoulder in an office, or "dumpster diving." But exploiting a computer's default log-ins and passwords can often be even simpler—as Nick Whiteley discovered when he hacked in to the QMC computer for the first time. A common default is "sysmaint," for systems maintenance, used as both the log-in and the password. Accessing a machine with this default would require no more than typing "sysmaint" at the log-in prompt and then again at the password prompt. Experienced hackers also know that common commands such as "test" or "help" are also often used as IDs and passwords.

Pat first accessed ARPANET by using a default code. "Back then there was no real need for security," he says. "It was all incredibly simple. Computers were developed for human beings to use. They have to be simple to access because humans are idiots."

ARPANET became a game for him—he saw it as "a new frontier to play in." He jumped from computer to computer within the system, accessing everything from the main computers regulating the network to mainframes at the Pentagon, air force, and army installations and research centers. "It was like going through an electronic road map, trying to get somewhere, without knowing where," he says. Pat talks in vague terms about downloading information from the computers he accessed, but is evasive about what he did with it. He says that some of it was sold, although what he sold and to whom and for how much remains unclear.

It is more likely that selling the data was of secondary concern; he was merely "fascinated" by the intricacies of the new technology. "This is the information age," he says. "Knowing about computers made me feel more intelligent. Very few people had access to them, and even fewer understood them."

At about the time that he was first hacking into ARPANET, a new program called Super Zap appeared which could bypass copy protection[2] on IBM PC-type software. Pat thought that its function mirrored his own activities, so he decided to call himself Captain Zap.

▪ ▪ ▪

By 1980 Captain Zap was becoming more and more adventurous. He had learned the dial-ups for the White House computer network, which he accessed regularly over the next year, and had also dialed directly into the Pentagon. He was going for prestige hacks.

He used to download information from the White House, reams and reams of computer paper, and bring it home to his wife. "Look what I've found!" he would shout, but she was less interested in what he had found than in the fact he could get caught. And whatever it was that he had discovered, he himself can't remember. "There was all sorts of bullshit," he says. Some of it was encrypted, some not, but none of it seems to have been very memorable.

There was another use for the White House phone number, however. He would sometimes call the central operator number—a voice number, not a dial-up—and in his best bureaucratic style say something like, "This is Mr. McNamara, admin counsel. I need a secure line to the American embassy in Germany." He swears that the operators would patch him through, and that once connected to the American embassy—on a secure line, from the White House—he could request another secure line to whatever local number he wanted to call. He claims that Mr. McNamara was just a name that he had made up, and that whether or not there was such a person, the operators never turned him down.

Captain Zap was a believer in "knowing the lingo"—the lingo being the language necessary, whether computer-speak, telco-speak, or even bureaucratese—to obtain information or to persuade people to help you. This practice, known as social engineering, is a by-product of hacking, simply getting information from someone by pretending to be someone else.

It works like this. Say you need the dial-up for a particular computer. You call the voice number of the target company and ask to speak to the computer operator. When you get through, you put on your best telco repairman's accent and say, "We're doing a few repairs on the computer lines in your area. Have you been having trouble with your terminal?" The answer is invariably yes. "Yeah, I thought so," you say. "Look, we need to check the line. Can you start up your system and run me through it? What's your dial-up?" And so on. In most cases the operator will volunteer not only the dial-up, but the log-in and password as well.

Social engineering takes a lot of the hassle out of hacking, and for adolescent hackers it has an additional attraction: it gives them a chance to put one over on an adult. Deceiving grown-ups has always been a youthful pastime; social engineering demands it.

While Captain Zap was hacking the White House and the Pentagon, he was also putting his skills to a more profitable use—theft. He and his friend, Doctor Diode, had learned how to crack the sales and invoicing systems of a number of large computer companies and equipment wholesalers. The system they had worked out was surprisingly simple. First they would create dummy corporations by hacking into a credit agency, listing their company on the register, and giving it a "triple-A" credit rating—the highest.[3] Then they would hack into a supplier's computer and create a real-paper trail: they would connect themselves to the sales department and cut an order, jump to the accounts department and "pay" the invoice, then skip over to shipping and write out a delivery manifest. The delivery address would be a mail drop—the address of an answering service, say, which would also receive all documentation from the target company. From the supplier's point of view the paper trail was complete: they had an order, a paid invoice, and a delivery manifest. The paperwork made sense. If they checked with the credit agency, they would find that the buyer had a triple-A credit rating. Of course the company didn't actually have the money to cover the equipment it had just delivered, but that wouldn't be discovered until they tried to balance their books.

The supplies that Captain Zap and his friend ordered included portable terminals, a Hewlett-Packard computer, peripherals, cameras, walkie-talkies, and other supplies. According to the authorities, the total amount of goods stolen in the scam amounted to over $500,000.

Pat insists that hacking into the supplier's computers was simple: "There was no security," he says. Using guesswork and knowledge of the default settings, they could make their way past the log-in and password prompts. For more recalcitrant computers they rigged up an adapted "war-dialing" system that would keep pounding at the door with one ID and password combination after the other until they got in. Even if a computer operator has assiduously removed default codes, there are still common combinations that people use over and over. There are said to be just a few of these combinations—such as name and surname, or company name and department—that, in a large system, someone will use. Knowing the names of employees and where they work greatly speeds up the process of hacking. People pick simple combinations for an obvious reason: they need to remember them. Choosing something completely off-the-wall increases the chance of forgetting the ID or password just as the prompt is flashing. And writing them down defeats the object.

The surveillance of Captain Zap began in May 1981. Pat knew he was being watched because he noticed a van with two men in it outside his apartment. By then his unorthodox buying spree had gone on for almost two years. Though each "order" was relatively small, the companies that had been robbed had been able to isolate the accounts that appeared to be paid but for which there was no corresponding check. Then they called the police.

There was a trail of connections the authorities could follow, which led from the companies that had sold the goods to the mail drops, and from there to Pat and the others he worked with. The bust came at ten A.M. on July 2, 1981. Agents from the FBI accompanied by state police from the White Collar Crime Unit, Bell Security representatives and two military policemen raided Pat's parents' home. The maid answered the door.

He lived in one of the wealthiest suburbs of Philadelphia; the homes are substantial, the residents well established. Pat's father owned and managed one of the largest and oldest shipping companies on the East Coast. When the newspapers carried the story, Pat and his friends would be castigated as "children of privilege."

The FBI presented Pat's mother with a thirty-seven-page document. "We have a search warrant," they said.

"For what?"

"For Pat. He's accused of computer fraud."

His mother looked aghast. "He couldn't pass mathematics. You're telling me he's a computer genius?"

The agents proceeded to tear apart Pat's room. They packed up all the computers, modems, and communications gear they could find. They went through the files, stuffing them in boxes. When Pat came home that night, he found that all of his equipment had been taken away.

Pat was indicted on September 21 in both Harrisburg, Pennsylvania, and Washington, D.C., for a number of offenses, including theft of equipment—the $500,000 worth of computers and supplies—and theft of telephone services. He was twenty-four years old at the time. In 1981 there was no comprehensive computer-fraud law, so Pat was "shoehorned"—his expression—into the existing criminal statutes.

There are advantages to being a child of privilege. Though Pat's colleagues were also arrested (there were five arrests in total, including Pat and Doctor Diode) and some turned state's evidence in exchange for a light sentence, Pat's father's money bought him the services of two of Philadelphia's biggest law firms. After looking at the evidence, one of the lawyers turned to Pat and said, "No jury will ever understand what you did and no jury will ever convict you for ripping off the phone company."

The lawyer's words were not put to the test. The charges against Pat were plea-bargained down to a $1,000 fine and two and a half years' "phone probation"—meaning that Pat had to report to his probation officer by calling in. He still finds it ironic that a convicted phreaker and hacker was required to report in by telephone.

In the wake of the Captain Zap case the American authorities quickly woke up to the threat of computer hacking. By the mid-1980s almost every state had criminalized "theft by browsing"—that is, hacking into computers to see what's there. The first federal law on computer crime, the Computer Fraud and Abuse Act, was passed in 1986.

The contrast between the leniency shown Captain Zap in the U.S. courts for what was, in the end, hacking for profit, and the judgment given to Nick Whiteley in England for schoolboyish pranks nine years later is illustrative of the changes in the authorities' perception of hacking over the decade. In 1981, when Captain Zap was arrested, his lawyer was probably correct in assuming that no jury would have understood the prosecution's case. In 1990, however, Nick was almost certainly right in saying the courts were determined to throw the book at him.

Over the course of a decade, both the authorities' awareness of hacking and the technological underground that committed this crime had grown. Hacking—though probably only dimly understood by most of the public—had become a fashionable threat, explained in long, analytical newspaper articles and described in detail by stylish magazines. Computer security experts (and some hackers) were invited onto TV talk shows to paint the threats to computer security in lurid terms. The sense of impending technological apocalypse was heightened by a number of well-publicized hacking cases during the 1980s, of which the best known was probably the Kevin Mitnick affair.

Mitnick was said to be obsessed with computers. In 1979 he and a friend had successfully hacked into the NORAD (North American Air Defense command) mainframe in Colorado Springs. Mitnick has since said that they didn't tamper with anything, but simply entered the system, looked around, and got out.

He first ran afoul of the law in 1981, when he and three friends were arrested for stealing technical manuals from the Pacific Telephone Company: he was convicted and served six months. In 1983 he was caught by the University of Southern California while trying to hack one of their computers. Later, he was accused of breaking into a TRW computer (the TRW Credit Information Corporation holds data on 80 million Americans nationwide). In 1987 he was arrested for stealing software from a southern California company and sentenced to thirty-six months' probation.

Mitnick belonged to a group of Los Angeles–area hackers called the Roscoe Gang. He and the gang allegedly used PCs to harass their victims, break into Defense Department computers, and sabotage businesses. He was also accused of breaking into a National Security Agency computer and stealing important information. More seriously, he was charged with defrauding the computer company Digital Equipment Corporation (DEC) and the long-distance phone company MCI, and with transporting proprietary software across state lines. The software was alleged to be a copy of DEC's Security Software System, which made it possible for Mitnick to break into DEC's computers and cause $4 million worth of damage.

Mitnick was again arrested in late 1988. He was refused bail by several federal judges, who said there would be no way to protect society if he were freed. He was also denied access to a phone while in jail, for fear that he may have preprogrammed a computer to remotely trigger off damaging programs. In 1989 he was sentenced to two years in prison.

The decision to deny Mitnick access to a phone was greeted with alarm by an increasingly nervous hacker community. "We must rise to defend those endangered by the hacker witch-hunts," wrote an unnamed contributor to *2600*, the hacker journal. The U.S. Attorney's office in Chicago, then in the midst of its own hacker case, responded by saying it intended to prosecute "aggressively."

The Chicago case, though less publicized than the Mitnick

affair, was the first test of the federal Computer Fraud and Abuse Act. In 1987 local law enforcement agencies began watching a sixteen-year-old hacker and high school dropout named Herbert Zinn, Jr., who used the handle Shadow Hawk. The law enforcement officials spent two months investigating Zinn, auditing his calls and monitoring his activities on computers.

He was subsequently accused of using a PC to hack into a Bell Laboratories computer in New York, an AT&T computer in North Carolina, another AT&T computer at Robbins Air Force Base in Georgia, an IBM facility in New York, and other computers belonging to the Illinois Bell Telephone Company. He was also accused of copying various documents, including what were called highly sensitive programs relating to the U.S. Missile Command.

Shadow Hawk was arrested in a raid involving the FBI, AT&T security representatives, and the Chicago police. He was eventually sentenced to nine months in prison and fined $10,000.

The Mitnick and Shadow Hawk cases fueled the growing concern among U.S. law enforcement agencies about hacking. By the end of the decade, the Secret Service—which is now charged with investigating computer crime, a responsibility partly, and not entirely amicably, shared with the FBI—was said to have established a unit for monitoring pirate bulletin boards. A number of state and local police forces had organized their own computer crime sections, while separate investigations of the underground were mounted by U.S. Attorneys' offices and local prosecutors. By the beginning of the 1990s, American law enforcement agencies had begun paying extraordinary attention to computer crime.

Across the Atlantic, away from the prying eyes of the American authorities, the biggest international gathering of hackers ever organized took place in Amsterdam in early August 1989.

The assembly was held in the seedy confines of the Paradiso, a former church that had been turned into a one-thousand-seat theater. The Paradiso was the home of Amsterdam's alternative culture; it specialized in musical events, underground exhibits, and drug parties. The Galactic Hacker Party—or, more grandly, the International Conference on the Alternative Use of Technology—brought together some 400 to 450 hackers, hangers-on, journalists, and, inevitably, undercover cops, to swap stories, refine techniques, gather information, or simply enjoy themselves.

The conference took place on all three floors of the Paradiso. On the top floor, above what had been the nave of the church, participants were provided with computers to play with. (Their popularity decreased after one wag programmed them to flash, THIS MACHINE IS BEING MONITORED BY THE DUTCH POLICE, when they were turned on.) The ground floor, the theater itself, was reserved for speakers and demonstrations; across the back of the stage drooped a white banner emblazoned with the words GALACTIC HACKER PARTY. The crypts in the basement of the Paradiso were reserved for partying.

At ten A.M. on Tuesday, August 2nd, the opening day, a large monitor displayed a computer-generated image of a head of a hacker. "Keep on hacking," urged the head in an American accent, as the multinational gathering milled about in the disorganized way of a crowd that clearly lacked a common language. Then, a bearded, bespectacled, balding figure shuffled unheralded onto the stage. He was the keynote speaker, the man who, more than anyone, had given rise to the whole hacking phenomenon.

At forty-six, Captain Crunch looked strangely out of place among the younger hackers. It had been eighteen years since he had first come to symbolize the new technological underground, ten years since he had last been jailed for a second time for phone phreaking. And here he was in Amsterdam, on a month's vacation in Europe, still spreading the word.

He began with a rambling discourse in English about the phone system in the former Soviet Union, information gleaned on an earlier visit there. Their phone network, the Captain reported, was old, of mixed origin, and, he suspected, had been continuously monitored by the KGB. He then began the slow process of demonstrating the newly established Sov-Am Teleport Union, a telephone link that connected San Francisco to Moscow via satellite. Using a phone on the stage the Captain first dialed San Francisco, where he linked to the Teleport, and then jumped via satellite to Moscow. Unusually for the Captain, he had a purpose to his call. He dialed a number in Moscow, where a group of ten hackers were waiting to address the conference about the underground in Russia.

The Russians then joined a multilingual babble of hackers on the line from a number of other countries, including Germany, France, Kenya, New Zealand, and the U.S. The Captain, reveling in his role as prophet for the whole movement, fielded calls about technology and the ethics of hacking—one caller wanted to know if it would be right to hack into South African computers at the behest of the African National Congress—and then related his own phreaking experiences.

The Captain was in Amsterdam representing what has been called the second generation of hackers. The kids he was talking to, the visitors to the Galactic Hacker Party, were dubbed the fourth generation. Though they had been separated by more than a decade in time and by thousands of miles in geography, the Hacker Party was their meeting place.

The concept of hacker generations was first suggested by Steven Levy, the man who also outlined the philosophy of "hacker ethics." In his book *Hackers,* he argued that the first generation of hackers was a group of students at MIT in the 1960s who had access to big, expensive mainframes; worked together to produce useful, new software; and, in doing so, bent the rules of the university. More than anything, they believed in freedom of information and unfettered access to technology. They abhorred security to the extent that they made sure they could pick every lock in the building they worked in.

The second generation of hackers, according to Levy, were people like Captain Crunch and Steve Wozniak, as well as the other members of the Bay Area's Personal Computer Company and its successor, the Homebrew Computer Club. These were the people who intuitively believed that the way to drive technology forward was to make the specifications for their machines freely available, a concept known as open architecture. They were hardware hackers, and their achievement can now be seen everywhere in the generality of the ubiquitous PC standard.

Each decade has brought a different twist of geography and motivation to the various generations of hackers: the 1960s hackers, the first generation, were based on the East Coast, developing software; the second-generation, 1970s hackers were on the West Coast, developing hardware.

The next generation, the third, was based both in North America and Europe. These were the kids who had inherited the gift of the personal computer and were copying and selling the first computer games. Their motivation was often a fast buck, and their instincts entirely commercial.

The Captain's audience, the fourth generation, had inherited a world in which technology was rapidly converging around the new standard-bearer, the IBM PC. This new generation shared the same obsessions as their predecessors, but now that they had everything that technology could offer, they hacked merely for the sake of hacking. Hacking had become an end in itself.

For many of the fourth generation, technology was merely a relief from boredom and monotony. Hacking was a pastime that varied the routine of school or university, or a dead-end job. To become proficient, they would typically devote most of their waking hours—80 to 100 hours a week was not uncommon, more time than most people give to their jobs—to working on PCs and combing the international information networks. Hackers, for the most part, are not those with rich and rewarding careers or personal lives.

Of course, hacking is also a form of rebellion—against parents, schools, authority, the state, against adults and adult regulations in general. The rebellion is often pointless and unfocused, often simply for the sake of defying the system. Ultimately there may be no point at all; it has simply become a gesture to ward off boredom or, perhaps, the banality of ordinary life in a structured society.

The higher principles of hackers were summed up in a draft declaration prepared by the Galactic Hacker Party's organizers and circulated among delegates for their signatures. "The free and unfettered flow of information is an essential part of our fundamental liberties, and shall be upheld in all circumstances," the document proclaimed. "Computer technology shall not be used by government and corporate bodies to control and oppress the people."

The language echoed the beliefs of the second generation of hackers. But the conversation among the kids in the crypt and in the halls belied the rhetoric of the organizers. For Lee Felsenstein, an American visitor, it was a disturbing experience. Lee was a confirmed second-generation hacker, one of the original founders of the Homebrew Computer Club. He remained a staunch believer in freedom of speech and an avid supporter of individual rights. But he felt that the fourth-generation hackers were "underage and underdeveloped"; they displayed "negative social attitudes." Hacking, he said, had degenerated from being a collective mission of exploration into an orgy of self-indulgence.

For Lee, evidence of degeneracy included the hackers who boasted about breaking into American computers to steal military information and then selling it to the KGB. He was also disheartened to learn about the exploits of the VAXbusters, a German group that had broken into NASA and over a hundred other computers worldwide by exploiting a loophole in the operating system of Digital Equipment Corporation's VAX computers. The VAX, very powerful but small machines, are widely used in science laboratories, universities, and military installations.

More to the point, from Lee's point of view, the fourth generation of hackers was becoming involved in a new facet of computer programming, one that threatened everything he believed in. Far from increasing access and creating freedom for computer users, this new development could only cause the door to be slammed shut on access, for freedom to be replaced by fortresslike security. During the Galactic Party, a number of hackers had been demonstrating new programs called computer viruses.

Lee left Amsterdam muttering about Babylon and ancient Rome. John Draper, alias Captain Crunch, was less bothered. He spent the remainder of his vacation traveling around Germany, taking his hacking road show to eighteen different cities.

There was, in fact, nothing new about computer viruses except their existence. Viruses had been foreseen in science fiction; the earliest use of the term has been traced to a series of short stories written in the 1970s by David Gerrold. In 1972 Gerrold employed the virus theme for a sci-fi potboiler called *When HARLIE Was One.* HARLIE was an acronym for Human Analogue Robot Life Input Equivalents computer, which meant simply that the fictional creation could duplicate every function of the human brain—a sort of mechanical equivalent of Dr. Frankenstein's monster. This robot could also dial up other computers by telephone and reprogram them or modify data. In so doing, HARLIE was emulating a computer program called simply Virus, which dialed up telephone numbers at random. When it found another computer at the end of the line, it loaded a copy of itself onto the new machine, which started dialing other computers to transfer copies of the program, and so on. Soon hundreds of computers were tied up randomly calling numbers.

The Virus program was fictional, of course, and simply part of Gerrold's convoluted plot, but the concept of a computer program reproducing itself had been foreseen as early as 1948. In that year John van Neumann, a Hungarian-born mathematician and computer pioneer who had designed one of the world's first computers, quaintly called Maniac, began theoretical work on what was then thought of as electronically created artificial life, which he termed automata. He predicted that the reproduction process for such automata would be fairly simple.

Later, in the 1960s, before the advent of computer games, university engineering students sometimes amused themselves by seeing who could write the shortest program that could reproduce an exact copy of itself. These were called self-replicating programs, but van Neumann would have recognized them as versions of his concept of electronic automata.

The first attempts to use self-replicating programs for something useful were made at Xerox's Palo Alto Research Center in the late seventies. Two researchers, John Shoch and Jon Hupp, devised what they called a worm program to help with the management of the center's computer network, which linked over one hundred medium-sized machines. They envisaged the program working automatically, archiving old files, making backup copies of current files, and running routine diagnostic checks; they hoped that it would be able to perform the endless housekeeping tasks that the researchers at Palo Alto were too busy to keep up with. They named the new program a worm, the two later said, in honor of their inspiration—another work of science fiction by the English writer John Brunner called *The Shockwave Rider,* published in 1975. Brunner's book heralded the existence of a computer program, which he called a "tapeworm," that reproduced itself endlessly and couldn't be killed.

Something very similar happened to Shoch and Hupp. Their worm program was expected to sit quietly on one computer during the day, then emerge at night to roam the computers in the research center, carrying out housekeeping chores.[4] Because it worked only at night, skeptical colleagues nicknamed it the vampire program.

In their first test, Shoch and Hupp left the worm program "exercising" on half a dozen designated machines in the lab. It wasn't programmed to do anything; it was just expected to travel to the designated machines and leave copies of itself. The next morning, though, when the two arrived back at their office, they found that the worm had escaped and had rampaged through all the hundred-plus networked computers in the center. More disturbing, it had reproduced so quickly that it had brought every machine to a halt, seemingly strangling them by taking up all available space in the computers' memory.

Worse, when they attempted to restart one of the computers, the worm was reactivated and proceeded to strangle the machine again. To destroy the worm, they had to write another program—a killer program. Fortunately, unlike Brunner's tapeworm, their program was not indestructible, but Shoch and Hupp later called its behavior "rather puzzling," and simply abandoned the experiment, leaving unsolved the problem of "controlling [its] growth while maintaining stable behavior."

In the early 1980s a number of computer science students succeeded in writing self-replicating programs for the new Apple II computers. Joe Dellinger, a student at Texas A&M University at the time, became intrigued by the idea that computer programs could become modified when copied. He had no trouble writing a self-replicating program for the Apple II, even though he didn't consider himself a particularly clever programmer. His biggest problem was in writing a program that wouldn't cause damage; he was surprised at how quickly the program could propagate, moving rapidly from computer to computer by diskette, eventually traveling to machines outside the A&M campus.

Though Dellinger was intrigued by the notion that programs change as they replicate and travel from computer to computer, there is nothing metaphysical about it. It is simply a computer error. The longer and more complex a program is, the more likely that a line of instruction, a command within the program, will be skipped or altered in the copying process. These tiny modifications rarely cause problems, but the potential for error is there.

What is more important is that Dellinger discovered that any self-replicating program, no matter how benign, carried with it the potential for damage, just as a fly buzzing about a room carries the possibility of disease. Unlike the software sold by commercial houses, self-replicating programs are untested, untried and generally unstable. The changes created when these programs transfer themselves from machine to machine can cause them to be damaging, and their very presence on a computer is inherently risky.

Equally intriguing is the speed at which they propagate. In an environment like a university campus, where anyone has access to any computer and programs are routinely carried from machine to machine on diskette, they can multiply exponentially. They are, after all, designed to replicate, so that one copy quickly becomes two, two become four, four become eight, and so on. Dellinger found that once let loose, the program's spread was almost unstoppable.

It was another four years, however, before self-replicating programs became "viruses." In 1983 and 1984 a graduate student at the University of Southern California named Fred Cohen was experimenting with these programs and, at the suggestion of his adviser, decided to call them computer viruses. It was a catchier name, and also became the title of his 1985 doctoral thesis, in which he offered an explanation of viruses. A virus, he wrote, is "a program that can infect other programs by modifying them to include a slightly altered copy of itself." Further, "every program that gets infected can also act as a virus and thus the infection grows." Cohen also indicated that viruses presented a threat to computer security and could modify or damage data.

The thesis did not break any new ground in terms of computer science: in essence, Cohen took the known characteristics of self-replicating programs and renamed them viruses. The term itself suggests that the programs are created in some kind of wild electronic biosphere and are capable of spreading incurable diseases from computer to computer—the high-tech equivalent of the biological viruses to which they are often compared. The sensationalistic use of the word would later prove to be fortuitous to computer security experts and have an irresistible appeal to rogue computer programmers. Though the word was perhaps chosen innocently, the metaphor was not entirely apt. Computer viruses, like biological viruses, are spread unknowingly, and they can mutate while spreading, but they are not created in the same way. Biological viruses are carried by small, natural organisms, over which man has little control; computer viruses, however, are simply programs—and computer programs are written by people.

Cohen's work quickly attracted attention, not least from a German computer system engineer named Ralf Burger. At the time, Burger was twenty-six and living in a small town near the Dutch-German border, not far from the city of Bremen. Burger became fascinated by the concept of viruses, and in July 1986 he had succeeded in creating his own, which he called Virdem. It was, to all intents and purposes, a simple self-replicating program, but with a small twist. For Burger, the "primary function of the virus is to preserve its ability to reproduce." After being loaded onto a computer, Virdem was programmed to hunt down and infect other files in the machine. When there were no more files to infect, the virus would begin "a randomly-controlled gradual destruction of all files."

In December 1986 Burger decided to attend the annual convention of the Chaos Computer Club in nearby Hamburg. The club had been founded in 1981 by Herwart Holland-Moritz—who prefers to be known as Wau Holland—and is a registered nonprofit organization. Holland, who was a thirty-two-year-old computer programmer at the time, set up the club as a hobby; despite the sinister implications of the name, it was chosen only because "there is a lot of chaos in the application of computers." According to the club's constitution, it is dedicated to freedom of information.

Since its foundation the club has proven itself adept at organizing media events, and this ability together with the connotations of its name have given the group a high profile. Like many clubs, Chaos unites people with a wide range of interests: there are members who see computers as a weapon for sociological change, others who simply want to play computer games, those who want to know how computer systems work, and those concerned with making a fast buck, legally or illegally. The Chaos members refer to themselves as data travelers, rather than hackers, but they all share the same obsession with computers and all vaguely subscribe to a vague notion of "hacker ethics." Their own unique understanding of that term is that they have a mission to test, or penetrate, the security of computer systems. Early Chaos Clubbers were allied with the VAXbusters, the group that sought to break through the security of VAX computers around the world. The club's first brush with notoriety, though, occurred in 1984, when they broke into Btx, or Bildschirmtext, an on-line text and information service patterned after Britain's Prestel. In 1986 they captured the media's attention again when, after the meltdown of the Soviet nuclear reactor in Chernobyl, they provided alternative information on contamination levels by hacking into government computers and releasing the data that they found. Their findings were sufficiently at odds with official reassurances to make them the darlings of Germany's Green movement.

The annual conferences of the Chaos Club were held in Hamburg, always in December. They attracted the cream of the German hacker community, as well as observers from throughout Europe and elsewhere; were always well covered by the media; and, without a doubt, were carefully watched by the local police. Each conference was given a theme that was designed to excite media attention, and in 1986 the theme was computer viruses.

Even though little was known about viruses at the time, the conference organizers hoped piously that the publicity given to the subject would help dispel myths. The organizers also declared: "The problem isn't computer viruses, but the dependence on technology," and they blamed the writing of viruses on "bad social condition(s) for programmers."

The star performer at the conference was Ralf Burger, simply because he had actually written a virus, which in those days was something of a feat. To prove that his virus, Virdem, would work, Burger handed out copies to some two or three hundred interested delegates. He said it would "give users a chance to work with computer viruses."

• • •

Technically, any virus is little more than a self-replicating program with a sting in its tail. This sting, usually known as the payload, is what the virus actually does to the computer, which is often nothing at all—apart from replicating, or performing a harmless joke, such as making a ball bounce around the screen or instructing the computer to play a tune. At another level, however, the payload can cause the destruction of data.

Computer viruses are carried from computer to computer by diskette or, in networked computers, by the wires that link them. They can also be transmitted on telephone lines, through modems, like ordinary computer programs. Viruses do not fly through the air and cannot jump from computer to computer without being carried by a physical medium. Moreover, all viruses are man-written: they aren't natural, or caused spontaneously by computer technology. The only "artificial life" inherent in a virus is its tendency to modify itself as it is copied, but that's possible with any computer program.

This explanation may seem simple to the point of absurdity, but when viruses first began to garner mentions in the press, and breathless reporters began to write lurid stories about "technological viruses," their properties were exaggerated into the realm of science fiction. Viruses made a good story—even when there was no evidence that they had actually damaged anything.

In 1986, when Burger made his presentation to the Chaos conference, there were almost no viruses in existence. Few people in the computer industry had ever seen one, despite increasing interest in the subject from security experts, who were touting them as the next big threat to computer systems. The simple fact was that Burger's Virdem was probably the only virus that most of them had even heard about.

The properties of viruses and the damage that they could cause were widely known, however. Even the nightmare scenario had been posited: that a plague of viruses would move swiftly through the computers of the world, wiping out data and devastating corporations, government agencies, police forces, financial institutions, the military, and, eventually, the structure of modern society itself. By 1986, however, actual attacks by viruses on computer systems had yet to occur.

The next year, 1987, Burger's book about computer viruses, *Das Grosse-computervirenbuch,* was published by Data Becker GmbH of Dusseldorf.[5] In the book Burger warned: "Traveling at what seems the speed of moving electrons, comical, sometimes destructive programs known as viruses have been spreading through the international computer community like an uncontrollable plague." There was in fact no hard evidence for this statement, and later in the book, contradicting the apocalyptic tone of the first section, Burger admitted: "So far it has been impossible to find proof of a virus attack."

Later that year, two new viruses appeared. The first was created by the Greek computer magazine *Pixel,* which had hired a local computer wizard named Nick Nassufis to write one. The magazine published the virus as a list of BASIC-language instructions in the April 1987 issue. Readers who keyed in the instructions found themselves with a fully functioning virus on their computers. It didn't do much apart from replicate, but from time to time it would display a poorly written English language message on the computer screen: PROGRAM SICK ERROR:–CALL DOCTOR OR BUY PIXEL FOR CURE DESCRIPTION. Three months later Pixel published instructions for wiping it out.

Then, as Burger was preparing the second edition of his book, he received a copy of a virus found in Vienna by a local journalist. This virus, now known as Vienna, was said to have appeared at a local university in December 1987. Its writer is unknown, as are the writers of most viruses.

Burger described Vienna as "extremely clever." But by the standards of virus writing today, it wasn't, though it was certainly the most advanced virus in existence at the time. Vienna is known as a file virus because it attaches itself to what are known in the computer industry somewhat tediously as executable files (i.e., the software, such as a word-processing program, that actually enables a computer to do something useful). When an infected program is loaded onto a computer from a diskette (or transferred through a network), Vienna comes with it and slips itself into the computer's memory. It then looks for other executable files to infect, and after infecting seven it damages the eighth, simply by overwriting itself onto the program code.

Although the payload of the Vienna virus was destructive—the eighth program that was damaged was irreparable—by present-day standards it wasn't particularly malicious. More dangerous was Burger's decision to publish a reconstruction of the Vienna program code in the second edition of his book. It became the recipe for writing viruses.

Programmers with access to the code could quite easily adapt it for their own purposes—by altering the payload, for instance. That's what eventually happened with Vienna.[6] Though Burger had deliberately altered his reconstruction to make it unworkable, programmers had little trouble finding their way around the alterations. Variants of Vienna have been found all over the world: in Hungary, a Vienna clone carries a sales message that translates roughly as POLIMER TAPE CASSETTES ARE THE BEST. GO FOR THEM. A Russian version was adapted to destroy the computer's hard disk, the internal memory and storage area for programs, after infecting sixty-four files. A Polish variant displays the message MERRY CHRISTMAS on infected computers between December 19th and 31st. A version from Portugal carries out the standard overwriting of the eighth program, but also displays the word AIDS. In the US a group of unknown American virus writers used Vienna as the basis for a series of viruses called Violator, all intentionally damaging to computer systems.

It is ironic that a book written to warn about the dangers of viruses should be the medium for distributing the recipe for writing them. But even though no one had yet documented a proven virus attack on a computer system anywhere in the world, and the predicted plague of computer viruses had not yet materialized, the potential threat of viruses was being aggressively hyped by computer engineers like Burger and by a small group of computer security consultants in America—and many people appeared remarkably eager to believe them. In what was probably the first press report of viruses, in February 1987, the editor of the international computer trade journal *Computers & Security* wrote, "Computer viruses can be deadly. . . . Last year a continuous-process industry's computer crashed causing hundreds of thousands of dollars' damage. A *post mortem* revealed that it had been infected with a computer virus. Another nationwide organization's computer system crashed twice in less than a year. The cause of each crash was a computer virus. . . . A computer virus can cause an epidemic which today we are unable to combat."

It has never been possible to trace either the "continuous-process" corporation or the "nationwide organization" whose computers had been so badly damaged by viruses. Like so many aspects of computer viruses, investigation only reveals myth and legend, rarely fact. But myth is self-perpetuating, and prophecies are often self-fulfilling.

4
■
VIRUSES, TROJANS, WORMS, AND BOMBS

The first documented computer virus attack was recorded on October 22, 1987, at the University of Delaware, in Newark, Delaware. According to a spokesperson for the Academic Computer Center at the university, the virus infected "several hundred disks, rendering 1 percent of them unusable, and destroying at least one student's thesis." Later a news report appeared in *The New York Times* that claimed, "Buried within the code of the virus . . . was an apparent ransom demand. Computer users were asked to send $2,000 to an address in Pakistan to obtain an immunity program." But that wasn't quite true. Researchers using specialized software were later able to call up the actual operating program of the virus onto a computer screen. Within the mass of instructions that controlled the bug, they found the following message:

WELCOME TO THE DUNGEON
© 1986 BASIT & AMJAD (PVT) LTD.
BRAIN COMPUTER SERVICES
730 NIZAB BLOCK ALLAMA IQBAL TOWN
LAHORE–PAKISTAN
PHONE: 430791, 443248, 280530.
BEWARE OF THIS VIRUS . . .
CONTACT US FOR VACCINATION . . .

There was no ransom demand.

Computer researchers now know the virus as Brain, though at the time it didn't have a name, and it was later discovered to have been programmed only to infect the first sector on a diskette. Diskettes are divided into sectors invisible to the naked eye, each holding 512 bytes (or characters) of information, equivalent to about half a page of typewritten material. The first sector on a diskette is known as the boot sector, and its function is something like that of the starter motor on a car: it kicks the machine into operation (hence the expression "booting up," or starting up, a computer). When a computer is switched on, the machine bursts into life and carries out some simple self-diagnostic tests. If no fault is found, the machine checks to see if there is a diskette in the disk drive. The disk drive, acting like a record player with the diskette as its record, begins to rotate if a diskette is in place, and the boot sector of the diskette directs the computer to the three actual start-up programs that make the computer operational.

The Brain virus was designed to hide in the boot sector waiting for the computer to start up from the diskette so that it can load itself into the computer's memory, as if it were a legitimate start-up program. But at around 2,750 bytes long, it is much too big to fit entirely within the boot sector, and instead does two things: it places its first 512 bytes in the boot sector and then stores the rest of its code, together with the original boot-sector data, in six other sectors on the diskette. When the computer starts up, the head of the virus jumps into memory, then calls up its tail and the original boot sector.

Brain is one of the most innocent viruses imaginable, though that wasn't known at the time. The University of Delaware spent a full week and considerable manpower cleaning out its computer system and destroying infected diskettes, only to find that the virus's payload is simply the tagging of infected diskettes with the label "Brain." A label is the name a user can give to a diskette, and is of no real importance. Most users don't even bother to label their diskettes, and if a virus suddenly names it for them, they are unlikely to notice or care.

However, like all viruses, Brain can cause unintended damage. If a diskette is almost full, it is possible for some sectors to be accidentally overwritten while the virus is attaching its tail, thereby wiping out all the data contained there. Also, copying can render the virus unstable, and could unintentionally overwrite systems areas (the sectors on diskettes that enable their use by computers), thus rendering them useless.

Paramount to the viability of a computer virus is an effective infection strategy. Brain was viable because it didn't do anything deliberately dangerous or even very obvious, so it wasn't likely to get noticed. Therefore, when it climbed into the computer memory, it could stay there until the computer was switched off, targeting any other diskettes that were introduced into the computer during that session.

Brain also contained a special counter, which permitted it to infect a new diskette only after the computer operator had accessed it thirty-one times. Thereafter, it infected at every fourth use. Yet another, particularly ingenious, feature was its ability to evade detection. Normally the boot sector, where the virus hides, can be read by special programs known as disk editors. But if someone tried to read the boot sector to look for it, Brain redirected them to the place where the original boot sector had been stored, so that everything looked normal. This feature, which now takes other forms, has become known as *stealth*, after the Stealth bomber that was designed to evade radar detection.

It wasn't difficult to trace the writers of Brain, since they had conveniently included their names, telephone numbers, and address on their virus. The programmers were nineteen-year-old Basit Farooq Alvi and his twenty-six-year-old brother, Amjad Farooq Alvi. Together they run a computer store in Lahore, Pakistan, called Brain Computer Services. They wrote the virus in 1986, they said, "for fun," and it was in all probability the first virus ever to be disseminated internationally.

Shortly after writing Brain, Basit had given a copy of the virus to an unidentified friend, and it traveled from Pakistan to North America via an unknown route, finally reaching the University of

Delaware. Like Joe Dellinger at A&M, who was surprised at how quickly his self-replicating programs had traveled, Basit and Amjad Alvi were startled that their little virus had emigrated all the way to America in less than a year.

The second documented virus attack occurred only a month later, in November 1987, on computers at Lehigh University in Bethlehem, Pennsylvania. Unlike Brain, the virus at Lehigh was deliberately damaging. It kept a count of the number of files that it infected and, when its counter reached four, it trashed the diskette by overwriting it with "garbage" collected from another part of the computer.

The university's senior computer consultant, Ken van Wyk, realized he had a problem when students began complaining that their diskettes didn't work. At first there was a trickle of bad diskettes, then a flood. Something was zeroing out the diskettes, and Van Wyk guessed that it was probably a virus.

Van Wyk worked for five days to isolate the bug and find a cure. He discovered that, unlike Brain, the Lehigh virus did not infect the boot sector; instead, it hid itself inside one of the three start-up programs that are triggered immediately after the boot had occurred. Like Brain, the virus jumped into memory whenever a computer was started from an infected diskette. Van Wyk also discovered that the antidote was extremely simple: all he needed to do was delete the infected start-up program and replace it with a clean one. The data on the trashed diskettes, however, was irrecoverable. Van Wyk notified colleagues at other colleges that the virus "is not a joke. A large percentage of our disks have been gonged by this virus in the last couple of days."

Later that year the university suffered another attack from a modified version of the same virus. This one trashed a diskette after infecting ten files, as opposed to four. The longer delay made the new version of what was by then known as the Lehigh virus much more insidious in that it infected more diskettes with versions of itself, and therefore propagated more widely, before unleashing its payload. But because the antidote was already known to Van Wyk, the cleanup operation was quick.

The writer of the Lehigh virus was never discovered, though he or she was assumed to be a student at the university. But by one of those concurrences that excite conspiracy theorists, the professor of electrical engineering and computer science at Lehigh when the viruses attacked was Fred Cohen, by then Dr. Cohen, the same student who two years earlier had written the dissertation that had first coined the term *computer virus.*

Early in 1988 two more viruses were discovered, both of them written for the Macintosh, a personal computer produced by Apple, which had become the successor to its historic Apple II. The first became known as MacMag or, sometimes, Peace, and contained the phrase "universal message of peace" signed by Richard Brandow, the publisher of *MacMag Magazine,* a Canadian publication for Macintosh users. It also included a small drawing of the world autographed by the author of the virus, Drew Davidson.

Later it was discovered that the virus had been included on a computer game shown at a meeting of a Macintosh users' group in Montreal. A speaker at the meeting had accidentally copied the virus onto a diskette, and subsequently infected a computer in the offices of Aldus, a Seattle-based software publisher, for whom he was doing some work. The company then unwittingly copied the virus onto what was later described as "several thousand" copies of a program called Freehand, which were distributed to thousands of computer stores. After complaints from consumers, who were quite bewildered at receiving a peace message with their software, the company recalled five thousand copies of the program.

The MacMag virus, though relatively widely distributed, was not malicious. After displaying its message, it removed itself from infected systems. Nevertheless, it was an unwanted extra and served to demonstrate the speed and ease with which self-replicating programs could propagate. When questioned about the morality of deliberately publishing Davidson's virus, Brandow was quoted as saying, "You can't blame Einstein for Hiroshima."

The second Macintosh virus to be reported in 1988 was called

Scores and was much more serious. On April 19, 1988 Electronic Data Systems (EDS) of Dallas, a subsidiary of General Motors, announced that twenty-four of its machines had been infected with a virus that was thought to have been written by a disgruntled ex-employee. The virus had infected the operating system and two standard files of each computer, and then hidden itself inside two more secret files that it had created. Two days after a system has been infected with Scores, the virus begins to spread to the other programs on the computer—in particular, it looks for two specific programs developed by EDS, and when it finds them, it prevents the computer user from saving his data, thereby causing the loss of whatever he was working on.

By early 1988 a small but potentially lucrative computer security industry had begun to specialize in protecting machines from viruses. A number of computer specialists offered their services as security consultants or sold computer software designed to track down and kill viruses. But despite Brain, Lehigh, and the two Macintosh viruses, there was little real evidence of the oft-hyped plague of computer bugs. It was understandable that writers of antiviral software and others in the new security industry would exaggerate the threat; they were like burglar-alarm salesmen in a community without very many burglars. They needed to convince the public that a slew of viruses was gathering, to be unleashed on defenseless computer users in the coming year.

The emotive term *virus* helped their case, as did the willingness of the press to publish dubious statistics and unverified, unsourced stories of virus incidents—particularly the computer magazines, which were then locked in a difficult circulation war and looking for something out of the ordinary to write about. Viruses made good copy, as did nightmarish stories about the effects of a plague. In essence, the burglars hadn't quite hit town yet, but by God they were on the way.

One of the earliest antiviral programs for IBM PC–type computers was the work of a New York–based programmer, Ross

Greenberg. He said that he had seen the impending virus threat coming for years, and had therefore created a program called Flu Shot.

During the summer of 1988 Greenberg was contacted by writer Ralph Roberts, who was researching a book about computer viruses. According to Roberts, Greenberg insisted that he had "about twenty viruses in quarantine." When asked to identify them, Greenberg told the writer, "I don't give the little suckers names." But he did describe his "favorite virus," which he said could randomly transpose two numbers on the screen. "Sounds cute," he reportedly said, "but it could be dangerous if you're using Lotus 1-2-3 [a program used for accounting] to run a multi-million-dollar company."

Roberts's book, *Computer Viruses,* was the first attempt to put the problem into perspective. In it he describes his interviews with the newly formed Computer Virus Industry Association (CVIA), a body representing virus researchers and consultants that had identified "twenty different types that attack IBM PCs and compatibles" and fourteen others that infect other types of computers. The CVIA also listed the names of the top five virus strains by reported incidence as Scores, Brain, SCSI, Lehigh, and Merritt. Yet the Lehigh virus seemed to be confined to Lehigh University; Brain was relatively harmless in that the damage it caused was infrequent and accidental; and the Merritt virus (sometimes called Alameda or Yale) was a benign virus that simply replicated and had been seen at only a few universities and colleges. The SCSI virus attacked only the Amiga, which was primarily a games machine. The most threatening virus on the list was Scores, even though it seemed to be directed against one particular company. Of the twenty-nine other reported viruses, either they had been seen only once or twice or their existence was unconfirmed. (The twenty viruses Greenburg claimed to have in quarantine were not on the list.) And that, according to the CVIA, was about the size of the virus problem in the summer of 1988.

In the following year Greenberg wrote an article for *Byte,* an eminently respectable American computer magazine, in which he described two of the viruses he had in quarantine: his favorite number-transposing virus, now named Screen, and a similar one that he had reported to researchers as dBase, which transposed characters within files. It was called dBase because it targeted records generated by a popular program of the same name.

In 1988 and even early 1989, viruses were exceedingly rare, so there was a growing suspicion about Greenberg's claims to have twenty unnamed bugs in some sort of quarantine. It was thought that Greenberg was exaggerating for effect. Other virus researchers understandably wanted copies of Greenberg's viruses and, in particular, the dBase virus he had described in detail.

Eventually Greenberg produced a copy of dBase. It wasn't quite as he had first described it; it had only been seen on one unidentified site, and only then by Greenberg, but at least its existence could be verified. However, the existence of the other nineteen viruses, including Screen, has yet to be confirmed.

Other early viruses were equally problematic. A virus researcher named Pamela Kane told writer Ralph Roberts about the Sunnyvale Slug, which flashed the message, "Greetings from Sunnyvale. Can you find me?" on infected machines. But it has never been confirmed as a virus, nor seen since Kane first reported it. Then there was the "retro-virus," reported to have been distributed with three popular but unnamed shareware (free, shared software) programs. It was said to have been programmed to detach itself from its infected hosts—a program or file—and then to reinfect them at some future date. It was "like a submarine rigged for silent running . . . the retro-virus waits until the destroyers have stowed their depth charges and gone back to port before returning to sink ships," it was claimed, somewhat colorfully, in the computing journal *Info World.* At the time, the retro-virus was without a doubt the most sinister virus ever reported, but it had only been seen once—by the researcher who reported it.

The CVIA was not averse to creating a few myths of its own. Its chairman, John McAfee, an ebullient and eminently quotable computer expert, was always available to fill in the press on the irresistible spread of viruses. He was a good interviewee, with a store of anecdotes about computer viruses and reports of virus attacks at generally unidentified companies and institutions, and he managed to give the impression that each anecdote could lead to a thousand more, that each incident was representative of a hundred others. In 1988 and 1989, reports about viruses always intimated that what was public knowledge was only the tip of the iceberg—that the problem was much bigger, much wider, and much more pervasive than anyone suspected. But far from being the tip of the iceberg, what had been reported was the whole problem—and even that was seen through a prism. The hype had its effect, however, and sales of antivirus software soared.

Born in science fiction, legitimized by academia and institutionalized by the Computer Virus Industry Association, the computer virus finally came of age on September 26, 1988, when it made the front cover of *Time* magazine.

Time was once derided as the publication "for those that can't think" (its sister publication, *Life,* was said to be "for those who can't read"). It has been accused of publishing middle-brow analyses and overwrought cover stories, and its ability to be out of touch has been so noticeable that in show business the offer of a *Time* cover story is considered a sure sign that the unfortunate star's career is on the wane. Not that anyone has ever turned down a cover story—*Time* is still one of the most influential publications in America, and for better or worse, what it says is often believed.

So, when *Time* headlined its cover about computer viruses "Invasion of the Data Snatchers!" its readers were more than certain that data was indeed being snatched. The magazine detailed an attack on a local newspaper office by the Brain virus, and called it a "deliberate act of sabotage." Brain, *Time* said, was "pernicious," "small but deadly," and "only one of a swarm of infectious programs that have descended on U.S. computer users this year." The magazine also announced, "In the past nine months, an estimated 250,000 computers have been hit with similar contagions."

The article captured perfectly the hyperbole about viruses: Brain was far from pernicious, and it certainly wasn't deadly. There was no swarm of viruses: the number then proven to have infected systems—as opposed to those conjured up in the imaginations of virus researchers—was probably less than ten. And as for the estimate that 250,000 computers had been hit by viruses, it was just that—an estimate. No one at the time had any real idea how many computer sites had been affected.

The *Time* writer also dug deep to unearth the Cookie Monster, which had appeared during the 1970s at a number of American colleges. Inspired by a character on the children's television show *Sesame Street,* this joke program displayed a message on a computer screen: I WANT A COOKIE. If the user typed in "cookie," it would disappear, but, if the message was ignored, it kept reappearing with increasing frequency, becoming ever more insistent. But the Cookie Monster wasn't a virus, even in the broadest definition of the term: it was a joke program introduced by a prankster on a single computer; it had no ability to replicate and it couldn't travel surreptitiously from machine to machine.

Time did recognize that "the alarm caused by these . . . viruses was amplified by two groups with a vested interest in making the threat seem as dramatic as possible"—the computer security specialists and the computer press, "a collection of highly competitive weekly tabloids that have seized on the story like pit bulls, covering every outbreak with breathless copy and splashy headlines." It was an apt description of the exaggerated coverage of the virus phenomenon. But the threat would soon become real.

On the evening of November 2, 1988, a little over five weeks after the *Time* story appeared, events occurred that seemed to fulfill all of the doomsday prophecies. Between 5:00 and 6:00 P.M., eastern standard time, on that Wednesday night, a rogue program was loaded onto the ARPANET system. Three hours later, across the continent at the Rand Corporation in Santa Monica, operators noticed that their computers were running down. Something was taking up computer space and slowing the machines to a crawl. At 10:54 P.M. managers at the University of California at Berkeley discovered what they thought was a hacker trying to break into their systems. As the attempts continued and the attacks increased, they realized to their horror that it wasn't a hacker. It was a program, and it was multiplying.

By that time the same program was attacking the computer at MIT's Artificial Intelligence Laboratory as well as sites at Purdue, Princeton, and Stanford. It was moving across networks, spreading from the ARPANET onto MILNET—the Department of Defense computer network—and then onto Internet, which itself links four hundred local area networks. It spread to the Lawrence Livermore National Laboratory, then to the University of Maryland, then across the country again to the University of California campus at San Diego, and then into the NASA Ames Laboratory, and the Los Alamos National Laboratory in New Mexico. Within a few hours the entire Internet system was under siege. Peter Yee, at Ames, posted the first warning on the network's electronic mail service at 2:28 A.M.: "We are currently under attack from an Internet virus. It has hit UC Berkeley, UC San Diego, Lawrence Livermore, Stanford, and NASA, Ames . . ."

Yee had earlier spotted what seemed to be an entire army of intruders attempting to storm his computer. He counterattacked, killing off some of the invaders. But then came another wave, and another, and he was soon overwhelmed. His powerful computer had started to slow down noticeably, its energy drained by the proliferation of vampire programs that were reproducing uncontrollably and monopolizing its resources.

The same attackers hit the MIT Media Laboratory in Massachusetts. Pascal Chesnais, a scientist who had been working late in the lab, thought he had managed to kill off his mysterious intruders, then went to grab a meal. When he got back, he found that more copies of the invaders were coming in with his electronic mail, so he shut down his network connection for a few hours. Then, at 3:10 A.M., he sent out his own warning: "A virus has been detected at Media Lab. We suspect that the whole Internet is infected by now. The virus is spread by [electronic] mail . . . So mail will not be accepted or delivered."

Just before midnight the rogue program had spread to the Ballistic Research Laboratory, an army weapons center in Maryland. The managers at the lab feared the worst: they could be under attack from hostile agents. Even if that proved not to be the case, they didn't know what the program was doing. It was certainly multiplying, that was clear, but it might also be destroying data. By the next morning the lab had disconnected itself from the network and would remain isolated for nearly a week. It wasn't alone in disconnecting—so many sites attempted to isolate themselves that electronic mail (the usual channel of communication between computer operators) was hampered, creating even more confusion about what was happening. At one point the entire MILNET system severed all mailbridges—the transfer points for electronic mail—to ARPANET.

By midnight the electronic freeways between the sixty thousand or so interconnected computers on Internet and ARPANET were so clogged with traffic that computer specialists were roused from their sleep and summoned to their offices to help fight the attack. Most of them wouldn't get back home until the next night.

At 3:34 A.M. on November 3rd, shortly after Yee had sounded the first alarm, another message about the virus was sent from Harvard. This message was much more helpful: it wasn't just a warning, but offered constructive suggestions and outlined three steps that would stop the virus. The anonymous sender seemed to be well informed about its mechanisms, but because of the chaos on the network, the message wouldn't get through for forty-nine hours.

At first the experts believed that all of the sixty thousand–plus computers on the besieged networks were at risk. But it quickly became apparent that the rogue program was attacking only particular models: Sun Microsystems, Series 3 machines, and VAX computers running variants of the UNIX operating system.[1] On infected machines unusual messages appeared in the files of some utilities, particularly the electronic-mail handling agent, called Sendmail. But what was most apparent was that the rogue program was multiplying at devastating speed, spreading from computer to computer, reinfecting machines over and over. As the reinfections multiplied, the systems became bogged down; then the machines ran out of space and crashed.

On the morning of Thursday, November 3rd, Gene Spafford, a computer science professor at Purdue University, sent the following message to his colleagues: "All of our Vaxen[2] and some of our Suns here were infected with the virus. The virus made repeated copies of itself as it tried to spread, and the load averages on the infected machines skyrocketed. In fact, it got to the point that some of the machines ran out of space, preventing log-in to even see what was going on!" Spafford did manage to capture part of the rogue program, but only the half that controlled its spread. The other half, the main operating system within the program, erased itself as it moved from computer to computer, so as not to leave any evidence. The deviousness of the program lent weight to the theory that it would also be damaging: that the rogue program could somehow have been tampering with systems, altering files, or destroying information.

The rogue program, it was subsequently discovered, moved from computer to computer by exploiting flaws in the Berkeley version of UNIX. The principal flaw was in Sendmail, the program designed to send electronic mail between computers in the interlinked networks. A trapdoor on Sendmail would allow commands (as opposed to actual mail) to be sent from computer to computer. Those commands were the rogue program. Once it had entered one computer through Sendmail, it would collect information about other machines in the system to which it could jump, and then proceed to infect those machines.

In addition to exploiting the Sendmail flaw, the rogue program could try to guess the passwords to jump to target computers. Its password routine used three methods: it tried simple permutations of known users' names, it tried a list of 432 frequently used passwords, and it also tried names from the host computer's own dictionary.[3] If one method didn't work, it would try another and then another until it had managed to prise open the door of the target computer. An early analysis of the program made at four A.M. on the morning after the initial attack described it as "high quality." Some twelve hours after its release, it was estimated that about 6,200 computers on Internet had been infected; the costs, in downtime and personnel, were mounting.

In the meantime, three *ad hoc* response teams, at the University of California at Berkeley, at MIT, and at Purdue, were attempting to put an end to the attack. At five A.M. the Berkeley team sent out the first, interim set of instructions designed to halt the spread. By that time the initial fears that the rogue program might destroy information or systems had proved unfounded. The program, it was discovered, was designed to do nothing more than propagate. It contained no destructive elements apart from its ability to multiply and reinfect to such an extent that it would take over all available space on a target computer.

Later on Thursday the team at Purdue sent out an electronic bulletin that catalogued methods to eradicate the virus. And at Berkeley they isolated the trapdoors it had used and published procedures for closing them.

Once the commotion had died down and computer managers had cleared out the memories on their machines and checked all the software, their thoughts turned to the reasons for the attack. That it was deliberate was certain: the rogue program had been a cleverly engineered code that had exploited little-known flaws in UNIX; it had erased evidence of its intrusions on the computers it had infected; and it was encrypted (written in code) to make it more difficult to tear apart. There was little doubt in anyone's mind that the program was the work of a very clever virus writer, perhaps someone who had a grudge against ARPANET or one of the universities, a computer freak outside of the mainstream attempting to get back at the establishment. But these suppositions were wrong.

Internet's rogue program became a media event. *The New York Times* called the incident "the largest assault ever on the nation's systems." The program itself became known as the Internet Virus or, more accurately, the Internet Worm.[4] At a press conference at MIT the day after the worm was released onto ARPANET, the university's normally reticent computer boffins found themselves facing ten camera crews and twenty-five reporters. The press, the MIT researchers felt, was principally concerned with confirming details of either the collapse of the entire U.S. computer system or the beginning of a new world war, preferably both. One participant had nightmarish visions of a tabloid headline: COMPUTER VIRUS ESCAPES TO HUMANS, 96 KILLED.

The incident received worldwide press coverage, and the extent of the damage was magnified along the way. One of the first estimates—from John McAfee, the personable chairman of CVIA—was that cleaning up the networks and fixing the system's flaws would cost $96 million. Other estimates ran as high as $186 million. These figures were widely repeated, and it wasn't until later that cooler heads began to assess the damage realistically. The initial estimate that about 6,200 machines, some 10 percent of the computers on Internet, had been infected was revised to roughly 2,000, and the cleanup cost has now been calculated at about $1 million, a figure that is based on the assumed value of "downtime," the estimated loss of income while a computer is idle. The actual restitutional cost has been assessed as $150,000; McAfee's exaggerated estimate of $96 million was dismissed.

By the time the real assessments had been made, the identity of the author of the worm had been discovered. He was Robert Morris, Jr., a twenty-three-year-old graduate of Harvard University and, at the time of the incident, a postgraduate student at Cornell. Far from being an embittered hacker or an outsider, he was very much the product of an "insider" family. His father, Robert Morris, Sr., was the chief scientist at the National Computer Security Center, a nationally recognized expert on computer crime, and a veteran of Bell Laboratories. He was, coincidentally, also one of the three designers of a high-tech game called Core Wars, in which two programs engage in battle in a specially reserved area of the computer's memory. The game, which was written in the early 1960s at Bell, used "killer" programs that were designed to wipe out the defenses of the opponent. The curious similarities between Core Wars and the Internet Worm were often cited in press reports.

Morris received an enormous amount of publicity after his identity became known. His motives have been endlessly reviewed and analysed, especially in a recent book, *Cyberpunk,* that was partly devoted to the Internet Worm. The consensus was that Morris wrote a program that fulfilled a number of criteria, including the ability to propagate widely, but that he vastly underestimated the speed at which it would spread and infect and then reinfect other machines. He himself called the worm "a dismal failure" and claimed that it was never intended to slow computers down or cause any of them to crash.[5] His intention, he said, was for the program to make a single copy on each machine and then hide within the network. When he realized, on the night of November 2nd, that his program was crashing computers on the linked networks, he asked a friend, Andrew Sudduth, to post an electronic message with an apology and instructions for killing the program. That was the message sent out at 3:34 A.M., the one overlooked in the general confusion.

Morris was indicted for "intentionally and without authorization" accessing "federal-interest computers," preventing their use and causing a loss of at least $1,000 (that figure being the minimum loss for an indictment). The charge, under a section of the 1986 Computer Fraud and Abuse Act, potentially carries a fine of $250,000 and up to five years in prison.

Morris was tried in January 1990. His defense lawyers said that he had been attempting to "help security" on Internet and that his program had simply gotten out of control. The prosecution argued that "the worm was not merely a mistake; it was a crime against the government of the United States."

On January 22nd a federal jury found Morris guilty, the first conviction under that particular section of the 1986 act. Despite the verdict the judge stated that he believed the sentencing requirements did not apply in Morris's case, saying the circumstances did not exhibit "fraud and deceit." The sentence given was three years' probation, a fine of $10,000, and four hundred hours' community service.

The type of program that Morris had released onto ARPANET, a worm, has been defined as a program that takes up residence in a computer's memory, similar to the way a real worm takes up residence in an apple. Like the biological worm, the electronic one reproduces itself; unlike the real-life worm, however, the offspring of a computer worm will live in another machine and generally remain in communication with its progenitor. Its function is to use up space on the computer system and cause the machine to slow down or crash.

To researchers there is a clear distinction between worms and viruses, which are a separate sort of malicious program that require a "host," a program or file on a disk or diskette that they can attach themselves to. Viruses almost always have a payload as well, which is designed to change, modify, or even attack the system they take residence on. Worms can also usually be destroyed by closing down the network.

The fact that worms can travel independently from one linked machine to another has always intrigued programmers, and there have been many attempts to harness this ability for beneficial purposes. Ironically, one of the first experiments was made on ARPANET. A demonstration program called Creeper was designed to find and print a file on one computer, then move to a second and repeat the task. A later version not only moved through computers performing chores, but could also reproduce, creating perfect clones of itself that would undertake the same chores and replicate again. The problem became obvious: the number of worms would increase exponentially as each generation replicated, creating a seemingly endless number of clones.

The solution was to create another, nonreplicating worm, called the Reaper, which would crawl through the system behind the Creeper and kill off the proliferating clones after they had performed their tasks. The experiment was abandoned when it became apparent that the Reaper would never be able to keep up with the proliferating number of Creepers.

There are other sorts of malicious programs, including what are known as trojans—after the Greek wooden horse. The first trojan incident was reported in Germany in 1987. On the afternoon of December 9th, several students at the University of Clausthal-Zellerfeld, just south of Hannover, logged in to their computers and found that they had received electronic mail in the form of a file called Christmas. On reading the file, they saw the message LET THIS EXEC RUN AND ENJOY YOURSELF! followed by a small drawing of a Christmas tree, crudely represented by asterisks. An "exec" is an executable file, or program, and the suggestion was that if they ran the program, a large Christmas tree would appear on their computer screens. By the side of the small drawing was the greeting: A VERY MERRY CHRISTMAS AND BEST WISHES FOR THE NEXT YEAR.

Underneath the drawing was a further message, in broken English: BROWSING THIS FILE IS NO FUN AT ALL JUST TYPE "CHRISTMAS," followed by some seventy lines of computer instructions. The students could recognize that these instructions were written in an easy-to-use programming language that was available on their IBM mainframe, but few could comprehend what the program was designed to do. Most of the students decided to give the program a try, typed in "Christmas," and were duly rewarded with a large drawing of a Christmas tree. Typically, they then deleted the file. However the next time they logged in to their computers, they found that they had received more copies of the

Christmas file, as had many other computer users at the university. What no one had realized was that as well as drawing a Christmas tree, the program had been reading the files containing the students' electronic address books with the details of their other regular contacts on the IBM mainframe computer. The program then sent a copy of itself to all the other names that it could find. It was an electronic chain letter: each time the program was run, it could trigger fifty, or a hundred, or even more copies of itself, depending on the size of each user's electronic address book.

The unidentified student who playfully introduced the Christmas file into the electronic mail system had probably visualized a little local fun. He hadn't realized that some of the university's computer users had electronic addresses outside Clausthal-Zellerfeld linked by EARNet, the European Academic Research Network. Or that when copies of the file started whizzing around EARNet, they would then find their way onto BitNet, an academic computer network linking 1,300 sites in the United States, and from there onto VNet, IBM's private worldwide electronic mail network, which links about four thousand mainframe computers and many more smaller computers and workstations. The electronic chain letter reached VNet on December 15th, just six days after it was launched.

IBM's corporate users typically carry more names and addresses in their files than university users. Soon thousands of copies of the file were circulating around the world; it quickly reached Japan, which, like all the addresses, was only seconds away by electronic mail. Within two days the rampaging programs brought IBM's entire network to a standstill, simply by sending Christmas greetings throughout the network. The company spent an unfestive Christmas season killing all copies of the file.

The program was later dubbed the IBM Christmas Tree Virus, but because it needed some user interaction—in this case, typing in the word *Christmas*—it isn't considered a true virus. User interaction implies inviting the intruder in behind your defenses, as the Trojans did with the Greek horse. But virus researchers have created a subcategory for trojans that replicate—as the IBM Christmas Tree did—called, naturally enough, replicating trojans.

The pervasive media coverage of the Internet Worm was probably one reason for the next major computer incident that year. On December 23, 1988, just six weeks after Morris's Internet Worm hit the front pages, a very different worm hit the NASA Space Physics Astronomy Network (SPAN) and the Department of Energy computer networks.

Like the IBM Christmas Tree Trojan, it carried a Christmas greeting, and like the Internet Worm, it also targeted Digital Equipment's VAX computers. What later became known as the Father Christmas Worm waited until midnight on December 24th before delivering its message to users on the network: HI HOW ARE YOU? I HAD A HARD TIME PREPARING ALL THE PRESENTS. IT ISN'T QUITE AN EASY JOB. I'M GETTING MORE AND MORE LETTERS. . . . NOW STOP COMPUTING AND HAVE A GOOD TIME AT HOME!! MERRY CHRISTMAS AND A HAPPY NEW YEAR. YOUR FATHER CHRISTMAS.

The Father Christmas Worm was considered nothing more than a nuisance, and did no damage. But in October 1989 the SPAN network was hit again, with a worm delivering a protest message. The new worm was a variant of Father Christmas, but this time when users logged in to their systems, they found that their normal opening page had been replaced with a large graphics display woven around the word *WANK*.[6] In ordinary characters, the symbolism was explained:

WORMS AGAINST NUCLEAR KILLERS
Your System Has Been Officially WANKed.
You talk of times of peace for all, and then prepare
for war.

The arrival of the worm coincided with reports of protestors in Florida attempting to disrupt the launch of a nuclear-powered shuttle payload. It is assumed that the worm was also a protest against the launch.

The WANK Worm spread itself at a more leisurely rate than the Internet Worm, sending out fewer alarms and creating less hysteria. But when Kevin Obermann, a computer technician at Lawrence Livermore Laboratories, took it apart, he reported, "This is a mean bug to kill and could have done a lot of damage."

The WANK Worm had some features that were not present in the Father Christmas Worm: to a limited extent it could evolve and mutate, allowing it to become just a little bit smarter as it made its way from machine to machine. In other words, the worm had been designed to mutate deliberately, to add to the problems that might be caused by accidental mutation or by unintentional programming errors. And, by not immediately announcing its presence, it had more time to spread.

A method for combatting the worm was developed by Bernard Perrot of the Institut de Physique Nucléaire at Orsay, France. Perrot's scheme was to create a booby-trapped file of the type that the worm could be expected to attack. If the worm tried to use information from the file, it would itself come under attack and be blown up and killed.

By the end of 1989 the prophecies of the computer virus experts seemed to have come true. Now not only were there viruses, but there was a whole panoply of malicious software to deal with: worms, trojans, and the programs known as logic bombs.

Bombs are always deliberately damaging but, unlike viruses, don't replicate. They are designed to lay dormant within a computer for a period of time, then explode at some preprogrammed date or event.[7] Their targets vary: some delete or modify files, some zap the hard disk; some even release a virus or a worm when they explode. Their only common feature is the single blast of intentional destruction.

What had started out as simple self-replicating programs had grown into a full-blown threat to computer security. Those who had warned about the potential danger for the past two years were entitled to say, "I told you so."

But the prophecies were self-fulfilling. The choice of the term *virus* to describe quite unremarkable programs glamorized the mundane; the relentless promotion of the presumed threat put ideas in the minds of potential virus writers; the publicity given the concept ensured that the writer's progeny would become known and discussed. Even if the writer himself remained anonymous, he would know that his creative offspring would become famous.

The computer underworld is populated with young men (and almost no women), mostly single, who live out their fantasies of power and glory on a keyboard. That some young men find computing a substitute for sexual activity is probably incontrovertible. Just as a handle will often hide a shy and frightened fifteen-year-old, an obsession with computing to the exclusion of all else may represent security for a sexually insecure youngster. The computer is his partner, his handle is his alter ego, and the virus he writes is the child of this alter ego and his partner.

A German virus writer once said, "You feel something wonderful has happened when you've produced one. You've created something that lives. You don't know where it will go or what it will do, but you know it will live on."

The antivirus industry, of course, had no thoughts of creating a hobby for insecure technology wizards when it began its campaign of publicity and hype in 1987 and 1988. But there was little question that by the end of 1989 a real threat to computer systems had been created, posed by what was indeed becoming a plague of viruses. The number of catalogued viruses in the West would grow exponentially: from thirty-odd in mid-1988, to a hundred at the end of 1989, five hundred in 1990 and over two thousand–plus at the end of 1992. Along the way the antivirus industry would lose all control of the plague—its security software overwhelmed, its confidence battered by the sheer number of new viruses confronting it. And the new viruses became much more destructive, malicious, and uncontrollable than anyone had ever imagined.

5
■
THE BULGARIAN
THREAT

In March 1990 the first attempt was made to quantify the extent of the threat posed by computer viruses. Dr. Peter Tippett, a Case Western University scholar and the president of Certus International, a software company, predicted that 8 percent of all PCs would be infected within two years, even if no new viruses were written. He estimated the cost of removing the infections at $1.5 billion over five years—not taking into account the value of the data that would be destroyed. In 1991 he estimated that organizations in North America with over four hundred computers had a 26 percent probability of being hit by a virus within the next year; they also had a 5 percent chance of that virus causing a "disaster," which he defined as an infection that spread to twenty-five or more machines. A more recent projection, made in late 1991, went farther. It suggested that as many as 12 million of the world's 70 million computers—or roughly 17 percent—would be infected within the next two years.

But predictions such as those made by Dr. Tippett have proved difficult to substantiate: most virus attacks simply aren't reported; there is no body that regularly collects reliable statistics about the virus problem, and estimates of costs are always just guesses. When Dr. Tippett made his predictions, the number of new viruses that were appearing made it seem possible that their sheer volume would overwhelm the world's computer systems. By 1992, there were over 1,500 catalogued viruses and variants in the West; by spring 1993, there could well be twice that number.

Tippett had based his predictions on the behavior of just one virus, called Jerusalem. It was first discovered in December 1987 at the Hebrew University in Jerusalem, though it is thought to have been written in Haifa, the country's principal port and the home of its leading technical college, Technion University. At least, that is one theory. No one has proved that the virus was written in Haifa, nor has anyone ever claimed authorship.

The Jerusalem virus was a malicious joke, which would delete any program files used on Friday the 13th. There are two Friday the 13ths in any given year; in between those dates the virus signaled its presence by displaying a little box in the lower half of the computer screen and then slowing down infected systems to an unacceptable crawl. It also contained a gremlin that, contrary to the programmer's intentions, caused it to reinfect—or add itself to—many of the same program files. Eventually the files would grow so big that the virus would take up all of the computer's memory.

The virus quickly acquired a fearsome reputation. *Maariv,* one of Israel's leading daily newspapers, heralded its discovery with an article on January 8, 1988, that warned, "Don't use your computer on Friday the 13th of May this year! On this day, the Israeli virus which is running wild will wake up from its hibernation and destroy any information found in the computer memory or on the disks."

The report was somewhat exaggerated. It wasn't true that Jerusalem could destroy "any information found in the computer memory or on the disks," as it had been written to delete only programs that were used on Friday the 13th. In practice, few users suffered any real damage. Most operators would delete the virus as soon as they saw the little box appear on the screen and noticed the system slow down—which generally happened about half an hour after the virus had infected a computer.

While Jerusalem may not have been as destructive as its publicity suggested, it was exceptionally virulent and spread quickly and widely. Unlike most previous viruses, Jerusalem could infect nearly any common program file, which gave it more opportunity to travel. (By contrast, the Pakistani virus, Brain, could only infect the boot sector on specific diskettes, and Lehigh could only infect one particular type of program file.)

Jerusalem's propagation rate was phenomenal. From Israel it spread quickly to Europe and North America, and a year after its discovery in Israel it had become the most common virus in the world. In 1989 it was said to have been responsible for almost 90 percent of all reported incidents of viral infection in the United States.

Because Tippett's predictions were based on the propagation rate of this particularly infectious bug, they probably overstated the potential growth rate of viruses.[1] One of the peculiarities of viruses that Tippett overlooked is that most remain localized, causing infection on a limited number of machines, sometimes on just a single site. So far only about fifty viruses have propagated rapidly and spread from their spawning ground to computers throughout the world. The rate of propagation seems to be a matter of luck. Through an unpredictable combination of circumstance and chance, some viruses are destined to wither away in parochial isolation, while others achieve a sort of international notoriety. There seems little logic to which remain localized and which propagate.

In March 1989 a new virus was discovered in the United States, which was reported to have come to North America via Venezuela. Its payload was simple: it displayed the words *Den* and *Zuk,* converging from separate sides of the computer screen. The word *Zuk* was followed by a globe resembling the AT&T corporate logo. Inevitably, the virus became known as Den Zuk.

The bug was found to be relatively harmless. Like Brain, it nestled in the boot sector of infected diskettes, but changed their volume labels to "Y.C.1.E.R.P." Its payload was set to trigger after what is known as a warm reboot—restarting the computer from the keyboard without using the power switch. Warm reboots are generally employed when the computer has frozen, or stopped—a fairly uncommon occurrence, so the payload wasn't triggered very often.

An Icelandic virus researcher, Fridrik Skulason, surmised that the character string "Y.C.1.E.R.P" could be an amateur radio call sign. He looked up the sign in the International Callbook and found that it was attributed to an operator in Bandung, a city on the island of Java, in Indonesia. Skulason wrote to the operator, Denny Ramdhani, who replied with a long and detailed letter. He was, he admitted, the author of Den Zuk: "Den" was an allusion to his first name; "Zuk" came from his nickname, Zuko, after Danny Zuko, the character played by John Travolta in the film *Grease*. He had written the virus in March 1988, when he was twenty-four, "as an experiment." He wanted, he said, "to 'say hello' to other computer users in my city. I never thought or expected it to spread nationwide and then worldwide. I was really surprised when my virus attacked the U.S.A."

If Denny was surprised, the computer industry was flabbergasted. Den Zuk was neither a particularly infectious bug, nor was it grown in a locale that could be said to be within the communication mainstream. Bandung, for all of its exotic charm, is not a city normally associated with high-technology industries. Denny's virus traveled simply because it got lucky.

Viruses are unguided missiles, so it seems almost as likely that a bug launched from an obscure Indonesian city will hit targets in North America as one set off from, say, Germany. Nor is the sophistication of the bug any arbiter of its reach: Den Zuk was a simple virus, without any real pretension to what is known as an infection strategy.

The universality of the PC culture is reflected by the provenance of viruses. In Britain, New Scotland Yard's Computer Crime Unit recently compiled a list of the country's most troublesome bugs, which originated in places as diverse as New Zealand, Taiwan, Italy, Israel (the Jerusalem virus), Austria, Pakistan

(Brain), Switzerland, India, and Spain—as well as a couple from the United States and even one that is believed to be from China.[2]

The increasing links between virus writers in different parts of the world is demonstrated by the growing number of adaptations of existing viruses. The Vienna virus, which Ralph Burger had included in his *Das grosse Computervirenbuch* spawned a whole series of knockoffs, with slightly differing payloads and messages. As did the Jerusalem virus: there are now perhaps a hundred variants, all based on the one prototype. The knockoffs come from all over the world: Australia, the Netherlands, the republics of the former Soviet Union, Britain, South Africa, Czechoslovakia, Malaysia, Argentina, Spain, Switzerland, the United States—the list is only slightly shorter than the membership of the U.N. Some of the new variants are just jokes, and play tunes, but others are even more destructive than the original.

Jerusalem's most fearsome variant came from Asia. Called Invader, this bug first appeared in Taiwan in July 1990, where it is presumed to have been written. Within a month it had swept through the Far East and was reported to have reached North America. Just four months later it was found at the Canadian Computer Show, where it was running amok on the PC displays. Invader is an exceptionally sophisticated variant. It would infect a target computer's hard disk, diskettes, and program files, and its payload was devastating: it would zap data stored on a hard disk or diskette to the sound of an exploding bomb whenever a particular, quite common, piece of drafting software, called Autocad, was loaded.

Invader is part of the new generation of viruses: destructive, malicious, and clever. Since 1988, as the number of bugs has grown exponentially, virus techniques have improved dramatically, and their infection strategies have become more effective, which means they have a better chance of traveling. They exploit obscure functions of computers in order to evade detection; they can trash data; and in some cases, they can zero out large-scale computer networks.

While the early viruses could cause damage, it was generally by accident; the new strains are programmed to be destructive. Some seem demonic and frenzied, as if the virus writer was driven by a personal animus.

On January 15, 1991, the principal bank on the Mediterranean island of Malta was attacked by a particularly vicious bug. The first warning of the virus was an announcement that popped up suddenly on the computer screen:

DISK DESTROYER—A SOUVENIR OF MALTA
I HAVE JUST DESTROYED THE FAT ON YOUR DISK!!
HOWEVER, I HAVE KEPT A COPY IN RAM, AND I'M GIVING YOU
A LAST CHANCE TO RESTORE YOUR PRECIOUS DATA.
WARNING: IF YOU RESET NOW ALL YOUR DATA
WILL BE LOST FOREVER!!
YOUR DATA DEPENDS ON A GAME OF JACKPOT
CASINO DE MALTE JACKPOT
+ L + □□ + ? + □□ + C +
CREDITS: 5
ANY KEY TO PLAY

The virus was, in essence, inviting operators to gamble with the data on their hard disks. It had captured the FAT, the File Allocation Table which, despite its unprepossessing name, is one of the most important components of a computer's hard disk: it is a master index that keeps track of where all the pages for each file are kept. On a hard disk, unlike in a filing cabinet, pages of a single file are not necessarily stored together; they are stored wherever there happens to be disk space, which often results in "fragmentation"—particularly of larger files. Whenever a user selects a particular file, the FAT is responsible for finding all of the file's parts and assembling them in the correct order. Once corrupted, the FAT takes on all the attributes of an unqualified temporary secretary: it can't find anything, it loses files, and the ones it doesn't lose are incomplete or presented in the wrong order.

The gamble the operators faced was more or less the same as on a slot machine—except that the computer user was playing with data instead of a coin. If he played and lost, the virus would zap the FAT, with disastrous consequences. If he played and won, the virus would replace the FAT it had captured with the copy it had sequestered in the RAM, or random access memory, the computer's principal memory, and the area where programs are run.

When the user followed the on-screen instructions and pressed a key, the characters in the three "windows" ran through a sequence, like a real slot machine. The operator had five "credits," or tries, and the game ended when three *L*s, *C*s, or *?*s came up. The operator could try again if a combination of characters came up. The jackpot was three *L*s. Then the operator would see the following message on his screen: BASTARD! YOU'RE LUCKY THIS TIME, BUT FOR YOUR OWN SAKE, SWITCH OFF YOUR COMPUTER NOW AND DON'T TURN IT ON UNTIL TOMORROW! Three *?*s was a loser: the virus would then announce NO FUCKING CHANCE and destroy the FAT. Three *C*s, unsportingly, was also a loser: the message was: HA HA! YOU ASSHOLE, YOU'VE LOST: SAY BYE TO YOUR BALLS. Once again, the FAT would be zapped.

The Maltese bank had no choice but to gamble. Once the virus had seized control of the FAT, there was no possible way of retrieving it other than by coming up with a jackpot, and the odds against that were three to one. The computer operators pressed their keys, losing two games to every one they won and having to rebuild the system and restore the damaged files on two thirds of their infected computers. They also had to track down and destroy the virus, which became known as Casino, on all of their machines, a process that required the help of a computer security expert from Britain.

From the spelling and the use of American expressions such as *asshole*, it was thought that the author of Casino was American, or perhaps a Maltese who had previously lived in the States. But, as in so many cases, his identity was never discovered.

Casino epitomized many of the characteristics of the new breed of viruses: it was vicious, destructive, and its payload was curiously spiteful. To date, the virus hasn't spread from its island home, though that doesn't mean that it won't travel in the future.

It is estimated that a virus that is going to travel will reach its peak propagation within eighteen months. (Casino is thought to have been written just a few weeks before it hit the bank.) About half of the viruses ever written are less than six months old: they are, in a manner of speaking, now waiting for their travel documents, for that odd confluence of luck and circumstance that will unleash them throughout the world.

As the world population of computer viruses grows exponentially, so does the potential for real disaster. Viruses will affect computer users first, but then, indirectly, many people who have never even touched a computer will be affected. A virus let loose in a hospital computer could harm vital records and might result in patients receiving the wrong dosages of medicine; workers could suffer job losses in virus-ravaged businesses; dangerous emissions could be released from nuclear power plants if the controlling computers were compromised; and so on. Even military operations could be affected. Already, during the 1991 Gulf conflict, Allied forces had to contend with at least two separate virus assaults affecting over seven thousand computers. One of the incidents was caused by the ubiquitous Jerusalem bug, the other by a "fun" virus from New Zealand called Stoned, which displayed the message YOUR PC IS NOW STONED on the screen. The two outbreaks were enough to cause computer shutdowns and the loss of data. The consequences for the military, now utterly dependent on computers, of an attack by one of the newer, more destructive viruses—perhaps one unleashed by the enemy—could be catastrophic.

In truth, there has been no major disaster, no loss of life or jobs due to a virus. The only losses to date have been financial. But hospitals have already found viruses lurking in their systems; the military has been affected; and a Russian nuclear power plant's central computer was once shut down because of a virus. None of the bugs were destructive, but it is probably only a matter of time before there is a real catastrophe.

It is now believed by many that the real threat from computer viruses will escalate in the mid-nineties when a new generation of bugs begins to spread throughout the industrialized countries of the West. The new viruses will attack from every corner of the world, but the biggest threat will come from one country—Bulgaria.

The first call came in to the Help Desk of a California magazine publisher just after five P.M. on Thursday, June 27, 1991.[3] The company has 1,500 interlinked computers spread around three buildings. The Help Desk, part of the technical-support department, works as a sort of troubleshooter for the entire networked system, dealing with routine problems and helping the less computer-literate staff with their hassles.

"My computer has started making a noise," said the caller.

In the normal run of events, noises, apart from the standard beep when starting up or the low-pitched whir of the machine's cooling system, are not part of a computer's standard repertoire. A noise usually suggests a problem—a high-pitched whine can be a warning that the computer's monitor is faulty; a loud hum can signal a difficulty with the hard disk.

"What sort of noise?" asked the girl at the Help Desk.

"I don't know, it's just a noise. I've switched it off. Can someone come over?"

Seconds later the Help Desk received a call from another user with the same problem. Then the switchboard lit up. There were callers from all over the company, all with the same complaint: their computers were making odd noises. It may be a tune, one of the callers added helpfully, coming from the computer's small internal speaker. The sixth caller recognized the melody. The computers were all playing tinny renditions of "Yankee Doodle."

To the specialists in the technical-support department, the discovery that the tune was "Yankee Doodle" was confirmation that they had been hit by a virus, and a well-known one at that. The Yankee Doodle virus had first been seen in 1989 and was said to be relatively harmless. There are a number of variants of the bug, but most simply cause computers to play "Yankee Doodle." This particular variant, known as Version 44, played the tune at five P.M. every eight days.

The company arranged for antiviral software to be shipped overnight by Federal Express. The publishers of the software assured the Help Desk that they would simply need to run the program on the computers to locate the infected files and kill the virus; the files wouldn't be damaged and no data would be lost. Yankee Doodle was a nuisance, they said, but not a major problem.

On Friday morning the technical-support staff began the time-consuming task of checking every computer in the company. They discovered that eighteen of their machines had been hit by the virus and that the killer function of the software they had just bought wouldn't work on their particular variant of Yankee Doodle. Instead, to clean the bug out, they would need to delete all infected files and replace them.

The virus they were fighting is generally transferred by diskette. It attaches itself to an executable file—a word-processing program or a game, for instance—then, once loaded on to a computer, it searches out other programs to infect. It is generally harmless in that it never attacks data files, the ones users actually work on, so it can't cause serious damage. Its nuisance value comes in eradicating it: deleting programs and then replacing them can be time-consuming.

In the meantime, to stop the virus from spreading any farther, the company decided to shut down the entire network of 1,500 computers, leaving machines and staff idle. The technical-support specialists estimated that killing the bug and replacing the programs would take them two or three hours at the most. But by mid-afternoon they realized that they had underestimated the size of the job, and arranged to come in over the weekend. In the end, the technical staff worked for four days, Friday through Monday, before they were satisfied that all the machines were free of the virus. During that time computers and staff were inactive, neither processing work in progress nor going ahead with anything else.

The computers worked well for the next three days, but then, at ten A.M. on Thursday, July 4th, the virus was rediscovered. In a routine scan of one of the computers with the new antiviral software, one member of a small crew working over the Independence Day holiday received a big shock: Yankee Doodle was back. The technical specialists, called into the offices from their homes, discovered to their horror that this time 320 machines had been infected and when they asked the maker of the antiviral software for an explanation, they were simply told, "You missed a spot."

The company was forced to shut down its computers again, and again staff and machinery sat idle while the support staff searched laboriously through every program on all 1,500 machines. There was no damage: the bug was eradicated and the programs reinstalled without even a byte of data lost. But the lack of damage disguised the virus's real cost in downtime. By the time Yankee Doodle had been completely eradicated, the company had suffered one week of lost production, one week in which 1,500 staff were idle, one week of irrecoverable business. The company never quantified its loss, but it is estimated to run into the hundreds of thousands of dollars—all from what was purported to be a harmless virus.

Since 1990 virus researchers have pieced together a history of Yankee Doodle. It was first spotted in 1989 in the United Nations offices in Vienna on a computer game called Outrun. The game is proprietary, though unauthorized pirate copies are often passed around on diskette. Someone, somewhere, is thought to have infected a copy of the game, accidentally or deliberately, and the virus began its travels, first to Vienna, then around the world courtesy of the United Nations. Though there are known to be fifty-one versions of the virus, they are all based on one original prototype. And that program, despite the virus's all-American name, was written in Bulgaria.

In the same month that the California publishing company was trying to eradicate Yankee Doodle, a major financial-services house on the other side of the country was hit by another bug. This one wasn't a joke; it was deliberately malicious.

The first symptoms appeared when one of the secretaries was unable to print out a letter she had just entered into her computer. In such cases people usually follow the same routine: the secretary checked the paper, switched both the computer and the printer off and on, and then fiddled with the connecting cables. Still nothing printed out. Finally she rang her company's technical-support office.

When the specialist arrived, he began running tests on the affected machine. First he created a new document and tried printing it out, but that didn't work. He then guessed that the word-processing program itself was defective, that one of its files had become corrupted and was preventing the machine from printing. He went to another computer and copied out the list of program files used by the company, which showed the names of the programs and their size, in bytes (or characters). He then compared the files on the problem machine with the list. Everything matched, except that eight of the files on the affected computer were slightly larger than on the other. He checked the differences, and in each case the files on the problem machine were exactly 1,800 bytes larger.

With that information, the specialist knew immediately that the company had been hit by a virus; he also knew it was 1,800 bytes long and attached itself to program files. He called his supervisor, who hurried over with a virus-detection diskette. They inserted it in the infected computer and instructed it to check the machine for viruses. Program file names appeared briefly, one by one on the screen, as the virus detector bustled through its checks, examining each file for known bugs. After five minutes, a message appeared on the screen: it stated that eighty-three files had been checked and no virus had been found. In exasperation, the supervisor called the vendor of the virus-detection program.

"It does sound like you've got a virus," the vendor agreed. "But if it's not getting picked up by our software, then it must be a new virus. Or a new strain of an old one."

Most virus-detection programs operate by looking for known characteristics of familiar viruses—in other words, for a string of text or a jumble of characters that is known to be contained within the program of a previously discovered bug. Such virus-detection kits are, of course, unable to detect new or modified viruses.

At the suggestion of the vendor, the technical-support staff began a search of one of the infected files, looking for text or messages. Specialized software is needed to inspect the inside of a program file; during the inspection the screen displays a jumble of computer code. But within the code the staff saw two strings of text: EDDIE LIVES . . . SOMEWHERE IN TIME! said the first. The second announced: THIS PROGRAM WAS WRITTEN IN THE CITY OF SOFIA 1988–1989 © DARK AVENGER.

The supervisor phoned the vendor again: "Who the hell is the Dark Avenger?"

The short answer, the vendor explained patiently, is that no one knows. The Dark Avenger is an enigma. Most virus writers remain anonymous, their viruses appearing, seemingly, out of the ether, without provenance or claimed authorship, but the Dark Avenger is different: not only does he put his name to his viruses, he also signals where they were written—Sofia, the capital of Bulgaria. The Dark Avenger's viruses began seeping into the West in 1989. They are all highly contagious and maliciously destructive.

"The virus you've been hit with is called Eddie, or sometimes the Dark Avenger, the vendor told the increasingly worried technical-support supervisor. "It must be a new strain or something. That's why it wasn't picked up. Is there any other text message, a girl's name?"

The supervisor took a closer look at the virus. "I missed it before. There's another word here, Diana P. What does this thing do?"

"Well, as it's a new version, the answer is I don't know. Until we've seen a copy, it's anybody's guess."

To discover what a virus actually does, it has to be disassembled, its operating instructions—the program—taken apart line by line. This is a difficult and time-consuming process and can be carried out only by specialists. In the meantime the technical-support staff could only wait and watch as the virus spread slowly through the company, bouncing from machine to machine via the network cables that interlinked the company's 2,200 computers.

Viruses like Eddie work by attaching a copy of themselves to an executable file; whenever an infected program is used, the virus springs into action. It usually has two tasks: first, to find more files to infect; then, after it has had enough time to spread its infection, to release its payload. It was obvious that Eddie was spreading, so it was already performing its infection task. What was worrying was what its payload would prove to be.

To arrest the spread of the bug, it was decided to turn off all the computers in the company and wait until the virus could be cleaned out. It was a difficult decision—it would mean downtime and lost business—but it was a sensible precaution. It was later discovered that the payload in the Eddie variant was particularly malicious. When unleashed, it takes occasional potshots at the hard disk, zapping any data or programs it hits. The effect is equivalent to tearing a page out of a book at random. The loss of the pages may not become evident until one can't be found. But on a computer, if the loss goes undetected over a period of time, then the backup files, taken as a security measure in case of problems with the originals, could also have pages missing. The slow corruption of data is particularly insidious. Any computer breakdown can cause a loss of data, necessitating some reentry of the affected transactions since the last backup. But if the backups are also affected, then the task could become impossible. At worst, the data could be lost forever.

In this instance some data was irrecoverably destroyed, even though only sixty machines were found to be infected. But, in a sense, the company had been lucky: because Eddie had taken a potshot at a secretary's word-processing program and knocked out its print capability, it was discovered fairly early on. Had it lurked undetected for longer, it could have destroyed even more data.

The process of checking all 2,200 computers in the company took four and a half days, with a team of twelve people working twelve hours a day. Every executable file on every hard disk on every machine had to be checked. The team had special programs to help with the task, but viruses could easily get wrapped up inside "archived" files—files that are compressed to save computer space—where they can escape detection. All archived files had to be expanded back to their full size, checked, and then packed away again. That took time. Also, all diskettes had to be checked, a nearly impossible task given the difficulty in finding them: diskettes have a habit of disappearing into black holes in desk drawers, in briefcases, in storage cupboards.

The computer diskette has now assumed the generality of paper as a medium for storing information. Staff with home computers often carry diskettes to and from their office, and it makes sense that diskettes containing valuable data should be stored off-site, as a precaution against problems with the office computer. But the home PC also encourages the transfer of viruses among families. A student might transfer a virus from college to home; a parent might transfer a virus from home to office. For the most part, viruses are spread innocently, but there is now such a large traffic in diskettes that it is usually impossible to trace the source of an infection.

After seven hundred hours of intensive effort, the technical-support staff felt confident they had eliminated all traces of Eddie. Their confidence was short-lived. Within a week Eddie was back. This time they lost a further one and a half days' work. (Because it is very difficult to remove all traces of a virus, 90 percent of victims suffer a recurrence within thirty days.)

After the final bout of Eddie was cleared away, executives of the company tried to quantify how much the bug's visit had cost them—not that any of it would be recoverable from insurance. "We lost $500,000 of business—really lost business, not orders deferred until we could catch up, but business that had to be done there and then or it went to a competitor," said the company's chief financial officer. "We also lost data. That cost us $20,000. But what really hurt was the lost business. If we force a customer into the hands of a competitor, he might go there again. I guess that could cost us another $500,000."

The company tried to find out how the virus had got into its machines in the first place. Sometimes disenchanted employees (or ex-employees) have been known deliberately to cause havoc on computer systems, but it seemed unlikely in this case. The company concluded that the infection was almost certainly accidental, probably introduced on a diskette brought in from outside. All they knew for certain was that some Bulgarian who called himself the Dark Avenger had cost them $1 million.

Meanwhile, across the Atlantic in England, computer operators in government offices in Whitehall and regional centers were confounded by a new virus that spread, seemingly unstoppably, from office to office and department to department.

The virus was first observed in the House of Commons library in the Palace of Westminster. In early October 1990, researchers at the library became concerned about one of their computer systems. The library operates a PC-based research service for members of Parliament, providing information, background, and documentation on subjects of concern. Part of the service uses a network of Compaq computers, and it was this system that was causing problems. Computer files that should have been available suddenly appeared to be missing, while others were corrupted or incomplete, and some of the file names were distorted.

As the days went by, the problems multiplied, and the head of computer systems at the library called in an outside specialist. A virus-detection program run on one of the affected machines came up clean, but from the way the computers were malfunctioning, the specialist was convinced that the House of Commons library had been hit by a virus. He compared the lengths of the program files on an infected machine with those on a clean computer. As expected, the programs on the infected computer were longer, which suggested the unknown virus was attaching itself to the ends of program files. A visual inspection of the virus followed, revealing one full word in the jumble of characters on the screen: NOMENKLATURA.

The word is of Russian origin, though in common use throughout Eastern Europe. It was the name given to the upper echelons of the Communist party and the high-ranking bureaucrats—the class that did well from the old system, those who had access to the special shops and the special rations, the cars and the country homes. It is a pejorative now and was almost certainly picked by the virus writer for its ironic overtones.

A copy of the virus, immediately nicknamed Nomenklatura, was sent to a British researcher, Alan Solomon, who runs a specialist computer data-recovery service from Berkhamsted, northwest of London. When he disassembled the bug, he found he was looking at one of the most destructive viruses he had ever seen.

The virus's target proved to be the FAT, the all-important File Allocation Table. With the FAT corrupted, the computer would be unable to reassemble data files in the correct order—hence the gaps in the information accessed in the House of Commons library. Solomon also noticed a string of text characters within the Nomenklatura program. It could be a message, he thought, except that the text was represented on his computer screen by a code that appeared to refer to non-English-language characters, which looked like Greek or Russian. Solomon guessed it was Bulgarian.

To confirm his hunch, Solomon dialed an electronic bulletin board in Sofia, linking to the East European country via Fidonet, an international public-access computer network run by hobbyists. The board he accessed was owned by MicroComm, a subsidiary of the Bulgarian public telephone company. Once linked to the board, he managed to make contact with one of the company's engineers, Veni Markovski, who spoke a little English. Solomon uploaded the code to Sofia, and Veni looked at it with his Cyrillic converter. If the code represented Cyrillic characters, the converter—a program that translates keyboard strokes into Cyrillic—would recognize them and display the message in the virus. The text, though, would be in Bulgarian, which was why Solomon needed Veni's help.

The converter rapidly deciphered the code, changing it to Cyrillic. Solomon had guessed correctly. The phrase, Veni reported, was an idiomatic Bulgarian expression. It took some time to translate—Veni's English is poor—and its meaning is obscure. But, Veni said, it translates to something like: "This fat idiot instead of kissing the girl's lips, kisses quite some other thing."

Solomon wasn't surprised that the message was in Bulgarian. By 1990 everyone involved in computer security had become aware that something odd was going on in that obscure East European country. Increasingly sophisticated and damaging viruses that affected IBM-type PCs were moving into the West, carried on diskette or transferred by electronic bulletin boards, and all had one thing in common: they had been written in Bulgaria.

Though only a few of the viruses had actually been seen "in the wild"—that is, infecting computers—reports from Bulgaria suggested that two new viruses were being discovered in that country every week. By mid-1990 there were so many reported Bulgarian viruses that one researcher was moved to refer to the existence of a "Bulgarian virus factory." The phrase stuck.

The origins of that factory go back to the last decade. In the early 1980s the then president of Bulgaria, Todor Zhivkov, decided that his country was to become a high-tech power, with computers managing the economy while industry concentrated on manufacturing hardware to match that of the West. Bulgaria, he decided, would function as the hardware-manufacturing center for Comecon (Eastern Europe's Council for Mutual Economic Assistance, now defunct), trading its computers for cheap raw materials from the Soviet Union and basic imports from the other Socialist countries. Bulgaria had the potential, in that it had many well-educated young electronics engineers; what it didn't have, with its archaic infrastructure and ill-managed economy, was any particularly useful application for its own hardware.

With the resources of the state behind Bulgaria's computerization, the country began manufacturing copies of IBM and Apple models. The machines were slow—very slow by today's standards—and were already obsolete even when they first started crawling off the production line. They had been "designed" at the Bulgarian Academy of Sciences, but without the help or blessing of either IBM or Apple. The Bulgarian machines were simply poorly manufactured clones that used the same operating systems and computer language as the real IBMs and Apples.

In the latter half of the 1980s shiny new computers started to appear in state organizations, schools, colleges, and computer clubs. Many were destined to sit on the boss's desk, largely unused, symbols of a high-tech society that never really existed. Few businesses had any real need for computers; some used them simply to store personnel records. It was a gloss of technology laid over a system that, at its core, wasn't functioning.

In addition, Bulgaria didn't have any software. While the factories continued to manufacture PCs, the most basic requirement—programs to make the machines function—had to be pirated. So the Bulgarians began copying Western programs, cracking any copy-protection schemes that stood in their way, and became more and more skilled at hacking—in the classic sense of the word. They could program their way around any problem; they learned the ins and outs of the IBM and Apple operating systems; they became skilled computer technicians as they struggled to keep their unreliable and poorly manufactured computers functioning. In short, they were assimilating all the skills they would need to become first-class virus writers.

The first Bulgarian viruses to arrive in the West were seen in

1989. They became increasingly sophisticated and malignant, progressing within a year from the relatively harmless Yankee Doodle to the more destructive Eddie and then to Nomenklatura, which was deadly.

Nomenklatura's attack on the House of Commons library had zapped data in the statistical section, rendering valuable information irrecoverable. From the House of Commons, the virus began to journey through other sectors of the British government, presumably carried on diskettes from the library. The virus traveled slowly, popping up first in one department, then spreading to another. As soon as it was wiped out in one office, it would reappear elsewhere; it has not been completely eradicated to this day. Alan Solomon, a computer security specialist who worked on the case, is convinced that Nomenklatura's creator is the Dark Avenger.

In November 1988 stories about Robert Morris, Jr., and the Internet Worm were published in Bulgaria. The news, already exaggerated in the American press, became even more fanciful by the time it was retold in Bulgarian newspapers.

The worm excited the curiosity of two young men, Teodor Prevalsky and Vesselin (Vesko) Bontchev. They had been close friends for many years, had gone to university together, and had served side by side as officers in the Bulgarian army. Aged twenty-seven, they were both engineering graduates from professional families, which made them part of the privileged class in Bulgaria at the time.

The Bulgarian computer industry was in full swing by then, but the country had few uses for the new machines. In response, a magazine was started called *Komputar za vas* ("Computer for You"), to show readers how to do something constructive on their relatively worthless PCs. The magazine needed technical writers who could explain how the machines worked, and Vesko, provided with desk space at the magazine's offices, found that he could double his income of $45 a month by writing the articles.

By Bulgarian standards his salary was already high; with the additional income from the magazine he was positively wealthy.

When news of the Internet Worm broke, Vesko and his friend Teodor discussed it at length. For Vesko, it would be the inspiration for an article; for Teodor, it was the catalyst for a new intellectual pursuit.

On November 10, 1988, Teodor sat down at a computer at the technical institute where he worked and started to write his first virus. He had managed to get a copy of Vienna, which had been copied from Ralf Burger's book, and he used it as a model for his own bug. On November 12th Teodor proudly made an entry in his diary: "Version 0 lives."

Version 0 was, in all probability, the first homegrown Bulgarian virus. It did very little except replicate, leaving copies of itself on what are called COM files—simple program files of limited length, used for basic computer utilities. When the virus infected a file, it beeped.

Just two days after writing Version 0, Teodor had prepared Version 2.[4] It was more clever than the original in that it could infect both common types of executable files: COM and EXE. The latter are the more sophisticated programs—like word-processing, for instance—and because they are structurally complex they are more difficult to infect. But Teodor's Version 2 employed a little trick that would convert the shorter EXE files into COM files. When the operator called up, or loaded, an EXE file, the lurking virus saw the load command, jumped in ahead and modified the structure of the EXE file so it resembled a COM file. The next time a restructured EXE file was loaded up, it could be successfully infected by the virus, just like an ordinary COM file.

Teodor was also experimenting with anti-virus software at the time, and developed a program that would hunt down and kill Versions 0 and 2. It was called "Vacsina," the Bulgarian word for vaccine. However, by Version 5 Teodor had adapted his virus so that it was immune to his own killer program. He accomplished this by simply adding the character string "Vacsina" to the virus.

When his anti-virus program saw the string, it would leave the bug alone.

It was shortly thereafter that Version 5 escaped. Like most Bulgarians, Teodor had to share his computer with colleagues at the Technical Institute; with four people using one machine, with software copying rampant, and with the casual transfer of diskettes, it was only a matter of time before one of the bugs began to propagate out of his control. Within weeks Version 5 had spread throughout Bulgaria. In less than a year it had reached the West—the first Eastern virus to jump the Iron Curtain. When the virus was examined, researchers discovered the text string "Vacsina," which immediately gave a name to Version 5.

Meanwhile, Teodor continued experimenting. By December 15, 1988 he had advanced to Version 8. On this variant the payload—the innocuous beep—now sounded only when an infected computer was restarted from the keyboard (a "warm reboot"), allowing it to remain hidden for longer. In the best programming tradition, all his improvements were duly documented and given version numbers as they appeared.

Later in December a new Bulgarian virus was discovered. It carried a text string which said it had been authored by a Vladimir Botchev. The bug was almost certainly written in response to one of Vesko's magazine articles: in November Vesko had stated that it would be "difficult" to write a virus that could infect all EXE files, including the longer ones, and Vladimir had presumably seen that as a challenge. His virus appeared less than a month after the article was published. It employed a novel and technically elegant device that enabled it to attach itself to any EXE file, no matter what length. After it infected a file it played the tune "Yankee Doodle"—in celebration, perhaps.

This virus was generally not damaging—its payload was the tune—and because it was easy to detect, it never spread. But the new bug's payload was immediately copied by Teodor in his new variant, Version 18, which appeared on January 6, 1989. This one didn't beep; instead it played "Yankee Doodle," which Teodor had lifted, note for note, straight from Vladimir's program.

Five days later, Teodor produced Version 21, which could remove the virus from infected files if a more recent version of this bug attacked the same system. Then, on February 6, 1989, Version 30 appeared. It incorporated a "detection and repair" capability, that would warn the virus if it had been modified or corrupted while replicating. Eerily, it could then fix the damage itself by changing the corrupted instructions back to their original form. It was a kind of artificial life, though the repair capability was limited (it could handle only changes of up to 16 bytes in length).

By the end of February Teodor was on to Version 39 and his virus was now full of tricks: it could infect EXE files of any size, it could even evade antiviral software. As soon as it noted the presence of a detection program, it would detach itself from the infected file and hide elsewhere in the computer's memory.

With Version 42, which appeared in March, his virus took on a new role: virus fighter. The Ping Pong boot-sector virus, which is believed to have been created at Turin University in Italy, had now reached Bulgaria. Ping Pong (also called Bouncing Ball) was a joke virus: from time to time it simply sent a dot careering around the screen, like a ball in a squash court. Teodor's new virus could detect Ping Pong and was able to modify it in such a way that, after a time, it destroyed itself, leaving behind its corpse. He persisted with the tune "Yankee Doodle" as his payload, but he varied the time and frequency it would play. One of his next variants was Version 44, which plays the tune every eight days at 5 P.M. This was the version destined to become the most widely traveled of all Teodor's viruses: once again, it escaped from his office machine, probably on a diskette, and spread through Bulgaria; on September 30, 1989 it was sighted in offices of the United Nations in Vienna; and from there, now known as Yankee Doodle, it traveled the world. It was this version which caused mayhem at the California publishing house in July 1991.

Teodor continued to develop his virus. The last variant was Version 50, by which time it had been given the additional power to detect and destroy the Cascade bug, which had just arrived in

Bulgaria from Austria. Cascade was another joke virus: it caused the letters on a computer terminal to fall down and pile up in heaps at the bottom of the screen to an accompanying clicking noise. After it had finished its performance, a user could resume his work—though he would need to replace the letters and words that had fallen from his screen. It wasn't particularly damaging, though the operator's nerves could well have been frayed.

After Version 50 Teodor began to explore some of his other ideas. One was a joke virus that hopped around a hard disk while challenging the operator to FIND ME! It was unusual in that it was nearly undetectable: unlike other viruses, Find Me! wouldn't infect the boot sector or a program file. It created its own home within infected systems by stealing the name of an EXE file and attributing it to a new COM file; this new COM file became its hiding place.[5]

It was a clever trick. Teodor knew that on computers with two files of the same name the COM file is always loaded prior to the EXE file. So his little bug would get to the screen first, to taunt the operator with "Find Me!" messages. If the operator looked at his list of files he might notice that he had an extra COM file with the same name as one of his EXE files, but he generally wouldn't realize the significance. Even if he did, the bug would probably be one step ahead of him. From time to time, Find Me! would create a new COM file (always with the same name as an EXE file) and transfer itself to a new home, deleting the old one as it did so. In that way it continued to hop around the hard disk, usually well ahead of the increasingly irritated operator. It was possible to remove the bug completely, but it invariably took a few manhours of frustrating chasing.

Teodor also experimented with "stealth" viruses—silent, deadly, and almost undetectable bugs that evade antiviral software in much the same way that the Stealth plane evades radar detection. Stealth technology has been exploited by virus writers since 1986 (the Pakistani Brain virus has some stealth capability in that it is able to camouflage its presence on the boot sector), but

Teodor's was the first that could add itself to a program file without, apparently, increasing the length of the file. Of course it was only an illusion: the virus would simply deduct its own length from the infected file whenever it was being examined.

With his stealth bug Teodor had more or less reached the pinnacle: there was little he could do to improve the programming of his latest virus except, perhaps, to add a destructive payload. But, for Teodor, destruction of data or programs was never the point. He wrote viruses as an intellectual challenge. None of his viruses had ever been intentionally damaging, though he had become aware that they could cause collateral losses. He had also realized that a completely harmless virus was an impossibility. All viruses, by their mere presence on a computer, can accidentally overwrite data or cause a system to crash. And the most dangerous of all, he thought, was an undetectable virus that could spread unstoppably, causing collateral damage without the operators even being aware they were under attack.

In 1989 Teodor decided to retire from virus writing. His own career up until then had, curiously, mirrored his friend Vesko's. While Teodor wrote viruses, Vesko wrote about them; as Teodor became more proficient at writing bugs, Vesko became more accomplished at analyzing them. By 1989 Vesko had become Bulgaria's most important virus researcher and a major contributor to Western literature on the subject. He had been invited to submit papers and to lecture at Western European computer security conferences: he was recognized as an authority on viruses, particularly those from Eastern Europe.

Vesko's reputation was due, in a large part, to having been in the right place at the right time. First, there were his friend Teodor's bugs. Teodor would often pass on the programming code to Vesko for analysis, who would then report on their capabilities in the local press and in Western journals. It was a convenient arrangement, and the resulting publicity would encourage other writers. Eventually, what became known as the Bulgarian virus factory started to pump out bug after bug, each more dangerous than the last, and Vesko was there to record it. He was in the eye of the storm, collecting viruses from all over Bulgaria as they spread from computer to computer. By 1991 he was reporting two new locally grown viruses each week.

In a country with so many bugs flying around, it was inevitable that Bulgarian computers would become overrun. Most computers in the country had been hit at least once; many had been hit with multiple viruses at the same time. Because Vesko was the country's leading authority on the malicious programs, he was eventually given responsibility for coordinating Bulgaria's effort to fight them off. He was constantly on call. Days he worked in his office in the Bulgarian Academy of Sciences, where he was given the dour title of Assistant Research Worker Engineer. Weekends and nights he continued the fight from his own cramped room on a borrowed Bulgarian clone of an IBM PC. He dealt with ten to twenty phone calls each day from institutions or firms that had been attacked by viruses.

By then the Bulgarian virus factory was in full production. It was no longer a matter of Vesko and his friend Teodor, one a researcher, the other a virus writer. Bulgaria had spawned some of the most skilled and prolific virus writers in the world.

In Plovdiv, Bulgaria's second largest town, a student named Peter Dimov produced a series of viruses "as revenge against his tutor" and another two "in tribute" to his girlfriend, Nina (it is not known if she was pleased). One of Peter's ambitions was to write the world's smallest virus: his first came to under 200 bytes. Later he wrote one only 45 bytes long. For a few weeks it was the shortest virus known—until another Bulgarian programmer produced one that was just 30 bytes. Peter was also the author of the first Bulgarian boot-sector virus as well as two ominous-sounding bugs that he called Terror and Manowar. But despite their names, neither was particularly damaging. In total, Peter wrote around twenty-five viruses.

In Varna, on the Black Sea, two students at the Mathematics Gymnasium (Upper School), Vasil Popov and Stanislav Kirilov, produced a series of viruses and trojans. Their most dangerous, called Creeping Death (or DIR-2),[6] was reported to be able to infect all the files on a hard disk within minutes.

Lubomir Mateev, then a twenty-three-year-old university student, and his friend Iani Brankov wrote a virus together to embarrass their professor when they were studying at Sofia University. Their first bug was programmed to make a shuffling noise while he was lecturing that sounded like the rustling of paper. This virus and a subsequent variant (which borrowed the bouncing-ball payload from Ping Pong) became known as Murphy 1 and Murphy 2.[7] Highly infectious, they spread throughout Bulgaria and reached the West in 1991.

Many other programmers and students took a stab at writing viruses, with varying degrees of success. It became something of a fad among computer freaks in Sofia and other Bulgarian cities in the late 1980s. There was, of course, no "factory" in the usual sense of the word—just a group of young men (they were all male), probably unknown to each other, who had learned the tricks of writing viruses through the techniques perfected while stealing Western software.

The value to Bulgaria of all the virus-writing activity was negligible. Though the programmers who compiled the bugs were, no doubt, honing their skills, and some of the viruses demonstrated a cleverness and technical dexterity that may have been admirable, viruses simply do not have any productive purpose. Indeed, Fred Cohen—the man who coined the term "computer virus" in the first place—once tried to find a role for them and organized a competition to write a beneficial virus. None was found.

In any event, in late 1990 and early 1991, Bulgaria itself, no longer Communist and not quite democratic, was going through an identity crisis. Public confidence in the government, in state institutions, and in the currency had evaporated, to be replaced by a deeply cynical, almost anarchic national ethos. Bulgaria had become a country of shabby, small-time dealers, of petty black-marketers and crooked currency changers. The symbols of the immediate past, of the near half-century of Communism, had been pulled down; little had been erected in their place. But the computers that President Zhirkov had decreed would turn Bulgaria into a modern technological power remained, and indeed offered themselves to the new generation of computer programmers as weapons to be turned against the state, to drive an electronic stake through the heart of the system. Viruses would cripple Zhivkov's dream. In this gray time of shortages and rationing, of cynicism and despair, writing viruses was a sort of protest—perhaps against the Communists, possibly against the transitional state, almost certainly against the lack of opportunity and hope. Writing viruses was a form of individualism, of striking out; it was also an opportunity for notoriety.

Since 1988 the Bulgarian virus factory has produced around two hundred new viruses. Most have yet to travel; only a few have reached the industrialized West. The scale of the problem may not become apparent for several years.

Some of those who created the viruses are known, some aren't, but the greatest threat is Bulgaria's most proficient and fearsome virus writer: the Dark Avenger.

The man who was to become known as the Dark Avenger began work on his first virus in September 1988. "In those days there were no viruses being written in Bulgaria, so I decided to write the first," he once said. "In early March 1989 it came into existence and started to live its own life, and to terrorize all engineers and other suckers."

The Dark Avenger had started work on the virus known as Eddie just weeks before Teodor had sat down to write the first of what became his Vacsina–Yankee Doodle series. Teodor's virus was ready first, but the Dark Avenger's bug was much more malicious and infective. "It may be of interest to you to know that Eddie is the most widespread virus in Bulgaria. I also have information that Eddie is well known in the U.S.A., West Germany, and Russia too," the Dark Avenger once boasted.

The Dark Avenger likes to leave teasing references to his identity in his viruses. As in the Eddie virus, he sometimes "copyrights" his bugs, and often gives Sofia as the source. The text string DIANA P. was assumed to be a reference to his girlfriend, except that Diana isn't a particularly Bulgarian name. It's now believed to be a reference to Diana, Princess of Wales.

The Dark Avenger also likes heavy-metal music: the other text string in his first virus, the mysterious EDDIE LIVES . . . , apparently refers to the skeletal mascot, Eddie, used by the British heavy-metal group Iron Maiden in their stage act. Heavy-metal symbols and motifs run through many of the other viruses written by the Dark Avenger. A family of perhaps twenty or more viruses can be attributed to him, all technically advanced, most deliberately malicious, some containing text strings that use the titles of Iron Maiden tracks: "Somewhere in Time," "The Evil That Men Do," and "The Good Die Young." His viruses also mimic the posturing Satanism of heavy-metal music. His Number of the Beast virus (the name is yet another reference to an Iron Maiden song) contains the 3-byte signature "666," the mystical number believed to refer to "the beast," the Antichrist in the Book of Revelations.

Perhaps appropriately, of all the viruses attributed to the Dark Avenger, Number of the Beast is considered the most technically accomplished. A stealth virus, it exploits an obscure feature of the standard PC operating system to evade detection and hide in unused space on program files so that it doesn't change the length of the host file. Oddly, the virus doesn't have a payload, though its mere presence on a PC is likely to cause it to crash.

The Dark Avenger has produced four versions of Eddie and six versions of Number of the Beast, as well as four variants of a virus called Phoenix and four of another one known as Anthrax (the name of an American heavy-metal group). He is also generally believed to have written Nomenklatura, the virus that attacked Britain's House of Commons library, principally because the bug is technically sophisticated and vicious and employs techniques that have been seen in his other viruses. In a way, the Dark

Avenger has become so well known that any particularly destructive and clever Bulgarian virus will almost automatically be attributed to him. The alternative is too dire for the computer security industry to contemplate.

The Dark Avenger's fame was evident from the response to his calls to the world's first "virus exchange" bulletin board, which was established in Sofia by twenty-year-old Todor Todorov on November 1, 1990. The idea was eventually copied by others in Britain, Italy, Sweden, Germany, the United States, and Russia, but Todorov was the first. The board describes itself as "a place for free exchange of viruses and a place where everything is permitted!"

Todorov built up a large collection of viruses after callers learned of his exchange procedures.

> IF YOU WANT TO DOWNLOAD VIRUSES FROM THIS BULLETIN BOARD, JUST UPLOAD TO US AT LEAST 1 VIRUS WHICH WE DON'T ALREADY HAVE. THEN YOU WILL BE GIVEN ACCESS TO THE VIRUS AREA, WHERE YOU CAN FIND MANY LIVE VIRUSES, DOCUMENTED DISASSEMBLIES, VIRUS DESCRIPTIONS, AND ORIGINAL VIRUS SOURCE COPIES! IF YOU CANNOT UPLOAD A VIRUS, JUST ASK THE SYSOP [SYSTEM OPERATOR] AND HE WILL DECIDE IF HE WILL GIVE YOU SOME VIRUSES.[8]

The Dark Avenger made his first call on November 28, 1990, four weeks after the bulletin board was set up. I'M GLAD TO SEE THAT THIS BOARD IS RUNNING, he wrote Todorov. I'VE UPLOADED A COUPLE OF VIRUSES TO YOU. I HOPE YOU WILL GIVE ME ACCESS TO THE VIRUS AREA. To which Todorov replied, THANK YOU FOR THE UPLOAD. YOUR SECURITY LEVEL HAS BEEN UPGRADED . . . AND YOU HAVE ACCESS TO THE VIRUS AREA NOW. IF YOU FIND ANY OTHER VIRUSES, PLEASE UPLOAD THEM HERE.

When it was learned that the Dark Avenger frequented Todorov's bulletin board, other users began leaving messages for him. HI, DARK AVENGER! WHERE HAVE YOU LEARNED PROGRAMMING?

AND WHAT DOES "EDDIE LIVES" MEAN? AND WHO IS "DIANA P."? IS SHE YOUR GIRLFRIEND OR WHAT? The queries were from Yves P., a French virus writer. Free Raider posted his salute on December 9th: HI, BRILLIANT VIRUS WRITER. Another message said, HI, I'M THE SYSOP OF THE INNERSOFT BULLETIN BOARD. SHOULD I CONSIDER MY BOARD NOT POPULAR BECAUSE YOU DON'T LIKE TO CALL IT? PLEASE GIVE IT A CALL.

The messages from his fans reflected the Dark Avenger's new status: he had become a star. In the two years since he created Eddie, he had become the computer underworld's most notorious virus writer. He had established a brand identity: the Dark Avenger's viruses were known to be the most destructive and among the best engineered ever seen. His fame, as he knew, had spread throughout Europe and to North America as well.

So it's not surprising that he wanted to be treated like the star he was, and reacted badly to criticism. In March 1991 he sent the following message to Fidonet, the international bulletin board network: HELLO, ALL ANTIVIRUS "RESEARCHERS" WHO ARE READING THIS MESSAGE. I AM GLAD TO INFORM YOU THAT MY FRIENDS AND I ARE DEVELOPING A NEW VIRUS, THAT WILL MUTATE IN 1 OF 4,000,-000,000 DIFFERENT WAYS! IT WILL NOT CONTAIN ANY CONSTANT INFORMATION. NO VIRUS SCANNER CAN DETECT IT. THE VIRUS WILL HAVE MANY OTHER NEW FEATURES THAT WILL MAKE IT COMPLETELY UNDETECTABLE AND VERY DESTRUCTIVE! Fidonet may not have been the best outlet for his boasting: its users are mostly ethical computer enthusiasts. The Dark Avenger received a flood of replies, from all over Europe. Most were critical; some were abusive. The Dark Avenger replied testily, I RECEIVED NO FRIENDLY REPLIES TO MY MESSAGE. THAT'S WHY I WILL NOT REPLY TO ALL THESE MESSAGES SAYING "FUCK YOU." THAT'S WHY I WILL NOT SAY ANY MORE ABOUT MY PLANS.

At thirty-one, Vesko Bontchev is surprisingly young looking, thin and somewhat frail. He is a serious man who speaks deliberately and intensely about the virus problem in Bulgaria. He lives with his mother in a shabby five-story 1950s block on a characteristically grim East European housing estate on the outskirts of Sofia. The apartment is large by Bulgarian standards: Vesko has his own room.

Although he is unassuming, it is apparent that he is proud of his reputation as the country's foremost virus fighter and of his contacts with other researchers in the West. His position is ensured by his oddly symbiotic relationship with the Dark Avenger, one that almost parallels his earlier relationship with Teodor. Because the Dark Avenger lives in Bulgaria, Vesko's position as a lecturer and researcher is secure. At the same time, Vesko contributes to the Dark Avenger's fame by publicizing his activities abroad. In a curious way the two need each other.

Cynics who have noticed this have argued that if the Dark Avenger hadn't existed, it would have been in Vesko's interest to have invented him. Some have even theorized that the two are one and the same: that the quiet, intense virus researcher has an alter ego—the demonic, heavy-metal fan, the admirer of Princess Diana, the virus writer called the Dark Avenger. The Avenger has himself contributed to the notion: one of his viruses contains Vesko's own copyright notice, and every so often he teases Vesko. Once, the Dark Avenger wrote: "To learn how to find out a program author by its code, or why virus-writers are not dead yet, contact Mr. Vesselin Bontchev. So, never say die! Eddie lives on and on and on . . ."

In an interview in a Bulgarian newspaper, Vesko was asked about the rumours. "Can you give me the name of Dark Avenger?" the reporter queried.

"No."

"Is it possibly you?"

"I have been asked similar questions both in the West and in the Soviet Union. But it is not true."

Despite the rumors, Vesko isn't the Dark Avenger—but he does provide the oxygen of publicity for the Bulgarian virus writer. It suits them both: for Vesko, the Dark Avenger provides the raw material for his reports; for the Dark Avenger, Vesko's watchfulness ensures his own reputation as the demonic scourge of computers.

The two young men—the hunter and the outlaw—are locked in an unfriendly embrace. The relationship between the two is one of mutual distrust, which neither attempts to disguise. It is the classic relationship between a cop and his adversary: hatred, tinged with a measure of respect.

On several occasions, Vesko says, he has tried to smoke out the virus writer. Once Vesko announced that he had carefully analyzed two viruses attributed to the Dark Avenger: the Number of the Beast and Eddie. He said that, in his view, they could not possibly be the work of the same writer. One was clever, the work of a professional, the other sloppy, the work of an amateur. Furthermore, he said that he intended to present his evidence at a lecture that would be held in Sofia. He guessed that the Dark Avenger would appear, if only to hear what Vesko had to say about his programs.

The meeting was well attended, particularly for a cold Friday night in early December. Vesko presented his evidence. Number of the Beast, he said, was obviously written by an extremely skilled specialist whose style contrasted in every way with the poor quality of Eddie. He watched the audience during his presentation, Vesko says, looking for someone who might be the Dark Avenger; during the questions and discussion afterwards he listened for anyone defending the programming of Eddie. He saw and heard nothing that gave him any clues.

But two days after the lecture he received a letter from the Dark Avenger. According to the letter, the virus writer had attended the meeting. Vesko published his comments in the magazine *Komputar za vas*. "The author of the Eddie virus is writing to you," the Dark Avenger began. "I have been reading your pieces of stupidity for quite a long time but what I heard in your lecture was, to put it boldly, the tops." The virus writer went on to complain about Vesko's critique of his programming skills. Then he added:

"I will tell you that my viruses really destroy information but, on the other hand, I don't turn other people's misfortunes into money. Since you [get paid to] write articles that mention my programs, do you not think I should get something?"

Virus writing is not a lucrative field. The Dark Avenger had once before alluded to getting paid for his skills, in a message to a local bulletin board operator, when he had suggested, none too hopefully, that "maybe someone can buy viruses." So far as is known, he has never sold any of his bugs.

In 1990 Vesko put together a psychological profile of the Dark Avenger, a compilation of all the known facts about him: his taste in music, his favorite groups, his supposed interest in the Princess of Wales, his need for money and so on. From his letter Vesko gleaned he had been a student at Sofia University and, from sarcastic remarks he had made about Vesko's engineering degree, that he was either a mathematics or science student (there is a traditional rivalry between engineering and the other two faculties). He sent the profile to seven former students at the university, asking if they knew anyone who fitted the criteria. All seven replied, Vesko says, and all seven mentioned the same name— that of a young man, then twenty-three, a programmer in a small, private software house in Sofia.

Vesko didn't turn him in. Even had he wanted to, there was little point: writing viruses is not illegal in Bulgaria.

6

■

HACKING FOR
PROFIT

Inevitably there are people in the computer underworld who use their skills to make money—legally or illegally. Hacking into suppliers to steal goods, or looting credit card companies, has become established practice. But there seems to be little commercial potential in viruses—unless it becomes part of a scam. In December 1989 the first such scam appeared. The virus was used as a blackmail weapon to frighten computer users into paying for protection. Jim Bates, a free-lance computer security consultant, was one of the first to examine the blackmail demand delivered on an apparently ordinary computer diskette. He had received a call earlier that day from Mark Hamilton, the technical editor of a British computer magazine called *PC Business World*. Mark had sounded worried: "There's apparently been a trojan diskette sent out to *PC Business World* customers. We don't know anything about it. If we send you a copy, can you look into it?"

Jim runs his little business from his home in a commuter suburb with the misleadingly bucolic name of Wigston Magna, near Leicester, in the English Midlands. Though he had other work to do at the time, he agreed to "look into it"—which meant, effectively, disassembling the bug. It would be a time-consuming task.

"What does it do?" he asked.

"We don't know. It may be some sort of blackmail attempt."

To Jim, the concept of viral blackmail sounded unlikely. As far as he knew, no one had ever made a penny out of writing viruses. It was said that if there was any money in writing bugs, Bulgaria would be one of the richest countries in Europe; but instead it remained one of the poorest.

At 5:30 that afternoon, December 12, 1989, the package from *PC Business World* arrived. As promised, it contained a diskette, of the sort sent out to the magazine's readers; it also contained a copy of a blue instruction leaflet that had accompanied the diskette.

Jim examined the leaflet closely. "Read this license agreement carefully [and] if you do not agree with the terms and conditions . . . do not use the software," it began. It then stated that the program on the diskette was leased to operators for either 365 uses at a price of $189, or the lifetime of their hard disk at a price of $389. "PC Cyborg Corporation," it continued, "also reserves the right [*sic*] to use program mechanisms to ensure termination of the use of the program [which] will adversely affect other program applications."

So far, Jim thought, it read much like a normal software licensing agreement, except for the warning that the program might "adversely effect other program applications."

But farther down in the small print on the leaflet was a paragraph that made him sit up. "You are advised of the most serious consequences of your failure to abide by the terms of this agreement: your conscience may haunt you for the rest of your life . . . *and your computer will stop functioning normally* [authors' italics]."

This, Jim thought, was carrying the concept of a licensing agreement too far. Licensing software was a perfectly acceptable business practice, as was making threats that unauthorized users of their products would be prosecuted for "copyright infringement." They never threatened to punish unauthorized users by damaging their computers.

Even more unusual, the diskette had been sent out like junk mail, unrequested, to computer users around Great Britain, inviting them to run it on their machines. Whoever had distributed the diskettes had obviously purchased *PC Business World*'s mailing list, which the magazine routinely rented out in the form of addressed labels. The magazine had seeded its list with names and addresses of its own staff, an ordinary practice that allows the renter to check that its clients aren't using the list more often than agreed. These seeded addresses had alerted the magazine to the existence of the diskette. If the publication had received copies from its seeded addresses, so had some seven thousand others on the mailing list. And Jim knew that many of these would have loaded the program without reading the blue leaflet—which was, in any case, printed in type so small that it was almost unreadable. Anyone who had already run the diskette, Jim thought, could well be sitting on a time bomb.

Later that evening an increasingly anxious Mark Hamilton phoned again: "We're now getting reports that this disk has been found in Belgium, Paris, Germany, Switzerland, Scandinavia, and Italy. Can you do anything with it?"

In fact, Jim was already working on an antidote. He had loaded the diskette on an isolated test computer in his upstairs office and had discovered that it contained two very large executable files: an "Install" program and an "AIDS" program. Jim had previously attempted to run the AIDS file on its own, but after a few seconds it aborted, displaying the message: "You must run the Install program before you can use the AIDS program."

He followed the instructions, warily loading up Install. It beeped into life, the light on the hard disk flickering off and on. When the installation was finished, Jim looked at the hard disk, using software designed to see all of the files listed in the computer's various directories. The software also allowed him to see any "hidden" files, those generally concealed from casual inspection to prevent them being deleted accidentally. There are always two hidden operating system files on a hard disk; but now, after running the Install program, there was suddenly a whole series of them, none of them named.

He decided to have a look at the hidden files, using another special program. This software went right into the heart of the files, penetrating the binary code, the building blocks of programs. It presented the contents on a vertically split screen: the left side displaying the files in computer code, the right in ordinary text. Jim went through them page by page. He discovered that the hidden files contained a counter, which kept track of the number of times the computer was turned on. After ninety start-ups the hidden files would spring to life and attack the computer's hard disk, encrypting working files and hiding programs.[1] Without access to programs and data, the system would be unusable.

The diskette Jim realized, was a huge trojan horse, a malicious piece of software that entered a system in the guise of something useful, then unleashed its payload. In this case the "useful" component was the "AIDS information" file; the payload was the scrambling of the hard disk.

Curiously, Jim found that the program had been written to behave almost like the real AIDS virus. It was opportunistic, just like its biological counterpart; it spread its infection slowly; and was ultimately fatal to its hosts. Whoever wrote the program must have been casually interested in AIDS, though perhaps he didn't know a great deal about the subject. Switching to the AIDS information file, Jim read through the material it offered, which described itself as "An interactive program for health education on the disease called AIDS. . . . The health information provided could save your life. . . . Please share this program diskette with other people so that they can benefit from it too."

The program offered "up-to-date information about how you can reduce the risk of future infection, based on the details of your own lifestyle and history." It required a user to answer thirty-eight questions—sex, age, number of sexual partners since 1980, medical history, sexual behavior, and so on—and according to the user's answers it provided "confidential advice," most of which was eccentric and misleading: "Scientific studies show that you cannot catch AIDS from insects," and "AIDS can be prevented by avoiding the virus" were two of the less helpful comments. Others included, "Danger: Reduce the number of your sex partners now!" "You are advised that your risk of contracting AIDS is so large that it goes off the chart of probabilities." "Buy condoms today when you leave your office." "Insist that your sex partner be mutually faithful to the relationship." "Casual kissing appears to be safe. Open-mouth kissing appears to be more dangerous. It is that which follows open-mouth kissing that is most risky." "The AIDS virus may appear in small quantities in the tears of an infected person."

The AIDS trojan, as it had quickly become named, also produced a variety of messages demanding payment for the license. In certain cases, if the computer was linked to a printer, it could cause an invoice to be printed out. The money for the license was to be sent to PC Cyborg Corporation at a post office box in Panama City, Panama. It was not specified what users would receive for the fee, apart from a license. But it was assumed that an antidote for the trojan would be included in the deal.

The AIDS information diskette was the largest and most complex trojan Jim had ever seen. He worked on it eighteen hours a day for seventeen days and later said that taking the program apart was "like peeling an onion with a paper clip." His final disassembly ran to 383 pages, each containing 120 lines of code. He had managed to produce a quick antidote to the AIDS trojan on the day he received it, but after he had disassembled the bug, he put together a program called ClearAid which would restore files and cleanse infected systems. The antidote and ClearAid were offered free to infected computer users by Jim and *PC Business World.*

Later, when the furor died down, Jim decided that the trojan had been written "by a young, inexperienced programmer with only scant knowledge of both the language and the machine capabilities at his disposal." Its tortuous complexity had been caused by incompetence rather than design.

This was little comfort for those who had suffered damage from the bug. Over twenty thousand of the AIDS diskettes had been sent out, using not only the *PC Business World* mailing list, but the delegate register to a World Health Organization (WHO) conference on AIDS in Stockholm. In the first few days, a number of recipients had panicked when they realized that they had just loaded a potentially destructive trojan onto their systems. The trojan had caused the loss of data at the U.N. Development Program offices in Geneva, and in Italy an AIDS research center at the University of Bologna reported the loss of ten years of research. Like many users, they had not kept backup copies of their valuable data. The trojan reached hospitals and clinics throughout Europe, and the Chase Manhattan Bank and International Computers Limited (ICL) in England both reported unspecified "problems" caused by the program. In every instance, scientists, researchers, and computer operators wasted days chasing down and eliminating the bug, even after Jim's antidote and ClearAid program became generally available.

At New Scotland Yard the Computer Crime Unit under Detective Inspector John Austen established that all twenty thousand diskettes had been posted from west and southwest London, between December 7 and 11, 1989, and that they had been sent to addresses in almost every country of the world, with one glaring exception: none had been sent to the United States.

The Computer Crime Unit does not have an easy job.

In many cases it has been frustrated by the unusual nature of computer crime, and with viruses it has been noticeably unsuccessful in bringing prosecutions. Most viruses are written abroad, by unknown and certainly untraceable authors, often in countries such as Bulgaria where the act itself is not a criminal offense. To prosecute a case against a virus writer, the unit must have a complaint against the author from a victim in Britain, evidence of criminal intent, proof of the author's identity, and finally, his presence in Britain, or at least in a country from which he can be extradited.

The legal problem with viruses, quite simply, is their internationality. They seep across borders, carried anonymously on diskettes or uploaded via phone lines to bulletin boards; their provenance is often unknown, their authorship usually a mystery. But inspector John Austen was determined that the AIDS diskette incident would be different. He viewed it as the "most serious" case the unit had faced: not only was it a large-scale attack on computers by a trojan-horse program, it was blackmail—or something very similar. In this case, he also had a complaint; indeed, he had a few thousand complaints. It was clearly time for the unit to throw its resources into tracking down the author of the trojan.

The publishers of *PC Business World* told the police that they had sold this particular mailing list for about $2,000 to a Mr. E. Ketema of Ketema & Associates, who purported to be an African businessman representing a Nigerian software company. The transaction had been carried out by post; no one had ever met Ketema.

Ketema & Associates operated out of a maildrop address in Bond Street, London. Company documents revealed that the firm had three other directors, supposedly Nigerian: Kitian Mekonen, Asrat Wakjiri, and Fantu Mekesse. The staff of the company that operated the maildrop had never seen the three Nigerians, but they had met Mr. Ketema. Far from being an African businessman, he was described as white, bearded, and probably American.

Computer Unit detectives then turned their attention to PC Cyborg Corporation of Panama City. Through inquiries to the Panamanian police, it was discovered that the company had been registered a year earlier. The Panamanians were also able to find the company's local telephone number.

Waiting until early evening in London, when it would be ten A.M. in Panama, a detective put a call through, and was rewarded by the sound of an American voice when the phone was answered. "Mr. Ketema?" asked the detective tentatively. "Who?" answered the voice. It turned out to be an American marine. Panama had been invaded on that very day.[2]

Simultaneous inquiries in Nigeria did not turn up evidence of the three Nigerian businessmen who were registered as directors of the company. Indeed, the Unit discovered that the three names didn't sound Nigerian at all. They might have been made up.

By then the Computer Unit's detectives were convinced that they were chasing one man, probably an American.

The arrest happened almost by accident. New Scotland Yard had routinely circulated details of the case to Interpol, the international police intelligence agency. Four days before Christmas in 1989, just two weeks after the diskettes had been posted from London, the Dutch police detained an American citizen at Schiphol airport in Amsterdam, who had been behaving strangely.

The American was Joseph Lewis Popp. He was en route from Nairobi, where he had been attending a WHO seminar, to Ohio, where he lived with his parents in the small town of Willowick, near Cleveland. Popp seemed to think that someone was trying to kill him: at Schiphol he had written "Dr. Popp has been poisoned" on the suitcase of another traveler, apparently in an attempt to notify the police. When he had calmed down, the authorities took a discreet look through his bags: in one, they found the company seal for PC Cyborg Corporation.

The police let Popp continue his journey to Ohio, then notified Austen in England about the seal. On January 18, 1990, Austen began extradition proceedings. The charge: "That on December 11, 1989, within the jurisdiction of the Central Criminal Court, you with a view to gain for another, viz. PC Cyborg Corporation of Panama, with menaces made unwarranted demands, viz. a payment of one hundred and eighty nine U.S. dollars or three hundred and seventy eight U.S. dollars from the victim." In Ohio the FBI began a surveillance of Popp's parents' home, and finally arrested him on February 3rd.

Neighbors in Willowick were said to have been surprised at his arrest. He was described as "quiet, intelligent, and a real gentleman." At the time of his arrest he was thirty-nine, a zoologist and anthropologist who had worked as a consultant on animal behavior with UNICEF and WHO. He was a soft-spoken man, dark-haired, with flecks of gray in his beard. He had graduated from Ohio State University in 1972 and obtained a doctorate in anthropology from Harvard in 1979. In the previous few years he had become passionately interested in AIDS.

Austen's extradition request ground through the American courts for nearly a year. In September 1990 Jim Bates was flown over to Cleveland for five days to give evidence at Popp's extradition hearing. It is unusual to have live witnesses at such hearings, but Jim brought the AIDS diskette. He was the principal witness, and it was his task to demonstrate to the court what the diskette was and what it did.

In the hallway outside the small courtroom, Jim sat beside Popp's parents, a friendly and courteous pair. "Do you like Cleveland?" Popp's mother asked. Jim wasn't sure; all he had seen by then was the airport, a hotel room, and the hallway. Inside the courtroom Jim had his first glance at Joseph Popp. His hair was long and unkempt, his beard had grown out, making the gray more emphatic. He shuffled around the courtroom, wearing a shabby jacket, a sweater, and faded jeans. He looked, Jim later said, "like a lost soul."

Popp's mental state was the crux of the defense's argument in the extradition hearings: his lawyers argued that he had suffered a nervous breakdown and was unfit to stand trial. Popp never denied writing the AIDS trojan nor sending out the diskettes. But at the time, his lawyers said, he was in the grip of mental illness and was behaving abnormally.

The lawyers also argued that the demand for a license fee for the use of the diskette was not tantamount to blackmail. It was, they agreed, somewhat extreme to wreck a computer's hard disk if the user didn't pay, but operators were warned not to load the diskette if they didn't accept the terms and conditions laid down in the instruction leaflet. And it was quite clearly stated on the same sheet that if they used the diskette and didn't pay, the computer "would stop functioning normally."

There was a basis in law to the argument. Software publishers have long struggled to stop the unauthorized use and copying of their copyright programs. Software piracy is said to cost American publishers as much as $5 billion a year, and many markets—Taiwan, Thailand, Hong Kong, Singapore, Brazil, India, and even Japan, among others—have become what are euphemistically referred to as "single-disk" countries: in other words, countries where one legitimate copy of a software program is bought and the rest illegally copied. To combat piracy, publishing houses have used a number of devices: some programs, for example, contain deliberate "errors," which are triggered at set intervals—say, once every year—and which require a call from the user to the publisher to rectify. The publisher can then verify that the user is legitimate and has paid his license fee before telling him how to fix it.

Other publishers have resorted to more extreme methods. One celebrated case involved an American cosmetics conglomerate that had leased a program from a small software house to handle the distribution of its products. On October 16, 1990, after a disagreement between the two about the lease payments, the software company dialed into the cosmetic giant's computer and entered a code that disabled its own program. The cosmetics company's entire distribution operation was halted for three days. The software house argued that it was simply protecting its property and that its action was akin to a disconnection by the telephone company. The cosmetics company said that it was "commercial terrorism."

The Cleveland District Court, however, rejected arguments that the AIDS diskettes simply contained some sort of elaborate copyright-protection device. It also ruled that Popp was fit to stand trial and ordered his extradition to Britain to face charges.

Popp was the first person ever extradited for a computer crime and the first ever to be tried in Britain for writing a malicious program. From the welter of complaints, the police had prepared five counts against him; he faced ten years in prison on each charge. According to the police, Popp had perpetrated a scam that could have grossed him over $7.5 million, assuming that each of the twenty thousand recipients of the diskette had sent the "lifetime" license fee. More realistically, it was estimated that one thousand recipients had actually loaded the diskette after receiving it; but even if only those one thousand had sent him the minimum license fee, he still would have earned $189,000.

The police also discovered a diskette that they believed Popp intended to send out to "registered users" who had opted for the cheaper, $189 license. Far from being an antidote, it was another trojan and merely extended the counter from 90 boot-ups to 365 before scrambling the hard disk. In addition, there was evidence that the London mailing was only an initial test run: when Popp's home in Ohio was raided, the FBI found one million blank diskettes. It was believed that Popp was intending to use the proceeds from the AIDS scheme to fund a mass, worldwide mailing, using another trojan. The potential return from one million diskettes is a rather improbable $378 million.

The police also had suspicions that Popp, far from being mentally unstable, had launched the scheme with cunning and foresight. For example, he had purposely avoided sending any of the diskettes to addresses in the United States, where he lived, possibly believing that it would make him immune to prosecution under American law.

But the case was never to come to trial. Popp's defense presented evidence that his mental state had deteriorated. Their client, his British lawyers said, had begun putting curlers in his beard and wearing a cardboard box on his head to protect himself from radiation. In November 1991 the prosecution accepted that Popp was mentally unfit to stand trial. To this day, the Computer Crime Unit has never successfully prosecuted a virus writer.[3]

For Popp, whatever his motives and his mental state, the AIDS scheme was an expensive affair—all funded from his own pocket. The postage needed to send out the first twenty thousand diskettes had cost nearly $7,700, the envelopes and labels about $11,500, the diskettes and the blue printed instruction leaflets yet another $11,500—to say nothing of the cost of registering PC Cyborg Corporation in Panama, or establishing an address in London. To add insult to injury, not one license payment was ever received from anyone, anywhere.

Popp's scheme was not particularly well thought out. The scam depended on recipients of his diskettes mailing checks halfway around the world in the hope of receiving an antidote to the trojan. But, as John Austen said, "Who in their right mind would send money to a post office box number in Panama City for an antidote that might never arrive?" Or that may not be an antidote anyway.

It seems unlikely that anyone will ever again attempt a mass blackmail of this type; it's not the sort of crime that lends itself to a high volume, low cost formula. It's far more likely that specific corporations will be singled out for targeted attacks. Individually, they are far more vulnerable to blackmail, particularly if the plotters are aided by an insider with knowledge of any loopholes. An added advantage for the perpetrators is the likely publicity blackout with which the corporate victim would immediately shroud the affair: every major corporation has its regular quota of threats, mostly empty, and a well-defined response strategy.

But at present, hacking—which gives access to information—has proven to be substantially more lucrative. Present-day hackers traffic in what the authorities call access device codes, the collective name for credit card numbers, telephone authorization codes, and computer passwords. They are defined as any card, code, account number, or "means of account access" that can be used to obtain money, goods, or services. In the United States the codes are traded through a number of telecom devices, principally voice-mail computers; internationally, they are swapped on hacker boards.

The existence of this international traffic has created what one press report referred to colorfully as "offshore data havens"—pirate boards where hackers from different countries convene to trade Visa numbers for computer passwords, or American Express accounts for telephone codes. The passwords and telephone codes, the common currency of hacking, are traded to enable hackers to maintain their lifeline—the phone—and to break into computers. Credit card numbers are used more conventionally: to fraudulently acquire money, goods, and services.

The acquisition of stolen numbers by hacking into credit agency computers or by means as mundane as dumpster diving (scavenging rubbish in search of the carbons from credit card receipts) differs from ordinary theft. When a person is mugged, for example, he knows his cards have been stolen and cancels them. But if the numbers were acquired without the victim knowing about it, the cards generally remain "live" until the next bill is sent out, which could be a month away.

Live cards—ones that haven't been canceled and that still have some credit on them—are a valuable commodity in the computer underworld. Most obviously, they can be used to buy goods over the phone, with the purchases delivered to a temporary address or an abandoned house to which the hacker has access.

The extent of fraud of this sort is difficult to quantify. In April 1989 *Computerworld* magazine estimated that computer-related crime costs American companies as much as $555,464,000 each year, not including lost man-hours and computer downtime. The figure is global, in that it takes in everything: fraud, loss of data, theft of software, theft of telephone services, and so on. Though it's difficult to accept the number as anything more than a rough estimate, its apparent precision has given the figure a spurious legitimacy. The same number frequently appears in most surveys of computer crime in the United States and is even in many government documents. The blunt truth is that no one can be certain what computer fraud of any sort really costs. All anyone knows is that it occurs.

Leslie Lynne Doucette has been described as "the female Fagin" of the computer underworld. In her mid-thirties, she was considerably older than the 150 or so adolescent Olivers she gathered into her ring. As a woman, she has the distinction of being one of only two or three female hackers who have ever come to the attention of the authorities.

In 1989 Doucette lived in an apartment on the north side of Chicago in the sort of neighborhood that had seen better days; the block looked substantial, though it was showing the first signs of neglect. Despite having what the police like to term "no visible means of support," Doucette was able to provide for herself and her two children, pay the rent, and keep up with the bills. Her small apartment was filled with electronic gear: personal computer equipment, modems, automatic dialers, and other telecom peripherals.

Doucette was a professional computer criminal. She operated a scheme dealing in stolen access codes: credit cards, telephone cards (from AT&T, MCI, Sprint, and ITT) as well as corporate PBX telephone access codes, computer passwords, and codes for voice-mail (VM) computers. She dealt mostly in MasterCard and Visa numbers, though occasionally in American Express too. Her job was to turn around live numbers as rapidly as possible. Using a network of teenage hackers throughout the country, she would receive credit card numbers taken from a variety of sources. She would then check them, either by hacking into any one of a number of credit card validation computers or, more often, by calling a "chat line" telephone number. If the chat line accepted the card as payment, it was live. She then grouped the cards by type, and called the numbers through to a "code line," a hijacked mailbox on a voice-mail computer.

Because Doucette turned the cards around quickly, checking their validity within hours of receiving their numbers and then, more importantly, getting the good numbers disseminated on a code line within days, they remained live for a longer period. It was a very efficiently run hacker service industry. To supplement her income, she would pass on card numbers to members of her ring in other cities, who would use them to buy Western Union money orders payable to one of Doucette's aliases. The cards were also used to pay for an unknown number of airline tickets and for hotel accommodation when Doucette or her accomplices were traveling.

The key to Doucette's business was communication—hence the emphasis on PBX and voice-mail computer access codes. The PBXs provided the means for communication; the voice-mail computers the location for code lines.

PBX is a customer-operated, computerized telephone system, providing both internal and external communication. One of its features is the Remote Access Unit (RAU), designed to permit legitimate users to call in from out of the office, often on a 1-800 number, and access a long-distance line after punching in a short code on the telephone keypad. The long-distance calls made in this way are then charged to the customer company. Less legitimate users—hackers, in other words—force access to the RAU by guessing the code. This is usually done by calling the system and trying different sequences of numbers on the keypad until stumbling on a code. The process is time-consuming, but hackers are a patient bunch.

The losses to a company whose PBX is compromised can be staggering. Some hackers are known to run what are known as "call-sell" operations: sidewalk or street-corner enterprises offering passersby cheap long-distance calls (both national and international) on a cellular or pay phone. The calls, of course, are routed through some company's PBX. In a recent case, a "call-sell" operator ran up $1.4 million in charges against one PBX owner over a four-day holiday period. (The rewards to "call-sell" merchants can be equally enormous: at $10 a call some operators working whole banks of pay phones are estimated by U.S. law enforcement agencies to have made as much as $10,000 a day.)

PBXs may have become the blue boxes for a new generation of phreakers, but voice-mail computers have taken over as hacker bulletin boards. The problem with the boards was that they became too well known: most were regularly monitored by law enforcement agencies. Among other things, the police recorded the numbers of access device codes trafficked on boards, and as the codes are useful only as long as they are live—usually the time between their first fraudulent use and the victim's first bill—the police monitoring served to invalidate them that much faster. Worse, from the point of view of hackers, the police then took steps to catch the individuals who had posted the codes.

The solution was to use voice mail. Voice-mail computers operate like highly sophisticated answering machines and are often attached to a company's toll-free 1-800 number. For users, voice-mail systems are much more flexible than answering machines: they can receive and store messages from callers, or route them from one box to another box on the system, or even send one single message to a preselected number of boxes. The functions are controlled by the appropriate numerical commands on a telephone keypad. Users can access their boxes and pick up their messages while they're away from the office by calling their 1-800 number, punching in the digits for their box, then pressing the keys for their private password. The system is just a simple computer, accessible by telephone and controllable by the phone keys.

But for hackers voice mail is made to order. The 1-800 numbers for voice-mail systems are easy enough to find; the tried-and-true methods of dumpster diving, social engineering, and war-dialing will almost always turn up a few usable targets. War-dialing has been simplified in the last decade with the advent of automatic dialers, programs which churn through hundreds of numbers, recording those that are answered by machines or computers. The process is still inelegant, but it works.

After identifying a suitable 1-800 number, hackers break into the system to take over a box or, better, a series of boxes. Security is often lax on voice-mail computers, with box numbers and passwords ridiculously easy to guess by an experienced hacker. One of the methods has become known as finger hacking: punching away on the telephone keypad trying groups of numbers until a box and the appropriate password are found. Ideally, hackers look for unused boxes. That way they can assign their own passwords and are less likely to be detected. Failing that, though, they will simply annex an assigned box, changing the password to lock out the real user.

VM boxes are more secure than hacker boards: the police, for a start, can't routinely monitor voice-mail systems as they can boards, while hackers can quickly move to new systems if they suspect the authorities of monitoring one they are using. The messaging technology of voice-mail systems lends itself to passing on lists of codes. The code line is often the greeting message of the hacker-controlled mailbox; in other words, instead of hearing the standard "Hello, Mr. Smith is not in the office. Please leave a message," hackers calling in will hear the current list of stolen code numbers. In this manner, only the hacker leaving the codes need know the box password. The other hackers, those picking up the codes or leaving a message, only need to know the box number.

It was ultimately a voice-mail computer that led the authorities to Doucette. On February 9, 1989, the president of a real estate company in Rolling Meadow, Illinois, contacted the U.S. Secret Service office in Chicago. His voice-mail computer, he complained, had been overrun by hackers.

The harassed real estate man became known as Source 1. On February 15th, two Secret Service agents—William "Fred" Moore and Bill Tebbe—drove from Chicago to the realtor's office to interview him. They found a man beset by unwanted intruders.

The company had installed its voice-mail system in the autumn of 1988. The box numbers and passwords were personally assigned by the company president. While the 1-800 number to access the system was published, he insisted that the passwords were known only to himself and to the individual box users.

In November 1988, during an ordinary review of the traffic on the system, he had been startled to discover a number of unexplained messages. He had no idea what they were about or who they were for; he thought they could have been left in error.

However, the number of "errors" had grown throughout November and December. By January 1989 the "errors" had become so frequent that they overwhelmed the system, taking over almost all of the voice-mail computer's memory and wiping out messages for the company's business.

The Secret Service recorded the messages over a period from late February to March. Listening to the tapes, they realized they were dealing with a code line.

The law on access devices prohibits the unauthorized possession of fifteen or more of such codes, or the swapping or sale of the codes "with an intent to defraud." (Fraud is defined as a $1,000 loss to the victim or profit to the violator.) On the tapes, the agents could identify 130 devices that were trafficked by the various unknown callers. They also heard the voice of a woman who identified herself alternatively as "Kyrie" or "long-distance information." It seemed as if she was running the code line, so they decided to focus the investigation on her.

In March security officials from MCI, the long-distance telephone company, told the Secret Service that Canadian Bell believed "Kyrie" to be an alias of Leslie Lynne Doucette, a Canadian citizen who had been hacking for six or seven years. In March 1987 Doucette had been convicted of telecommunications fraud in Canada and sentenced to ninety days' imprisonment with two years' probation. She had been charged with running a code line and trafficking stolen access codes. Subsequently, the Canadians reported, Doucette had left the country with her two children.

Later that month an MCI operative, Tom Schutz, told Moore that an informant had passed on the word that a well-known hacker named Kyrie had just moved from the West Coast to the Chicago area. The informant, Schutz said, had overheard the information on a hacker "bridge" (a conference call). At the beginning of April an MCI security officer, Sue Walsh, received information from another informant that Kyrie had a Chicago telephone number.

By mid-month, Moore was able to get court authorization to

attach a dialed-number recorder (DNR), to Doucette's phone. A DNR monitors outgoing calls, recording the number accessed and any codes used. From the surveillance, agents were able to detect a large volume of calls to various voice-mail systems and PBX networks.

The authorities traced the other compromised voice-mail systems to Long Beach, California, and Mobile, Alabama. They discovered that Kyrie was operating code lines on both networks. It's not unusual for hackers to work more than one system; sometimes Hacker A will leave codes for Hacker B on a voice-mail computer in, say, Florida, while Hacker B might leave his messages for Hacker A on a system in New York. By rotating through voice-mail computers in different states, hackers ensure that local law enforcement officials who stumble upon their activities see only part of the picture.

The agents also realized that Kyrie was running a gang. From other sources they heard tapes on which she gave tutorials to neophyte hackers on the techniques of credit card fraud. Over the period of the investigation they identified 152 separate contacts from all over the country, all used as sources for stolen codes. Of the gang, the agents noted seven in particular, whom they identified as "major hackers" within the ring: Little Silence in Los Angeles; the ironically named FBI Agent in Michigan; Outsider, also in Michigan; Stingray from Massachusetts; EG in Columbus, Ohio; Navoronne, also from Columbus; and Game Warden in Georgia.[4] DNRs were also attached to their telephones.

The agents assigned to the case described the group, imaginatively, as "a high-tech street gang." By then the Secret Service had turned the enquiry into a nationwide investigation involving the FBI, the Illinois State Police, the Arizona Attorney General's Office, the Chicago Police Department, the Columbus (Ohio) Police Department, the Cobb County (Georgia) Sheriff's Office, the Royal Canadian Mounted Police, and the Ontario Provincial Police. Security agents from MCI, Sprint, AT&T, and nine Bell phone companies provided technical assistance.

On May 24th the Secret Service asked local authorities in six cities for assistance to mount raids on Doucette's Chicago apartment and the addresses of the five other major hackers in the ring. Prior to the raids the authorities compiled a list of equipment that was to be seized: telephones and speed-dialing devices; computers and peripherals; diskettes; cassette tapes; videotapes; records and documents; computer or data-processing literature; bills, letters, invoices, or any other material relating to occupancy; information pertaining to access device codes; and "degaussing" equipment.[5]

The raid on Doucette's Chicago apartment produced a lode of access codes. Moore found a book listing the numbers for 171 AT&T, ITT, and other telephone cards, as well as authorization codes for 39 PBXs. In addition, the agents found numbers for 118 Visa cards, 150 MasterCards, and 2 American Express cards.

Doucette admitted that she was Kyrie. Later in the Secret Service offices, she confessed to operating code lines, trafficking stolen numbers, and receiving unauthorized Western Union money orders. She was held in custody without bond and indicted on seventeen counts of violating federal computer, access device, and telecom fraud laws between January 1988 and May 1989.

Estimates of the costs of Doucette's activities varied. On the day of her arrest, she was accused of causing "$200,000 in losses . . . by corporations and telephone service providers." Later it was announced that "substantially more than $1.6 million in losses were suffered" by credit card companies and telephone carriers.

Doucette's was a high-profile arrest, the first federal prosecution for hacking voice-mail systems and trafficking in access devices. The prosecution was determined that she would be made an example of; her case, the authorities said, would reflect "a new reality for hackers" in the 1990s—the certainty of "meaningful punishment." If convicted of all charges, Doucette faced eighty-nine years' imprisonment, a $69,000 fine, and $1.6 million in restitution charges.

The case was plea-bargained. Doucette admitted to one count;

the other charges were dismissed. On August 17, 1990, Doucette, then aged thirty-six, was sentenced to twenty-seven months in prison. It was one of the most severe sentences ever given to a computer hacker in the United States.[6]

Willie Sutton, a U.S. gangster, was once asked why he robbed banks. "Because that's where the money is," he replied.

Little has changed; banks still have the money. Only the means of robbing them have become more numerous. Modern banks are dependent on computer technology, creating new opportunities for fraud and high-tech bank robbery.

Probably the best-known story about modern-day bank fraud involves the computation of "rounded-off" interest payments. A bank employee noticed that the quarterly interest payments on the millions of savings accounts held by the bank were worked out to four decimal points, then rounded up or down. Anything above .0075 of a dollar was rounded up to the next penny and paid to the customer; anything below that was rounded down and kept by the bank. In other words, anything up to three quarters of a cent in earned interest on millions of accounts was going back into the bank's coffers.

Interest earned by bank customers was calculated and credited by computer. So it would be a simple matter for an employee to write a program amending the process: instead of the rounded-down interest going back to the bank, it could all be amalgamated in one account, to which the employee alone had access. Over the two or three years that such a scam was said to have been operational, an employee was supposed to have grossed millions, even billions, of dollars.

The story is an urban legend that has been told for years and accepted by many, but there has not been a single documented case. However, it certainly could be true: banks' dependence on computers has made fraud easier to commit and harder to detect. Computers are impersonal, their procedures faster and more anonymous than paper-based transactions. They can move money around the world in microseconds, and accounts can effortlessly be created and hidden from a computer keyboard.

Like any corporate fraud, most bank fraud is committed by insiders, employees with access to codes and procedures who can create a "paper trail" justifying a transaction. In such cases the fraud is not really different from illegal transactions carried out in the quill-pen era: the use of a computer has simply mechanized such fraud and made it more difficult to track.

The new threat to banks comes from hackers. In addition to the familiar duo of the bank robber and the criminal employee—the one bashing through the front door with a shotgun, the other sitting in the back room quietly cooking the books—banks now face a third security risk: the adolescent hacker with a PC, a modem, and the ability to access the bank's computers from a remote site. Unlike traditional bank robbers, hackers don't come through the front door: they sneak in through the bank's own computer access ports, then roam unseen through the systems, looking for vulnerable areas. Unlike crooked employees, hackers aren't a physical presence: they remain unseen and undetected until it's too late.

Though banks spend millions protecting their computer systems from intruders, they aren't necessarily that secure. Bank employees, particularly those who work in dealing rooms, are notorious for using the most obvious passwords, generally those that reflect their own ambitions: *Porsche* and *sex* are perennial favorites. Sometimes even the most basic security precautions are overlooked. Recently two hackers demonstrated this point for a London newspaper. They targeted the local headquarters of "a leading American bank"—one that was so well known for its laxity that its systems had become a training ground for neophyte hackers. The two had first hacked into the bank's computer in March 1988, and in October 1990 the pair did it again, using the same ID and password they had first employed in 1988. The bank hadn't bothered to modify its most basic procedures, and its first line of defense against hackers, for over two and a half years.

Given such opportunity, it could be assumed that banks are regularly being looted by hackers. The mechanics appear straightforward enough: operating from home a hacker should be able to break into a bank's central computer quite anonymously, access the sector dealing with cash transfers, then quickly move the money to an account that he controls. However, in practice the procedure is more complex. Banks use codes to validate transfers; in addition, transactions must be confirmed electronically by the recipient of the funds. Because of such safeguards, the plundering is probably limited.[7]

But the threat from hackers is still real. There may be a hundred hackers in the United States with the necessary skills to break into a bank and steal funds, which is a sizable number of potential bank robbers. And of course it would be the dream hack, the one that justifies the time spent staring at a video terminal while learning the craft.

The most successful bank robbery ever carried out by hackers *may* have occurred two years ago. The target was a branch of Citibank in New York. The identity of the two hackers is unknown, though they are thought to be in their late teens or early twenties.

The scheme began when the two became aware that certain financial institutions, including Citibank, used their connections on the various X.25 networks—the computer networks operated by commercial carriers such as Telenet or Sprint—to transfer money.[8] (The process is known as Electronic Fund Transfer, or EFT.) The two decided that if the funds could be intercepted in mid-transfer and diverted into another account—in this case, a computer file hidden within the system—then they could be redirected and withdrawn before the error was noticed.

The hackers began the robbery by investigating Telenet. They knew that Citibank had two "address prefixes" of its own—223 and 224—on the network; these were the prefixes for the seven-digit numbers (or "addresses") that denoted Citibank links to the system. By churning through sequential numbers they found a series of addresses for Citibank computer terminals, many of which were VAXen, the popular computers manufactured by DEC. One weekend they hacked into eight of the VAXen and found their way to the Citibank DECNET, an internal bank network linking the DEC computers. From there they found gateways to other banks and financial institutions in the New York area.

They ignored the other banks. What had particularly intrigued them were references in the computer systems to an EFT operation run by Citibank: in various files and throughout the electronic mail system they kept turning up allusions to EFT, clues that they were convinced pointed to a terminal that did nothing but transfer funds. They began sifting through their lists of computer access numbers, looking for one among hundreds that belonged to the EFT computer, and by a laborious process of elimination they whittled the lists down to five machines whose function they couldn't divine: Of those, one seemed particularly interesting. It could be entered by a debug port (a computer access port used for maintenance) that had been left in default mode—in other words, it could be accessed with the standard manufacturer-supplied password, because yet again no one had ever bothered to change it.

The system they entered contained menus that guided them through the computer. One path took them directly into an administration area used by system operators. After an hour of exploration they found a directory that held a tools package, allowing them to create their own programs. With it, they wrote a procedure to copy all incoming and outgoing transmissions on the terminal into their own file. They named the file ".trans" and placed it in a directory they called "..■ ■" (dot, dot, space, space), effectively hiding it from view. What they had created was a "capture" file; from the transmissions that were copied, they would be able to divine the functions of the computer terminal.

The capture file was created late on a Sunday night. At about nine P.M. on the next evening they logged on to the system again, and from the day's transmissions they could tell that the targeted machine was indeed an EFT terminal. They discovered that the computer began transactions by linking itself to a similar computer at another bank, waiting for a particular control sequence to be sent, and then transferring a long sequence of numbers and letters. They captured about 170 different transactions on the first day and several hundred more in the following week. At the end of the week they removed the ".trans" file and its directory, killed the capture routine, and went through the system removing any trace that they had ever been there.

From the captured transmissions they were able to piece together the meaning of the control sequence and the transfers themselves. They also noticed that after the Citibank computer had sent its transfer, the destination bank would repeat the transaction (by way of confirmation) and in ten seconds would say TRANSACTION COMPLETED, followed by the destination bank ID. The two guessed that the bank IDs were the standard Federal Reserve numbers for banks (every bank in America that deals with the Federal Reserve system has a number assigned to it, as do several European banks). To confirm the hunch, they called up Citibank and asked for its Federal Reserve number. It was the same as the ID being sent by the computer.

The two hackers then realized that they had collected all of the technical information they needed to raid the bank. They had discovered the codes and the procedures for the control sequence and the transfers; they knew what the bank IDs signified; and from the Federal Reserve itself they got a listing of all the national and international bank ID numbers. Now they had to organize the downstream: a secure process of getting money into their own pockets.

One of the duo had a friend, an accountant of questionable moral character, who opened a numbered Swiss account under a false name for the two hackers. He had originally laughed at the idea, explaining that an initial $50,000 was required to open a numbered account. But when he was told to get the forms so that the money could be wired to Switzerland, he began to take the scheme seriously. A few days later the accountant delivered the paperwork, the account number, and several transaction slips. He also raised his usual $1,000 fee to $6,500.

The two hackers flew to Oklahoma City to visit the hall of records and get new birth certificates. With these they obtained new Oklahoma IDs and Social Security numbers. Then, using the false IDs, they opened accounts at six different banks in Houston and Dallas, with $1,000 cash deposited in each.

The next day, armed with one Swiss and six American accounts, they began the attack. They rigged the Citicorp computer controlling the EFT transfers to direct all of its data flow to an unused Telenet terminal they had previously discovered. They took turns sitting on the terminal, collecting the transmissions, and returning the correct acknowledgments with the Federal Reserve IDs. The transmissions each represented a cash transfer: essentially, the money was being hijacked. But by sending the required acknowledgments the hackers were giving Citibank "confirmation" that the transactions had reached the destination banks. By noon the two had $184,300 in their limbo account.

The two then disabled the "data forwarding" function on the Citibank computer, taking control of the EFT machine themselves so that they could redistribute the captured funds. By altering the transmissions, they transferred the money to the Swiss account. To the Swiss, it looked like a normal Citibank transmission; after all, it had come through the Citibank's own EFT computer.

Once the two hackers had received the standard confirmation from the Swiss bank, they immediately filled out six withdrawal forms and faxed them to its New York branch, along with instructions detailing where the funds should be sent. They told the Swiss bank to send $7,333 to each of the six U.S. accounts. (The amount was chosen because it was below the sum requiring notification of the authorities.) They followed the same procedure for three days, leaving the Swiss account with a little over $52,000 remaining on deposit.

Over the next week they withdrew $22,000 from each of the Dallas and Houston banks in amounts of $5,000 per day, leaving just under $1,000 in each account. At the end of the week they had each taken home $66,000 in cash.

You can believe this story or not as you wish. Certainly Citibank doesn't believe a word of it; it has consistently denied that anything resembling the events described above have ever happened, or that it has lost money in an EFT transfer due to hacking. The only reason anyone knows about the incident is that the two hackers who did it—or say they did—posted the details on a pirate board called Black ICE. The board was used by the Legion of Doom, at one time the most proficient and experienced hacker gang in the United States, and the two hackers-cum-robbers are thought to be LoD members—or at least to consider themselves LoD members.

Hackers are generally boastful. They gain credibility by exaggerating their abilities and glamorizing their exploits. It's the issue of identity: just as meek little Harvey Merkelstein from Brooklyn becomes the fearsome Killer Hacker when he gets loose on a keyboard, he also gains points with his peers by topping everyone else's last hack, and robbing a bank would be considered a pretty good hack.

The report from the two hackers could have been a fantasy, a means of impressing other LoD members. But, if they had managed to pull the robbery off, they would still have wanted to boast about it. And the perfect crime is the one that even the victim doesn't realize has happened. In the report posted on Black ICE, one of the two "bank robbers" wrote,

IT WILL BE INTERESTING TO SEE HOW THE CITICORP [CITI-BANK'S PARENT] INTERNAL FRAUD AUDITORS AND THE TREASURY DEPARTMENT SORT THIS OUT. THERE ARE NO

TRACES OF THE DIVERSION, IT JUST SEEMS TO HAVE HAP-
PENED. CITIBANK HAS PRINTED PROOF THAT THE FUNDS
WERE SENT TO THE CORRECT BANKS, AND THE CORRECT
BANKS' ACKNOWLEDGMENT ON THE SAME PRINTOUT. THE
CORRECT DESTINATION BANKS, HOWEVER, HAVE NO RECORD
OF THE TRANSACTION. THERE IS RECORD OF CITIBANK SEND-
ING FUNDS TO OUR SWISS ACCOUNT, BUT ONLY THE SWISS
HAVE THOSE RECORDS. SINCE WE WERE CONTROLLING THE
HOST [THE EFT COMPUTER] WHEN THE TRANSACTIONS WERE
SENT, THERE WERE NO PRINTOUTS ON THE SENDING SIDE.
SINCE WE WERE NOT ACTUALLY AT A TERMINAL CONNECTED
TO ONE OF THEIR LINE PRINTERS, NO ONE SHOULD FIGURE
OUT TO START CONTACTING SWISS BANKS, AND SINCE CITI-
BANK DOES THIS SORT OF THING DAILY WITH LARGE EURO-
PEAN BANKS, THEY WILL BE ALL TWISTED AND CONFUSED
BY THE TIME THEY FIND OURS. SHOULD THEY EVEN GET TO
OUR BANK, THEY WILL THEN HAVE TO START THE LONG AND
TEDIOUS PROCESS OF EXTRACTING INFORMATION FROM THE
SWISS. THEN IF THEY GET THE SWISS TO COOPERATE, THEY
WILL HAVE A DEAD END WITH THE ACCOUNT, SINCE IT WAS
SET UP UNDER THE GUISE OF A NONENTITY. THE ACCOUNTS
IN DALLAS AND HOUSTON WERE ALSO IN FAKE NAMES WITH
FAKE SOCIAL SECURITY NUMBERS; WE EVEN CHANGED OUR
APPEARANCES AND HANDWRITING STYLES AT EACH BANK.

I'M GLAD I'M NOT THE ONE WHO WILL HAVE THE JOB OF
TRACKING ME DOWN, OR EVEN TRYING TO MUSTER UP
PROOF OF WHAT HAPPENED. NOW WE WON'T HAVE TO
WORRY ABOUT DISPOSABLE INCOME FOR A WHILE. I CAN
FINISH COLLEGE WITHOUT WORKING AND STILL LIVE IN
RELATIVE LUXURY. IT'S KIND OF WEIRD HAVING OVER SIX
HUNDRED $100 BILLS IN THE DRAWER, THOUGH. TOO BAD
WE CAN'T EARN ANY INTEREST ON IT!

Needless to say, the anonymous authors of this report have
never been traced.

▪ ▪ ▪

It wasn't until later that anyone in the LoD realized that Black ICE had been compromised. The board had been regularly monitored by the authorities, particularly the U.S. Secret Service, as part of a continuing investigation of the LoD, an investigation that was just about to blow open.

The authorities tended to take reports of hacker exploits seriously. The various federal agencies, police forces, and prosecutors who had dealt with the computer underworld knew that computer security had been undermined by hacking. Everything was at risk: hackers had entered the military computer networks; they had hacked NASA and the Pentagon; they had compromised credit agencies and defrauded credit card companies; they had broken into bank systems; and they had made the telecom system a playground. But it wasn't just fraud that concerned the authorities. It was now also apparent that some hackers were selling their services to the KGB.

7

■

THE ILLUMINATI CONSPIRACY

Karl Koch was last seen alive on May 23, 1989. That morning he had turned up to work as usual at the Hannover office of Germany's ruling Christian Democratic party. Just before twelve o'clock he drove off alone to deliver a package across town, but he never arrived. In the late afternoon his employers notified the police of his disappearance.

Nine days later the police went to a woods on the outskirts of the small village of Ohof, just outside Hannover, on a routine enquiry. They were investigating a report of an abandoned car, its roof, hood, and windscreen thick with dust. In the undergrowth near the car, the police stumbled on a charred corpse lying next to an empty gasoline can. The vegetation around the body was scorched and burned. The police noticed that the corpse was barefoot—but no shoes were found in the car or in the surrounding area.

The investigators were perplexed. There had been no rain for five weeks, and the undergrowth was as dry as matchwood. But the scorched patch around the body was contained, as if the fire that consumed the victim had been carefully controlled.

The body was later identified as that of the twenty-four-year-old Karl Koch. The police assumed he had committed suicide. But still there were questions: principally, if Koch had killed himself, how had he been able to control the fire? Why had it not spread outside the confined perimeter?

Then there were the shoes: Koch had obviously been wearing shoes when he left his office. If he had taken them off, what had he done with them? It seemed as if someone had taken them.

But there were no clues to a killer, and the death was deemed to be suicide.

Four years previously Karl Koch had been the first hacker in Germany recruited by agents working for the KGB. At the time he was living in Hannover, a dropout from society and school who had recently squandered the small inheritance he had received following the death of his parents. A small-time drug habit helped him through his bereavement, and beyond, but his life was going nowhere.

Apart from drugs, Koch's only interest was hacking. His handle was Hagbard, an alias taken from the *Illuminati* trilogy by Robert Shea and Robert Anton Wilson. According to the books, the Illuminati is a secret cult that has been in existence since the beginning of time and has orchestrated every major crime, misfortune, and calamity. Only one man had ever emerged who could fight the cult: the hero, Hagbard Celine. Koch was drawn by the conspiracy theories nurtured in the books; he believed there were parallels in real life.

That year Koch met an older man named Peter Kahl. Kahl was then in his mid-thirties, a small-time fixer who was looking for a big break. He worked nights as a croupier in a Hannover casino and during the day was occupied with putting together his latest scheme.

Kahl's idea was simple: he planned to recruit a gang of hackers who could break into West European and American computer systems, particularly those on military or defense-industry sites. Then he would sell the data and information they had gathered to the KGB.

Kahl first encountered Koch at a hacker's meeting in Hannover. The young man seemed an ideal recruit: malleable, drifting, amoral. Later, when Kahl explained his scheme to Koch, the hacker appeared receptive. Two weeks later Koch agreed to become a member of the Soviet hacker gang.

In 1985 the computer underworld was a growing force in Germany. Hacking had become prevalent at the beginning of the decade, as low-cost personal computers became increasingly available. It had grown in popularity with the release of *War Games*—the 1983 film in which Matthew Broderick nearly unleashes the next world war by hacking into NORAD—which proved peculiarly influential in Germany. By the mid-1980s the Germans were second only to the Americans in the number of hackers and their audacity. The national computer networks had all been compromised; German hackers would later turn up on systems all over the world.

The growth of the computer underworld was nurtured by sustained media coverage and the quasi-institutionalization of hacking. Nearly everything in Germany is organized, even anarchy. So, in a parody of Teutonic orderliness, hackers assembled into clubs: there was the BHP (the Bayrische Hackerpost) in Munich, Foebud-Bi in Bielefeld, Suecrates-S in Stuttgart, and HICop-CE (the Headquarters of the Independent Computer-Freaks) in Celle. Of course the most famous and best-organized of all was the Chaos Computer Club in Hamburg. Since its inception in 1981, it had spawned affiliates in other towns and cities, even a branch in France, and in 1984 hosted the first of its annual conferences, an event that served to keep the Chaos name in the press. In between the annual congresses, Chaos also held smaller hacker meets at the various computer conventions held around Germany. Whatever the event, the venue for the hacker meet was always next to the stand occupied by the Bundespost, the German Post Office, and the time was always four P.M. on the first Tuesday of the exhibition.

Chaos was never a huge organization—even now it only has about 150 registered members—but it is very accomplished at self-promotion and zealous in disseminating information on hacking. It publishes a bimonthly magazine, *Die Datenschleuder* (literally, "the Distribution of Data by Centrifuge") with sixteen to twenty pages an issue. It also promotes *Die Hackerbibel* ("The Hacker Bible"), a two-part set of reference books detailing hacker techniques.

Chaos first came to the notice of the general public in 1984, when it hacked into the German computer information system, Btx (Bildschirmtext).[1] Like all telephone and data services in Germany, the system is run by the Bundespost, an unloved, bureaucratic institution that is obsessive in its attempts to control all national telecommunications links. The company added to its unpopularity with hackers when it began licensing telephone answering machines and regulating the use of modems.

At first, Chaos was just another "information provider" on Btx. Subscribers to the service could dial up and read pages of information supplied by Chaos on their home computers. Users were charged at a premium rate for the calls, with proceeds shared between the Bundespost and Chaos. This seemed a good recipe for making money—until one of the computer wizards at Chaos discovered that security on the system was hopelessly weak. He realized that if a hacker broke into Btx, he could get hold of the Chaos ID and password (used by the club to access and update the information on its pages), then dial up other services and saddle Chaos with the cost. With a minimum of 10 marks per call, about $6.80, the amount involved could soon become astronomical.

Chaos's founder, Wau Holland, and a younger member of the club, Steffen Wernery, then aged twenty-two, decided to go public with the discovery. The two contacted Hans Gliss, the managing editor of the computer security journal *Datenschutz-Berater* ("Data Security Adviser"). Gliss invited Holland and Steffen to attend an upcoming conference on data security and present their information. But at the meeting Bundespost representatives disputed the club's claims, unwisely stating that its Btx security was impenetrable. It was the cue for Chaos to demonstrate otherwise.

The Chaos team hacked into the Btx system and into the account of their local savings bank, the Hamburger Sparkasse.
They then introduced a computer program they had written,
causing the bank to call up the Chaos Btx pages repeatedly over
a ten-hour period. The program was simple: it merely called the
Chaos Btx number, waited for an answer and then hung up. Over
and over again. After ten hours, the bill for the bank came to
almost $92,000. But although the bill was never presented, the
ensuing publicity—carefully orchestrated by Chaos through the
German press agency—forced the Bundespost to improve its
computer security, and Holland and Steffen became national
heroes.

The publicity increased Chaos's notoriety; its first annual congress was organized as a result of the coverage engendered by the
Btx hack. Chaos became a byword for high-tech mischief, and its
congresses became an important breeding ground for the German
computer underworld. These congresses were always held during
the week after Christmas at the Eidelstedter Burgerhaus on Hamburg's Elbgaustrasse. The events lasted for three days, and press
and visitors were welcome, provided they paid the entrance fee.

In 1985 one of the paying visitors was Karl Koch. Steffen
remembers seeing him there and being introduced briefly. He is
also certain that they also met on one other occasion, at a hacker
conference at an exhibition in Munich. Koch was an unmistak-
able figure: tall, emaciated, and invariably spaced out.

For the next three years their lives would crisscross in a complex dance. If Koch had seen the pattern, he would have understood. It was the Illuminati, faceless, unknown, all-powerful,
conspiring to take control of Steffen's life.

Koch's purpose in visiting the 1985 Chaos congress was to seek
out certain information on computer systems and networks. Despite his years of practice, he himself was a second-rate hacker. He
had come to realize that he was not a born computer wizard; he
needed assistance. He was coming under increasing pressure from

Kahl to find and copy classified material from computers in the West, and his money was running out just as his dependency on drugs was increasing: from the relatively harmless hashish favored by many hackers, he had graduated to LSD and cocaine.

At first the Soviets had seemed incredibly naïve: Koch was able to pass Kahl public-domain software, programs he had simply downloaded for free from electronic bulletin boards. The KGB had accepted the software, and Koch had received payment. It seemed very simple, and he assumed he wasn't doing anything illegal: after all, public-domain software is freely available to anyone who wants it.

But then the Soviets became more demanding. The KGB had produced lists of programs it wanted to obtain and sites it wanted cracked. They also wanted dial-ups, user IDs, passwords, and instructions on how to gain system-operator privileges in computer systems. In short, the KGB wanted to learn how to become hackers.

The Soviet secret service's list of sites included the Pentagon, NORAD, the research laboratories at Lawrence Livermore and Los Alamos, Genrad in Dallas, and Fermilab in Illinois, as well as MIT, Union Carbide, and NASA's Jet Propulsion Laboratory. It was a shopping list of top-secret defense contractors and installations. The list continued with names of companies in the U.K. and Japan. The KGB stipulated that it was interested in microelectronics projects for military and industrial purposes—specifically in programs for designing megachips, the electronic brains that were responsible for the military strength of the Western allies. Two French companies in particular attracted the KGB's attention: Philips-France and SGS-Thomson, both known to be involved in megachip research.

Koch knew that on the sites picked by the KGB he would be confronted with VAX computers, which were made by DEC, but he had no experience with VMS, the proprietary operating system used by VAXen. It was VAX expertise he was hunting for at the Chaos congress: someone to make up for the skills he lacked.

It was lucky, then, that he met a seventeen-year-old hacker from West Berlin named Hans Hubner. Hubner, a tall, slender young man with the paleness that comes from staring at a computer screen too long, had been fascinated by computers since he was a child. He was also addicted to an arcade game that involved a little penguinlike character called Pengo. He liked it so much that he adopted Pengo as his handle.

When he met Koch, Pengo was unemployed and desperately needed money. He also shared Koch's liking for drugs, but more important, he had experience with VMS. Since 1985 he had been playing on Tymnet, an international computer network run by the American defense contractor McDonnell Douglas, and had learned to use the VAX default passwords—the standard account names that are included with the machines when they're shipped out from the manufacturer. Pengo was also one of the first German hackers to break into CERN, the European Nuclear Research Center in Geneva, Switzerland, and was a caller to the Altos bulletin board in Munich—where, coincidentally, he had met Fry Guy, the Indiana hacker.

Koch befriended the young Berliner, invited him to Hannover, and introduced him to Peter Kahl. Before long Pengo had become the second member of the gang, operating from what was then West Berlin, while Koch continued his activities in Hannover. Kahl later involved a contact in West Berlin, Dirk Brescinsky, whose job it became to run Pengo.

Koch and Pengo had some early successes hacking into VAX machines. They discovered that DEC's Singapore computer center was exceptionally lax about security. From there they were able to copy a VMS program called Securepack, which allowed system managers to alter user status.

It was a useful piece of software for the KGB. But it wasn't military data. To get into defense sites, Pengo and Koch knew they needed to find a more certain way into VAXen.

They didn't have long to wait: within six months security on VAX systems worldwide would be blown wide open.

. . .

Steffen Wernery became entangled in the conspiracy because of his peripheral involvement in compromising VAX security. In the autumn of 1986 Hans Gliss, the editor of *Datenschutz-Berater* who had been so helpful to Chaos over the Btx affair, contacted Steffen. Gliss needed help and told the young hacker the following story:

Gliss had been working as a consultant for SCICON, one of the largest computer software companies in Germany. SCICON had been awarded a lucrative contract by the government for work that was "very important, high security, requiring maximum reliability." It involved three networked VAX computers in three locations, with the head office in Hamburg.

During the final phase of testing SCICON was contacted by a computer manager in northern Germany and asked to explain the messages—short bursts of characters and digits in no discernable order—that had been seen on his computers. From the computerized routing information it was clear that the messages were emanating from SCICON in Hamburg, but they made no sense to him or anyone at his institute, or to anyone at SCICON.

The SCICON researchers checked through their security logs— computer files that record all the comings and goings of users on the system—and quickly realized that the dated and timed messages had all been originated "out-of-hours," at times when no authorized users would be active. Further investigation showed that some new user IDs and passwords had been added to their system that no one could account for. The implications, Gliss said, were all too obvious: hackers had penetrated SCICON security and were using their computers as a launching pad to other systems.

What Gliss now needed to know was if Steffen had any idea who might be involved. If SCICON couldn't guarantee the security of the system, the entire contract with the German government would be at risk. Gliss needed to find out who the hackers were, how they got on, and how to stop them. Contacting Steffen was a long shot, but he was a leading member of Chaos and knew most of the hackers in Germany. Perhaps he could make some calls.

Steffen thought about it: He reasoned that because the hackers were breaking into the SCICON site in Hamburg, they were probably based in the city. It made sense to call a nearby computer; that way the phone bills were cheaper.

Two days later he called Gliss and said that he had identified the hackers—two Hamburg students. They had agreed to meet Gliss and help—provided that he promise not to prosecute, so Gliss gave his word.

Later that week he met the two students, code-named Bach and Handel,[2] in Hamburg. Their story was worrying: the two students had exploited a devastatingly simple flaw in the VMS operating system used on VAX. The machines, like most computer systems, required users to log in their ID and then type their password to gain access. If the ID or the password was wrong, the VMS system had been designed to show an "error" message and bar entry. But the two hackers told Gliss that if they simply ignored all the "error" messages, they could walk straight into the system—provided they continued with the log-on as though everything was in order. When confronted with the "error" message after keying in a fake ID, they would press Enter, which would take them to the password prompt. They would then type in a phony password, bringing up a second, equally ineffectual "error" message. By ignoring it and pressing Enter again, they were permitted access to the system. It was breathtakingly easy, and left the VAX open to any hacker, no matter how untalented.

For SCICON staff the situation was disastrous. To deliver their contract on time, they would need to find the flaw in the operating system and fix it. At first they turned to DEC for help, but with time running out, SCICON's programmers began looking for a solution themselves, tearing apart the VAX operating system line by line. They were looking for a bug in the program that would prevent it from operating correctly,[3] or an omission in the commands that would allow hackers to simply ignore the "error" message.

To the SCICON team's surprise, they didn't find one. What they discovered instead was a piece of program code that appeared to have been deliberately added to the operating system to provide the secret entrance. To the SCICON researchers it looked like a deliberate "back door."

Back doors are often left in computer programs, usually to facilitate testing. Generally, they allow writers of things like computer games to jump quickly through the program without having to play the game. For example, in the mid-1980s a game called Manic Miner involved maneuvering a miner level by level from the depths of his mine up to the surface, the game becoming progressively harder at each level. The programmer whose job it was to test the game needed a shortcut between levels, so he introduced back doors that would take him directly to any one of his choosing. Inevitably, some players stumbled onto the hidden routes, which—ironically—increased the game's popularity.

Often back doors, or "cheat modes," are deliberately built into games, encouraging the player to try to break the rules. Some computer magazines give tips on how to find the cheat modes; some games, such as the popular Prince of Persia, are said to be impossible to win without using them. Back doors might also be introduced for more mercenary reasons: legend has it that programmers include back doors on arcade games they create, and then supplement their incomes by playing the games at venues such as nightclubs and casinos, which offer prizes.

Some arcade back doors are well known. Occasionally, players stumble across them by making some noninstinctive move: for example, on certain computer gaming machines the instinct is to "hold" two lemons (if three lemons wins a prize) and then spin for the third lemon. But this strategy almost never wins. However, if the player doesn't hold the two lemons and simply respins, the three lemons will automatically come up. On another arcade game, one which offers a sizable jackpot, it is said that the player brave enough to refuse it and start the machine again will be rewarded by winning two jackpots.

On a more sophisticated level, back doors are also provided on operating systems for emergencies. Access to these back doors is reserved for the computer manufacturer; procedures for gaining entry to the system from the emergency back doors are highly confidential, highly complex, and not the sort that could be stumbled over by accident.

The back door on the VAXen, though, was out in the open. It wasn't simply for emergencies; its security was far too trivial.

The VAX operating system, VMS, had been subjected to stringent tests and was supposed to comply with the exacting "orange book" security standards established by the U.S. Department of Defense.[4] Under the orange-book testing program, technically qualified intruders attempt to break through the security features of a computer; the tests can take up to six months, depending on the level of security required. It strained belief that VMS could have gone through such testing without the back door being discovered.[5]

Responding to complaints from its users, DEC issued a "mandatory patch," a small program designed specifically to close the back door, in May 1987. But despite the "mandatory" order, many users didn't bother to install it, and for a short time, VAX computers across the world provided hackers with an open house if they knew about the security gap.

Back doors are, of course, deliberate. They aren't simple bugs in the program or errors in the system: they are written by a programmer for a specific purpose. In the case of the VAX back door, the who and why remains mysterious, though it is clear that whoever created it had to have access to the VMS source code, its basic operating instructions. One rather farfetched, though not impossible, idea is that hackers broke into DEC and amended VMS to make it more hospitable. Or perhaps a programmer put the commands in without the knowledge of the company so that he could access VAX machines throughout the world without IDs or passwords. Another more intriguing theory is that the back door was built by the National Security Agency for its own use, though this presupposes that the NSA is in the business of spying on computer users.

Yet some people do suppose precisely that. In their view it is a myth that the NSA is interested in protecting computer security. Instead, it may be actively engaged in penetrating computers—or more bluntly, hacking—all over the world by exploiting back doors that only the agency knows about.

It is likely, though, that had the NSA been involved in the VAX scheme, it would have chosen a more devious means of access. Whoever put the back door in, and for whatever purpose, it was probably not intended for German hackers. But by 1986, when Koch and Pengo were trawling for information about VAX, the secret of the back door had traveled across the Atlantic and had become known by a small group of hackers in Germany. Bach and Handel, the two students who broke into the SCICON company's VAX, are generally thought to have been among the first to exploit the trick. It was later discovered that their mentor was a student at Karlsruhe University named Steffen Weihruch.[6]

That same year, Karl Koch made contact with Weihruch as well. He had managed to track down the VAX wizard to Karlsruhe and had prevailed on him to tell him his technique. It wasn't difficult: Weihruch was known to be obliging and was rather pleased that his discovery was useful.

Weihruch had also perfected a "tool" to make hacking VAXen even easier. The problem with the back door was that it didn't entirely bypass all security checks: a would-be hacker still had to contend with the security log, which collated the IDs of all users as they entered the system. It was this log—which was kept on a computer file and could be examined by the system operator—that had alerted SCICON to Bach and Handel. A hacker coming in the back door would be conspicuous because the ID and password used—the ones entered in the log—could be any combination of random characters; they wouldn't necessarily be a real ID and password, and their inclusion in the log was a clear sign of an intrusion.

The solution was to capture the identity of legitimate users, especially ones with high privileges. Then hackers could roam through the system secretly, masquerading as authorized users.

To this end Weihruch had developed a special tool to capture IDs and passwords as they were entered. This tool—in reality, a program—replaced the real entry screen with a phony, a complete replica that was indistinguishable to a user. On seeing the screen, the unsuspecting user would enter his ID in the normal way, followed by his password. The program captured that information, saving it on a secret file. Then, because it wasn't able to allow entry, the phony screen displayed the message INVALID—PLEASE REENTER. The user would think he had simply miskeyed his password. For his next attempt, the user would be presented with the proper screen; if all was in order, he would be able to gain access.

The hacker could then pick up the secret file, containing all the IDs and passwords that it had collected, on his next visit. It was like using traps to catch rabbits, except that the rabbit felt no pain. The program had automated hacking, and with legitimate IDs and the back-door entry system, hacking became simply a matter of finding VAX computers, going in through the back door, leaving the trap program to function until it had captured some legitimate identities, then taking the real IDs and passwords from the file.

With the back door and the trap program, Pengo and Koch were able to supply the Soviets with better material. Koch passed Kahl computer log-ins and passwords to military systems. In return, Kahl passed back money.

But despite the success with VMS, the KGB was upping the ante again. The Soviets wanted Koch and Pengo to hack into computers that used the UNIX operating system. UNIX was becoming increasingly popular because it could be used on a wide range of computers; many VAX users preferred UNIX to DEC's VMS, much to the computer giant's chagrin.

However, neither Koch nor Pengo knew anything about UNIX; they needed to recruit yet another hacker to their team. Once again, Kahl and Koch made the rounds of various hacker meets, and soon found Marcus Hess, who at the time was working for a specialist UNIX systems company in Hannover. He was an ideal choice: local, experienced, and with an addiction almost as potent as drugs—he loved fast sports cars.

Now they were three. Hess soon became invaluable; shortly after becoming a member, he was able to download a copy of the UNIX source code. Kahl took it to the Soviets, who seemed impressed; they paid Kahl DM25,000, about $16,000, the most he had ever received from them.

Hess soon discovered that many American computer users were relaxed about security. Indeed, if their computers contained nothing secret or classified, some U.S. sites actually tolerated an occasional visiting hacker; sometimes system operators would even have time for a chat. In America, the nucleus of the mythical Worldnet, the concept of the "Global Village," where everybody would be friendly neighbors, courtesy of the computer networks, was born. It was easy to forget that computers, which themselves don't contain classified information, can provide entry points to a network with more interesting machines—and that was what Hess was looking for.

He soon found a particularly hospitable computer in California, which contained no classified material but did provide a convenient launching pad to other systems. For the cost of a domestic phone call, Hess could hack into the University of Bremen, where computer security was slack, hop across the Atlantic by satellite at the university's expense, and due to the hospitality of the computers at Lawrence Berkeley Laboratories, at the University of California in Berkeley, travel to other sites.

Some system operators tolerate hackers, some threaten them, but most don't even know they've got them. Very few actually chase them: it's a very time-consuming and generally unrewarding task. Clifford Stoll, the system administration manager at Lawrence Berkeley Laboratories, detected the activities of Hess in August 1986, after investigating a seventy-five-cent discrepancy in the accounting records of the lab's computers. (The seventy-five-cent fee couldn't be attributed to an authorized user, so the charge had to have been run up by an outsider.) Other system operators might not have bothered, but Stoll was an astronomer by vocation and was only filling in time until grant money could be found to allow him to pursue his chosen career. To Stoll, chasing a hacker seemed exciting.

Once he had detected Hess, he was faced with the classic dilemma: should he lock him out or watch him? If he were to lock him out, there was a chance that he might sneak in some other way and not be noticed; it was also likely that he might penetrate some other system. Stoll decided to keep a watch, setting up an intricate alarm system that would tip him off whenever the hacker appeared. On some occasions, he even slept at the lab. His principal intruder was Hess, whom he knew only through his various aliases—but he also noted the presence of both Pengo and Hagbard (Koch) on other occasions. These two, with their interest in the VAXen that used VMS, would not be a major source of worry for Stoll on his UNIX site.

It eventually became obvious that Lawrence Berkeley had nothing to interest Hess; it was just a convenient jumping-off place. Stoll tried to make things look a bit more exciting and concocted a "secret" file as bait, and the hacker gobbled it up.

Stoll subsequently recounted his experiences in an academic paper ("Stalking the Wily Hacker," 1988) and a best-selling book, *The Cuckoo's Egg* (1989). He would record the heavy artillery that was eventually wheeled out to deal with his German hackers: the FBI, the CIA and, the superspooks themselves, the National Security Agency.

The reaction of the various agencies at first ranged from apathy to annoyance. Stoll was hard-pressed to interest the authorities at all: losses in hacking incidents are generally estimated in nice large numbers, and chasing seventy-five cents seemed like a joke. But he persisted, and eventually the authorities became nervous and mounted an operation to catch the intruder. Finding him was a matter of tracing his calls back to their source. However, the calls were routed through several different computer networks, a practice known as network weaving, so that each time the authorities traced the calls back, they realized they had farther to go—from one network to another, across the country, and across the Atlantic.

Slowly, the calls were traced back to Germany, down to the University of Bremen, across to Hannover, and eventually to Marcus Hess's address. Under pressure from the Americans, the German authorities arrested and questioned Hess in June 1987. The Germans had little to go on—the loss of seventy-five cents didn't appear to be an extraditable offense—but they decided to tap his phone just in case.

But while the police were watching Hess, the Illuminati were moving in on Steffen Wernery.

The saga began when Bach and Handel, the two student hackers who broke into the SCICON computer, decided to set up a hacker gang known as the VAXbusters. The team used the backdoor technique to get into VAX computers throughout Europe and North America. They traveled on SPAN, NASA's Space Physics Analysis Network, which links computers involved in physics research around the world. From the ever-obliging Steffen Weihruch they were also able to get a copy of the "trap" program, giving them legitimate identities on the systems they hacked.

For ten months the team wandered through VAX sites with impunity. Unlike Koch and Pengo, the VAXbusters weren't spying, nor were they interested in damaging hacked computers. They were just tourists, browsing through the network, looking for sites of interest.

Despite their precautions and their benign intent, no hack is entirely undetectable. In July 1987 the curtain came down on the VAXbusters. Roy Omond, the particularly diligent manager of a VAX system in Heidelberg, discovered from a routine scrutiny of his security logs that he had been hacked. Even though the hackers had been using legitimate IDs, Omond guessed from the nocturnal timings that many of the entries in his visitors' book had not been posted by authorized users. Furious, he mounted his own investigation, and by sounding out various people he believed might be in contact with the hackers, he discovered the real names of Bach and Handel. He immediately posted an electronic message to all other users on SPAN, and named the two students involved.

Bach and Handel panicked. They assumed they would be prosecuted by the German authorities and called Steffen at Chaos for advice; Steffen who called Hans Gliss, who in turn contacted the Verfassungsschutz, the German secret service.[7] The agency said it would be interested in talking to the two hackers.

Prior to meeting the agents, Bach and Handel prepared a report, dated August 17, 1987, detailing all the installations that had been penetrated by the VAXbusters. The list comprised 135 sites in total, all on SPAN, and included nineteen installations at NASA, including two VAX sites at their headquarters in Washington, D.C., six at the Goddard Space Flight Center, and ten at the Marshall Space Flight Center. It also included a large number of systems at CERN in Switzerland, and others at the European Space Agency in the Netherlands, the Meudon Observatory and the Institut d'Astrophysique in Paris, and various Max Planck Institute sites in Germany.

There was a full exchange of information at the meeting, and in return for Bach and Handel's cooperation, the authorities declined to prosecute. The secret service then contacted the CIA in Bonn, as well as NASA, DEC, and other groups that the agency felt should be informed.

In the hope of defusing the situation for the VAXbusters, it was decided that their story should be released to the press on September 15th. The delay, it was thought, would give all the affected sites enough time to repair their defenses. Gliss would cover the technical aspects in the *Datenschutz-Berater* and two journalists who were known to Wernery would handle the media. On the designated day, the journalists told the full story on the evening news; the next morning it made newspaper headlines around the country.

A few days later the two journalists had a second chance at the story when it was realized that NASA had still not removed the VAXbusters' programs (the "trap" programs) from its two computers at its Washington headquarters. Nor had it installed the mandatory patches. So another event was staged for German television audiences. This time, in front of the cameras, Bach and Handel broke into the two NASA computers in Washington, D.C., and installed the mandatory patches that DEC had issued four months earlier. It took a matter of minutes in each case. The hackers had fixed the security flaw that NASA could not be bothered to fix for itself.

A spokesman for NASA in Washington, D.C., was not impressed. The loophole in the operating system was not a "security flaw," he insisted. The information on the computers was not classified: it was just scientific data, for the use of scientists. The two computers were, he said, "like a public library."

The VAXbusters knew differently. With the higher privileges they had been able to manipulate from the multitude of IDs and passwords they had copied, they had the authority of the chief librarian in NASA's library. They had roamed through the off-limits sections of the shelves; one of the files they had copied was a fifty-two-page document outlining the security within the entire NASA computer system.

The story, despite the Americans' professed indifference, got heavy play. Steffen found himself on television more than once, explaining the arcana of hacking and his own role in the VAX-buster saga. Eventually the media interest waned; and that, Steffen assumed, was that. He was not aware of the Illuminati.

▪ ▪ ▪

The French were less phlegmatic than the Americans. They had been suffering some "very serious" hacking incidents that had begun in 1986 and were still continuing in 1987. The incidents included the theft and destruction of important programs and data from VAX computers at Philips-France and SGS-Thomson—the two French companies targeted by the KGB. Their total losses, they claimed, reached an astronomical level, some hundreds of millions of dollars.

When the French authorities were told about the VAXbusters, they became convinced that the German hackers were the culprits. The penetration techniques used on the French VAXen were the same as those described in the August report made by the German secret service. The same back door and the same sort of program to collect legitimate user IDs and passwords were used.

At the instigation of the French, Germany's federal police raided the homes of a number of known Chaos Computer Club members in Hamburg on September 27th and 28th, impounding their computer equipment. Ironically, the police overlooked the VAXbusters, who were not Chaos members. To a large extent, Chaos had become a victim of its own publicity: the police, not aware the VAXbusters were a separate group, had simply raided the homes of the most notorious hackers in Germany. It was a case of rounding up the usual suspects—one of whom was Steffen Wernery, who told them about his own role in the matter and of his previous cooperation with the secret service. Within four months the police had completed their investigations. They concluded that Steffen was simply a "switching center"—a conduit for information—and nothing more. Neither he nor the other Chaos members were involved in hacking into the French computers.

This information was passed to the French—who didn't believe it. The methods used to hack into the French sites were too similar to the techniques employed by the VAXbusters to be mere coincidence. And even though the gang's list of all the VAX computers it had hacked did not include either Philips-France or

SGS-Thomson, the French authorities remained convinced that the trail from the two companies led back to Hamburg.

At about the same time, the secret service contacted Hans Gliss about the incidents in France and asked if he could help. Gliss discussed the matter with Steffen, and suggested that they both go to Paris for the forthcoming annual Securicom conference, in March 1988, and present a report on computer security—particularly VAX security. Securicom was the ideal forum: it attracted the top computer security specialists in the world. Steffen could tell the delegates about the back door on the DEC machines and how to fix it.

Steffen acquiesced; he had found the limelight agreeable, and the visit to Securicom would give him another chance to bask in its glow. He arranged to go to Paris with a colleague from Chaos. Gliss would drive to Paris from his holiday home in the south of France.

Steffen also offered to meet representatives of Philips-France, one of the companies hit by the unknown hackers. Philips agreed, and asked Steffen to confirm the names so that security passes could be arranged.

Steffen arrived at Paris's Orly Airport on March 14th. He approached immigration control and handed his German passport to one of the officers on duty, a woman. She looked at the photo and his name and hesitated.

"There has been a problem," she said. "Please wait a moment."

She reappeared a few minutes later with three men in civilian clothing who claimed to be from the Brigade Financière, France's revenue service. Steffen now suspects that they were from French Intelligence.

"Where is your friend?" they wanted to know. His friend, the colleague from Chaos, was coming in later by train. Steffen was immediately concerned: how did they know about his friend? And why should he tell them where he was? Steffen was arrested and taken to the police cells.[8]

Under French law an investigating judge can order the detention of a suspect for twenty-four hours and then for an additional twenty-four hours if necessary. During that period the suspect is not allowed to make contact with anyone at all, not even a lawyer. The police began interrogating Steffen: they asked him about Chaos, about the VAXbusters, and about the two sites in France. They also went through his belongings and papers, looking at names and addresses. In his diary they found the Paris contact address for Hans Gliss.

Gliss had checked into the Pullman St. Jacques Hotel, having driven up from his house in the Dordogne. When he arrived at the hotel, he found three members of the "Brigade Financière" waiting for him. Fortunately for Gliss he was with his wife, Ursula, who, seeing her husband arrested and escorted away, started telephoning for help.

Gliss was taken to the police station, and his passport was impounded. The police began asking him about the Chaos Computer Club. Gliss, whose French is poor, demanded an interpreter. The police told Gliss they had arrested Steffen—unnecessarily, as it happens, because Gliss could hear him being questioned in a nearby cell.

Gliss was interrogated for two and a half hours before his passport was returned. Half an hour after that he was set free. On his return to the hotel, Ursula told him she had phoned their friends in Paris, who had contacted the German police, who in turn had called the secret service. The agency, it was presumed, had prevailed on the French authorities to release him.

Steffen wasn't so lucky. He was held in the police cells for two days, under continuous interrogation. He says he was allowed to sleep for only three to four hours each day. Steffen told them all he knew, including the fact that a full list of computers penetrated by the VAXbusters had been presented to the German authorities and didn't include the two French sites. He also insisted that all Chaos members had stopped hacking.

While Steffen was being interrogated, Gliss told the five hundred delegates at Securicom of his experience and of Steffen's incarceration. He also read Steffen's paper, which had been written to help the French improve their computer security. Later he contacted the German authorities on Steffen's behalf, but they were powerless to intervene: the French were holding Steffen as an "accessory" to the break-ins at Philips-France and SGS-Thomson.

Three times Steffen was brought before a judge, and each time he was remanded in custody for further questioning. The German foreign office discreetly pressured the French government over the case, until finally Steffen's dossier reached the desk of the French president.

Mitterand presumably had enough problems: he ordered the German hacker's release. On May 20th, at five minutes past midnight, Steffen was driven to the airport and unceremoniously bundled aboard the night plane to Hamburg. He had spent over two months in a French jail.

While Steffen was incarcerated in Paris, the real culprits remained in Germany, safely beyond French jurisdiction.

Despite the French authorities' suspicions about Chaos and the VAXbusters, despite the raids in Hamburg, it was in reality the Soviet hacker gang—ensconced in Hannover and Berlin—who had penetrated the sites at Philips-France and SGS-Thomson. They were looking for information on megachip research, just as the KGB had requested. Surprisingly, in view of the importance the French authorities attached to the sites, Pengo remembers them as simple systems to get around in once they had been breached.

Koch and Pengo had penetrated the security at Philips-France and SGS-Thomson using the back door and the trap program they had learned about from Weihruch, the Karlsruhe student. It was understandable that the French would blame the VAXbusters: both teams had used the same techniques, having learned them from the same source.

Koch and Pengo had downloaded data from the two French

companies, and supposedly passed a computer tape to the KGB in East Berlin. Without revealing exactly what was on the tape, Pengo has suggested that it might have contained details of a design program for advanced microprocessors. But although the hackers were able to pass on the French material to their Soviet paymasters, the KGB was again demanding more. By the end of 1987 they wanted information on Western military computer networks, including the operating specifications of the interconnected machines. It appeared that the KGB wanted to infiltrate the military systems.

However, the pressure was beginning to tell on Pengo and Koch, and the two had other things on their minds. They were frightened by the arrests of the Chaos members in Hamburg; they felt that it wouldn't be long before the police stumbled over their own operation. And they had also heard about Steffen's interrogation in Paris, which meant that the French were also chasing them.

In the summer of 1988 both Pengo and Koch independently approached the authorities, hoping to take advantage of an amnesty provision in German espionage legislation. This provision guaranteed lenient treatment to those who had not previously been under suspicion and now confessed, provided they cooperated fully. The two confessed to espionage, the only offense covered by the amnesty. Paradoxically, confessing to any lesser offense could have resulted in a severer penalty.

Both were interrogated regularly and at length by the authorities. By early 1989 the Germans felt that they had enough evidence to support a case against the other members of the Soviet hacker gang. On March 2nd, eighteen people were interrogated and eight arrested. The latter included Hess, Pengo, and Koch, as well as Dirk Brescinsky and Peter Kahl. The others were local hackers caught up in the wide-ranging investigation. All the hackers were released after a few days; Kahl and Brescinsky were dispatched to a high-security prison in Karlsruhe. Pengo and Koch could expect to escape prosecution due to their earlier confessions under the amnesty.

Just two months after his arrest Karl Koch would be found dead, his burned body lying in a wood on the outskirts of Hannover.

In January 1990 Marcus Hess, Dirk Brescinsky, and Peter Kahl stood trial in Celle, in northern Germany. Clifford Stoll and Pengo were witnesses for the prosecution. The problem facing the court was establishing proof that anything of value had been sold to the KGB. That was compounded by the fact that the German police had neglected to apply for a judge's consent for the wiretapping of Hess. None of the material they had recorded "just in case" could be admitted in court.

Without concrete proof that espionage on any significant scale had actually occurred, the sentences were light. Hess received twenty months plus a fine of about $7,000, Brescinsky fourteen months and about $3,500, and Kahl two years and about $2,000. All the jail sentences were suspended and substituted with probation.

Steffen Wernery is now thirty, an intense, outspoken man. He is calm about the man whose activities caused him to spend sixty-six days in a French prison. His ire is reserved for the French authorities, who, he says, have "no regard for people's rights." His time in jail, he says, cost him $68,000 in lost income and legal fees— roughly what the Soviet hacker gang earned in total from the KGB. But he doesn't blame Koch, and he doesn't believe that he committed suicide either:

> Suicide did not make sense. It was unbelievable. Karl Koch had disclosed himself to the authorities and had cooperated fully. He had provided them with some good information and they had found him accommodations and a job with the Christian Democratic party. He was also getting help with his drug dependency and seemed on his way to rehabilitation. Murder seemed much more likely than suicide. And there were many people who could have had a motive.

There was much speculation. He was murdered to prevent him testifying; it was a warning to other hackers not to disclose themselves; perhaps it was even to embarrass Gorbachev, who was due for a visit. Or perhaps to protect people in high places.

After the unification of Germany the authorities gained access to police files in what had been East Germany. According to Hans Gliss, who maintains close contacts with the intelligence services, there was "a strong whisper" that the Stasi—East Germany's secret service—was responsible for Koch's death. The motive remained a mystery, though there were any number of arcane theories: that the agency was jealous of Koch's ties to the KGB; that they were protecting the KGB from a source who was proving too talkative; that they wanted to embarrass the KGB; that they had also been getting information from Koch, and so on.

The Staatssicherheit, or Stasi, has acquired a formidable reputation. Its foreign service, led by the legendary Marcus Wolf, was reported to have planted thousands of agents in West Germany's top political and social circles, most notoriously Gunther Guillaume, who became private secretary to Chancellor Willy Brandt. The revelation caused the fall of the Brandt government.

The Stasi has become a convenient villain: since the collapse of East Germany the shadowy secret service's reputation for skulduggery has grown to mythic proportions. In mysterious cases, such as the death of Karl Koch, the sinister hand of Stasi will be detected by all those who want to see it.

Nonetheless, murder can't be ruled out. There is the evidence— the missing shoes, the controlled fire—that suggests that another party was involved in Koch's death. Then there is the motive. Koch had little reason to kill himself. He had a job; he was getting treatment for his drug problem. He was in no danger of being prosecuted for his part in the "Soviet hacker" affair: like Pengo, he would have been a witness for the prosecution, protected from punishment by the terms of the amnesty provision. After the trial he would have resumed his life (like Pengo, who is now married and living in Vienna).

Some who knew Koch think the young hacker got in over his head. He, Pengo, and Hess were pawns in the espionage game, amateur spies recruited by the Soviets to break into Western computers. It is now thought possible that the Soviets were running other hackers at the same time, testing one gang against the other. For the KGB, it was low-risk espionage: they paid for programs, documents, and codes that would otherwise have been inaccessible—unless of course their own operatives were prepared to sit for days or even weeks in front of a computer, learning the rudiments of hacking.

It was an opportunistic intelligence-gathering operation. The Soviet hacker gang had quite literally walked through the KGB's front door, offering to sell military secrets. Given that the agency paid $68,000 for the data, it must be assumed they were satisfied with what they had received.

Espionage is a curious trade. Those who claim to know how intelligence agencies work say that computer penetration has become a new and useful tool for latter-day spies. The Americans are said to be involved, through the NSA, as are the British, through GCHQ, the General Communications Headquarters, which gathers intelligence from diverse sources. Hacking, at this rarefied level, becomes a matter of national security.

Of course the Americans and the British aren't the only ones suspected of involvement. Mossad, the Israeli secret service, is said to have penetrated the computer systems of French defense contractors who had sold weapons to its enemies in the Middle East. The Israeli service then altered some of the data for the weaponry, rendering it vulnerable to their own defense systems. In this case, the Israelis may have been merely copying the French. During the Gulf War it was widely reported that certain French missiles—the Exocets, which had previously been sold to the Iraqis—included back doors to their computer guidance systems. These back doors would allow the French military to send a radio signal to the Exocets' on-board computers, rendering the weapons harmless.

The scheme, neat as it appears, was never put to the test. The Iraqis never used their Exocets during the conflict—perhaps because they, too, had heard the stories. On the other hand, the entire scenario could well have been French disinformation.

It was in this murky world of spying and double-cross that the Soviet hacker gang found itself. In the wider sphere of international and industrial espionage the Germans were ultimately only minor irritants. The technology now exists to access the computer systems of competitors and rivals, and it would be naïve to presume that these methods are not being used. It is possible, for instance, to read a computer screen with a radio signal from a site hundreds of feet away. And, during the Cold War, a small truck believed to be equipped with such a device was shipped from Czechoslovakia to Canada. It entered the United States under the guise of diplomatic immunity and traveled, in a curious and indirect way, to the Mexican border. The route took the van close to a sizable number of American defense installations, where the driver would stop, often for days. It was assumed by the small army of federal agents following the truck that it was homing in on computer screens on the bases and sending the material on to the Soviet Embassy in Washington.

It's not known if the Czechs and the Soviets found any information of real value, but with the increased use of technology, and the vulnerability of networked computer systems, it is probable that corporations and governments will be tempted to subvert or steal data from rivals. And, under these circumstances, there is inevitably another explanation for the break-in at Philips-France and SGS-Thomson. In 1986 and 1987 Mossad was becoming increasingly worried about deliveries of French weaponry to Iraq and other Arab states. Some of the electronic components for these weapons were designed at the two companies. The Israelis wanted to destroy or steal the data for these components, and to do so, hacked into the companies' computers, using the same techniques being used by the Germans. Mossad knew that the German hackers would get the blame. Indeed, they knew that Pengo and Koch were wandering about the same computers. But the two Germans wouldn't have destroyed information—that would have drawn attention to their activities; nor did they ever manage to steal anything worth hundreds of millions of dollars. That was Mossad.

Koch, with his love of conspiracies, would have appreciated such a theory. The Illuminati—the French police, the KGB, the Stasi, and Mossad—were real after all.

8

■

CRACKDOWN

The Soviet hacker gang wasn't the only reason for the subsequent U.S. government crackdown on the computer underworld. But the threat of a Communist plot to steal top-secret military data was enough to focus the attention of the previously lethargic investigators. The federal authority's lack of urgency in dealing with what appeared to be a threat to national security had been documented by Clifford Stoll in *The Cuckoo's Egg,* and the diffidence displayed by the FBI and the Secret Service in that case had caused them a great deal of embarrassment. After Stoll's disclosures, the authorities began monitoring hacker bulletin boards much more closely.

One of the boards staked out by the Secret Service was Black ICE, the Legion of Doom's favorite, located somewhere in Richmond, Virginia. On March 4, 1989, two days after the arrest of the Soviet hacker gang, intrigued Secret Service agents recorded the following exchanges:

I SAW SOMETHING IN TODAY'S PAPER THAT REALLY BURNS ME, growled a Legionnaire known as Skinny Puppy, initiating a series of electronic messages.[1] He continued:

SOME WEST GERMAN HACKERS WERE BREAKING INTO SYS-
TEMS AND SELLING INFO TO THE RUSSIANS. IT'S ONE THING
BEING A HACKER. IT'S ANOTHER BEING A TRAITOR. IF I FIND

OUT THAT ANYONE ON THIS BOARD HAD ANYTHING TO DO WITH IT, I WILL PERSONALLY HUNT THEM DOWN AND MAKE THEM WISH THEY HAD BEEN BUSTED BY THE FBI. I AM CONSIDERING STARTING MY OWN INVESTIGATION INTO THIS INCIDENT AND DESTROYING A FEW PEOPLE THE BKA [German federal police] DIDN'T GET. DOES ANYONE CARE TO JOIN ME ON THIS CRUSADE? OR AT LEAST GIVE SUPPORT? CAN I CLAIM AN ACT UPON THESE CREEPS AS LOD VENGEANCE FOR DEFILING THE HACKERS' IMAGE?

An hour and a half later the Prophet uploaded his response:

DON'T FROTH AT THE MOUTH, PUPPY; YOU'LL PROBABLY JUST ATTRACT THE ATTENTION OF THE AUTHORITIES, WHO SEEM TO HAVE HANDLED THIS WELL ENOUGH ON THEIR OWN. TOO BAD THE IDIOTS AT NASA AND LOS ALAMOS COULDN'T HAVE DONE THE SAME. HOW MANY TIMES ARE THEY GOING TO ALLOW THEIR SECURITY TO BE PENETRATED? HOW DO YOU THINK THIS IS GOING TO AFFECT DOMESTIC HACKERS? MY GUESS IS, THE FEDS ARE GOING TO BEAR DOWN ON US HARDER.

The Highwayman, one of the bulletin board's system operators, suggested, LET'S BREAK INTO THE SOVIET COMPUTERS AND GIVE THE INFO TO THE CIA. I KNOW YOU CAN GET ON A SOVIET PSN [Public Switched Network, the public telephone system] FROM AN EAST GERMAN GATEWAY FROM WEST GERMANY.

Other Legionnaires were less patriotic. Erik Bloodaxe said, MAKE MONEY ANY WAY YOU CAN! FUCK IT. INFORMATION IS A VALUABLE COMMODITY, AND SHOULD BE SOLD. IF THERE IS MONEY TO BE MADE, THEN MAKE IT. FUCK AMERICAN SECRETS. IT DOESN'T MATTER. IF RUSSIA REALLY WANTED SOMETHING, THEY WOULD PROBABLY GET IT ANYWAY. GOOD FOR WHOEVER SOLD IT TO THEM!

The last message was posted late that same night. THIS GOVERNMENT DESERVES TO BE FUCKED, said the Urvile. I'M ALL FOR A

GOVERNMENT THAT CAN HELP ME (HEY, COMRADE, GOT SOME SE-
CRETS FOR YOU CHEAP). FUCK AMERICA. DEMOCRACY IS FOR LOSERS.
DICTATORSHIP, RAH! RAH!

At this early date there were rumors that Chaos had been involved with the Soviet hackers, even that some of its members had been arrested. One of the Legionnaires tried calling up Altos—the board in Munich that had become an international hacker hangout—to find out what was going on, but the board was down due to some sort of technical fault.

To the watching Secret Service agents, at least some of the messages suggested that American hackers might well follow in the footsteps of the Soviet hacker gang and go into business selling military or industrial secrets. It was disquieting—even if the characteristic hacker bravado was taken into account.

But in reality, the Soviet hacker gang was only a momentary distraction for the Legion of Doom. By the next day the flurry of interest had died out; the bulletin board messages resumed the usual pattern—technical queries; reports on hacking sites; postings about police surveillance, about Secret Service monitoring, about the FBI and the CIA.

Black ICE was the LoD's principal board, and was restricted to twenty users (mostly LoD members). It was accessed by remote call forwarding, which kept it—or so it was believed—one step ahead of the law.[2] The name Black ICE came from a novel by the science-fiction writer William Gibson. ICE, for Intrusion Countermeasures Electronics, was a program that kept watch for hackers; when it detected them, it literally "fried their brains"—the deadly "black" countermeasure.

The author William Gibson is an icon in the computer underworld, and his imaginative sci-fi thrillers have acquired cult status. In his best-known book, *Neuromancer* (1984), Gibson created a world he called Cyberspace, populated by computer cowboys who roamed the space's electronic systems. *Neuromancer* forecast the world of hackers—the networks and communication links that they inhabit—and gave them an alternate, more glamorous identity. The networks became known as Cyberspace, and the hacker became a Cyberpunk.

The conceit became common in the late 1980s. The Cyberpunk image complemented the secrecy and role-playing of handles, and it gave a whole new identity to fifteen-year-old computer wizards sitting in front of their computer screens. They weren't just teen-agers, or even hackers—they were Cyberpunks, the meanest, toughest technology junkies in the world.

The Legion of Doom was the best-known Cyberpunk gang in America; certainly it generated the most press. Like Chaos in Germany, the gang was conscious of the publicity value of a sinister, slightly menacing name. One of its members was once asked why they picked it: "What else could we have called our-selves?" he answered. "The Legion of Flower Pickers?"

The LoD's origins go back to the summer of 1984, when a hacker named Lex Luthor set up one of the first specialist hacker bulletin boards, based in Florida. It was an elite, invitation-only board, with detailed files on hacking and related crafts, such as social engineering and dumpster diving.

The first Legion of Doom had nine members, with handles such as Karl Marx, Agrajag the Prolonged, and King Blotto. The gang has been re-formed three times since. It went into decline when five of the original Legionnaires were busted, but bounced back in 1986 and again in 1988. The latest re-formation took place in late 1990. It was never a large group, and although the original LoD board had more than 150 users, admission to the bulletin board was not the same as gang membership.[3] The LoD was the elite of the elite, a sort of inner circle. The real LoD generally hovered between nine and eleven members; it has never had more than twelve at any one time. Between 1984 and January 1992 there were only forty confirmed LoD members in total.

The LoD was eulogized by the hacker bulletin *PHRACK* after one of its periodic demises:

LoD members may have entered into systems numbering in the tens of thousands, they may have peeped into credit histories, they may have snooped into files and buffered [stolen] interesting text, they may still have control over entire computer networks, but what damage have they done?

The answer is none—well, almost none. There are the inevitable exceptions: unpaid use of CPU [Central Processing Unit] time and network access charges.

What personal gains have any members gained? Again, the answer is none—apart from three instances of credit fraud that were instigated by three separate greedy individuals without group knowledge.

The bulletin concluded, "The Legion of Doom will long be remembered as an innovative and pioneering force."

But the LoD was not the only group on the electronic block: it had rivals, other high-tech gangs that contested LoD's reputation as the best hackers in Cyberspace. One of these other gangs was MoD—which, depending on whom you ask and what time of day it is, stands for either Masters of Destruction or Masters of Deception—or sometimes Mom's on Drugs. The MoD membership was centered in New York; the gang included hackers such as Corrupt, Julio, Renegade Hacker, and, from Philadelphia, the Wing.

But LoD's most serious rival was DPAC, a gang with members in both Maryland and New Jersey. The group had taken its name from a Canadian data communications system (a contraction of "Data Packet") and was led, off and on, by a hacker called Sharp. Membership in DPAC varied, but included Remob (after the device that allows phones to be tapped remotely), Meat Puppet, the Executioner, Supernigger, and GZ. Despite the handle, Supernigger wasn't black; and GZ, very unusually, was female.

The LoD disparaged the abilities of DPAC members. One of the Black ICE sysops, the Mentor, messaged, SUPERNIGGER AND

GZ ARE BOTH BLATANT IDIOTS WHO LIKE TO SHOOT THEIR MOUTHS OFF. GZ DOES STUFF LIKE HACK MCI FOR DAYS FROM HER HOUSE.

The Urvile, though, was less sanguine. In a message to Black ICE, he reported having received a phone call from someone named Mike Dawson, who claimed to be a special agent with the Secret Service, telling him that "We'll be visiting you tomorrow." The Urvile thought the voice sounded too young for a Secret Service agent; he was also bothered that Mike didn't know his address or last name.

"Are your parents going to be home tomorrow between two and three?" Mike persisted.

"Gee, I guess so."

His parents probably would be home, he thought—but at their home, not his. The Urvile, at the time, was a university student and lived in his own apartment. When he asked if the agent knew how old he was, Mike answered, "All will be made apparent tomorrow."

The next day the Urvile removed all his notes and files, just in case. But the Secret Service never appeared. "I'm betting five to one odds that it's DPAC, and I don't like it one bit," he said.

Ordinarily the Urvile's concerns could be dismissed as just another bout of hacker paranoia. But by 1989 the LoD had become involved in a "hacker war" with DPAC and MoD—a fight for control of Cyberspace, over phone lines and computer networks, with threatening messages left on bulletin boards or answering machines. In one case, an LoD member who worked (somewhat incongruously) for a telephone company's security department found taunting messages on his computer terminal at work. On a more serious level, there were attempts to reprogram switches to land opponents with astronomical phone bills; there was one instance of breaking into a credit bureau to destroy a gang member's credit rating. But while the three gangs were squabbling among themselves, the biggest crackdown on hacking in the United States had just begun.

▪ ▪ ▪

The catalyst was an anonymous phone call to an unlisted residential number in Indianapolis at eight P.M. on June 29, 1989.

As security manager for Indiana Bell, Robert S. was accustomed to anonymous calls: he was a prime target for hackers attempting to impress him with their ability to break into his system and find his home number. And the caller this night didn't seem much different from the others. He sounded like a young man trying to seem older, his voice a mix of swagger and menace. The caller presented his credentials by repeating Robert's credit history to him—which meant only that the anonymous hacker could also break into credit bureau computers.

"Tell you something else, Bob—you don't mind if I call you Bob, do you? I'll tell you, somebody like me who really knows the phone systems could really fuck things up. I mean I could put your 5ESS's into an endless loop. You know what I mean? You know what that would do?"

The 5ESS's were a type of electronic switching system. There were hundreds in Indiana Bell, thousands around the country. An endless loop is caused by changing the coding of the switch so that it no longer puts forward calls. The calls instead just loop around the switch, like a record needle caught in the same groove. The result would be paralysis: no calls from the switch could get out.

"It could cause a lot of problems. Is that what you're threatening?"

"Sort of. But I've made it better than that. I've planted computer bombs in some of the 5ESS's—time bombs—they're going to fuck up your switches. The game is to see if you can find them before they go off. And all I'm going to tell you about them is that they're programmed to blow on a national holiday. They could be anywhere in the country—it's sort of a competition, a security test, it'll give you something interesting to do for a change. You know what I mean?"

The line went dead. Of all the hacker calls Robert had received—most a mix of braggadocio and hubris—this was one of the few he would think of as threatening.

The threat was the bomb—a piece of computer programming, probably only a short program, that would be hidden among the thousands of instructions on any 5ESS switch, anywhere in the country. A computer bomb is a one-shot explosion. It could throw a switch into an endless loop, it could overload the system—or, indeed, it could create havoc by releasing a self-replicating program such as a worm, which would move through the network, knocking out switch after switch.

In a nightmare scenario the country could effectively be closed down for days, leaving its citizens with no means of communication and cut off from emergency fire, police, and ambulance services. The cost in terms of lives would be unthinkable and the revenue losses would be incalculable: crime would soar and businesses could be forced to shut down.

Robert couldn't know where the bombs had been hidden, nor did he know how many there were or what they would do when they went off. All he knew was that they had been set to explode on a national holiday—and five days later it would be Independence Day, the Fourth of July.

He reported the call to his superiors at Indiana Bell and to Bellcore (Bell Communication Research), which coordinates network security. Given the imminence of the Fourth of July, Bellcore had little choice but to take the threat seriously. The company organized an alert, assembling a security task force consisting of forty-two full-time employees. They would work around the clock in two twelve-hour shifts examining the 5ESS's, checking through each and every program for a few lines of code that could cause disruption.

The threat to the phone system was also reported to the United States Secret Service. The agency, part of the Treasury Department, had been assigned national responsibility for computer crime in 1984, after a long bureaucratic battle with the FBI. The limits of its responsibilities and those of the FBI have never been strictly defined; there have always been areas where the two agencies overlapped. The Secret Service's responsibility is to investigate access device fraud that affects interstate and foreign commerce if there is a minimum loss of $1000. Their mandate, though, is subject to agreement between the secretary of the Treasury (their boss) and the Attorney General, who runs the FBI. The effect has been to leave the two agencies to fight out their responsibilities between themselves.

The Secret Service was already in the midst of an in-depth investigation of the computer underworld. In 1988 the agency had become aware of a new proposal, one that seemed to signal an increase in hacker activity. Called the Phoenix Project, it was heralded in the hacker bulletin *PHRACK* as "a new beginning to the phreak/hack community where knowledge is the key to the future and is free. The telecommunications and security industries can no longer withhold the right to learn, the right to explore, or the right to have knowledge." The Phoenix Project, it was announced, would be launched at SummerCon '88—the annual hacker conference, to be held in a hotel near the airport in Saint Louis.

The Phoenix was the legendary bird that rose from its own ashes after a fiery death. To the hackers it was just a name for their latest convention. But to the telephone companies and the Secret Service, the Phoenix Project portended greater disruption—as well as the theft of industrial or defense secrets. The implications of "the right to learn, the right to explore, or the right to have knowledge" appeared more sinister than liberating, and the article was published just as the Secret Service was becoming aware of an upsurge in hacker activity, principally telecommunications fraud. The increase appeared linked to the hacker wars, then spluttering inconclusively along.

Coincidentally, in May 1988, police in the city of Phoenix, Arizona, raided the home of a suspected local hacker known as the Dictator. The young man was the system operator of a small pirate board called the Dark Side. The local police referred his case to the district attorney for prosecution, and he in turn notified the Secret Service.

No one was quite sure what to do with the Dictator—but then someone had the bright idea of running his board as a sting. The Dictator agreed to cooperate: in return for immunity from prosecution, he continued to operate the Dark Side as a Secret Service tool for collecting hacker lore and gossip and for monitoring the progress of the Phoenix Project. That the scheme to investigate the Phoenix Project was based in the city of Phoenix was entirely coincidental: it was established there solely because the local office of the Secret Service was willing to run an undercover operation.

Dubbed Operation Sundevil, after the Arizona State University mascot, it was officially described as "a Secret Service investigation into financial crimes (fraud, credit card fraud, communications service losses, etc.) led by the Phoenix Secret Service with task force participation by the Arizona U.S. Attorney's office and the Arizona Attorney General's office." The Arizona assistant attorney general assigned to the case was Gail Thackeray, an energetic and combative attorney who would become the focal point for press coverage of the operation.

But the impetus for Operation Sundevil—the Dark Side sting—only provided the authorities with a limited insight into the computer underworld. Reams of gossip and electronic messages were collected, but investigators were still no nearer to getting a fix on the extent of hacking or the identities of the key players. They decided on another trick: they enlisted the Dictator's help in penetrating the forthcoming SummerCon '88, the event that would launch the Phoenix Project.

Less a conference and more a hacker party, SummerCon '88 was held in a dingy motel not far from the Saint Louis airport. Delegates, usually adolescent hackers, popped in and out of one another's rooms to gossip and play with computers.

The Dictator stayed in a special room, courtesy of the Secret Service. Agents next door filmed the proceedings in the room through a two-way mirror, recording over 150 hours of videotape. Just what was captured in this film has never been revealed (the Secret Service has declined all requests to view the tapes), but cynics have suggested that it may be the most boring movie ever made—a six-day epic featuring kids drinking Coke, eating pizzas, and gossiping.

Nonetheless, the intelligence gathered at SummerCon and through the Dark Side had somehow convinced the Feds that they were dealing with a national conspiracy, a fraud that was costing the country more than $50 million in telecom costs alone. And that, said Gail Thackeray, was "just the tip of the iceberg."

Then the Phoenix Secret Service had a lucky break.

In May 1989, just a year after ousting the Dictator, police investigating the abuse of a Phoenix hotel's private telephone exchange stumbled across another hacker. He was no small-time operator. Questioned by the Secret Service, he admitted that he had access to Black ICE. He wasn't an LoD member, he added, merely one of the few non-Legionnaires allowed to use the gang's board. Under pressure from the Secret Service, who reminded him of the penalties for hacking into a private telephone exchange and stealing services, he, too, agreed to become an informant. He would be referred to only as Hacker 1.

A month later the Secret Service learned about the anonymous call to the Indiana Bell security manager and the threat to the telephone switches. At this stage there was still no evidence of an attack. Similar hoax calls are received every day by the phone companies. But then, on July 3rd, four days after the anonymous call, the Bellcore task force discovered that this wasn't just an idle threat. Three computer bombs were found, just hours before the Fourth of July public holiday. The bombs, as the caller had warned, were spread across the country: one was discovered in a switch in BellSouth in Atlanta, Georgia; another in Mountain Bell's system in Denver, Colorado; and the third in Newark, New Jersey. The devices were described by the Secret Service as "time bomb[s] . . . which if left undetected, would have compromised these computers (for an unknown period) and effectively shut down the compromised computer telephone systems in Denver, Atlanta, and New Jersey." In plainer language, had the bombs not been discovered and defused, they could have created local disasters.

In the Secret Service offices in Phoenix, the interrogation of Hacker 1 acquired more urgency. The agents now knew that somewhere out there was a computer freak—or perhaps a gang of freaks—with the ability and inclination to plant bombs in the telephone system. It could happen again, and the next time there might not be any warning. The agents probed Hacker 1 about his contacts in the Legion of Doom, particularly those Legionnaires who might have access to the compromised phone companies.

He told them about the Urvile, the Leftist, and the Prophet, three members who had the expertise to plant bombs, and were all based in Atlanta, the home of BellSouth.

This information was enough for the Georgia courts to authorize the placing of Dialed Number Recorders (DNRs) on the three hackers' phone lines.

For ten days the Secret Service monitored every call and recorded the hackers looping around the country to gain free telephone service and to avoid detection.[4] The Atlanta hackers often started their loops by dialing into the computer system at Georgia Tech, using IDs and passwords provided by the Urvile, a student there. From Georgia Tech they could tour the world, if they felt the inclination, hopping from one network to another, wherever lax security or their own expertise permitted. With the evidence from the DNRs, the Secret Service executed search warrants on the three LoD members, and eventually raided their homes.

The investigators uncovered thousands of pages of proprietary telephone company information, hundreds of diskettes, half a dozen computers, and volumes of notes. The three Legionnaires and their fellow hackers had been dumpster diving at BellSouth, looking for telco manuals. With the information gleaned, they had developed techniques for accessing over a dozen of BellSouth's computer systems, and from these they downloaded information that would allow them to get into other computer systems—including those belonging to banks, credit bureaus, hospitals, and businesses. When the Leftist was interviewed, he nonchalantly agreed that the Legionnaires could easily have shut down telephone services throughout the country.

Among the masses of information that the investigators found were files on computer bombs and trojan horses—as well as one document that described in detail how to bring down a telephone exchange by dropping a computer program into a 5ESS switch. The program simply kept adding new files to the switch's hard disk until it was full, causing the computer to shut down.

What the investigators didn't uncover was any *direct* evidence linking the Atlanta Three to the computer bombs. Simple possession of a report that details how a crime could be committed does not prove that it has been. But they did find one document that seemed to portend even greater destruction: during the search of the Prophet's home they discovered something called the "E911 file." Its significance escaped the Treasury agents, but it immediately caused the technicians from BellSouth to blanch: "You mean the hackers had this stuff?" The file, they said, described a new program developed for the emergency 911 service: the *E* simply stood for enhanced.

The 911 service is used throughout North America for handling emergency calls—police, fire, and ambulance. Dialing 911 gives direct access to a municipality's Public Safety Answering Point, a dedicated telephone facility for summoning the emergency services. The calls are carried over an ordinary telephone switch; however, incoming 911 calls are given priority over all other calls. From the switch, the 911 calls travel on lines dedicated to the emergency services.

In March 1988 BellSouth had developed a new program for enhancing the 911 service. The E911 file contained information relating to installation and maintenance of the service, and was headed, "Not for use or disclosure outside BellSouth or any of its subsidiaries except under written agreement." It had been stored in a computer in BellSouth's corporate headquarters in Atlanta, Georgia. While hacking into the supposedly secure system, the Prophet had found the file and downloaded it to his own PC.

In the hands of the wrong people, the BellSouth technicians said, the critical E911 document could be used as a blueprint for widespread disruption in the emergency systems. Clearly, hackers were the wrong sort of people. According to BellSouth, "any damage to that very sensitive system could result in a dangerous breakdown in police, fire, and ambulance services." Mere computer bombs seemed childish by comparison.

Just seven months later, on the public holiday in honor of Martin Luther King, Jr., the most sophisticated telephone system in the world went down for nine hours. At 2:25 P.M. on January 15, 1990 the nationwide network operated by AT&T was hit by a computer failure. For the duration of the breakdown, the only voice responding to millions of long-distance callers was a recorded message: "All services are busy—please try again later."

It was estimated that by early afternoon as many as half the long-distance calls being dialed in every major city were blocked. Some twenty million calls were affected, causing chaos in many businesses, especially those such as airlines, car rental companies, and hotels which rely on free 1-800 numbers. It was the most serious failure since the introduction of computer-based phone systems thirty years earlier.

Robert E. Allen, AT&T chairman, emerged the following day to explain that "preliminary indications are that a software problem occurred, which spread rapidly through the network." Another spokesman said that while a failure in the software systems was probably to blame, a computer bomb could not be ruled out. The problem had been centered in what was called a signal node, a computer or switch attached to the network. According to AT&T, the errant system "had told switches it was unable to receive calls, and this had a domino effect on other switches." The effect was not dissimilar to the endless loop, which causes all incoming calls to circle idly around the switch.

Software problems are not uncommon, but few have such spectacular effects. And coming so soon after the computer bomb threat, rumors flourished that AT&T had been hit by hackers. In the course of researching this book, the authors were told more than once that the AT&T failure had been caused by a computer bomb. One source even claimed he could identify the culprit. The rumors continue to circulate, as they do about everything in the computer underworld.

However, there is absolutely no proof that it was a computer bomb, and AT&T's final, official explanation remains that the shutdown was caused by an errant piece of software.

The attack did not affect the emergency 911 numbers, which are handled by local carriers. Nor, even if it was a bomb, was it likely to have been linked to the previous incident. But it had taken place on a national holiday—Martin Luther King Day—and the coincidence bothered the authorities.

On January 18th, three days after the AT&T system collapsed, the Secret Service began a nationwide sweep, targeting hacker gangs—in particular the Legion of Doom—and anyone who appeared to be a threat to the phone system.

Their first call was on Knight Lightning. The handle belonged to Craig Neidorf, a twenty-year-old prelaw student at the University of Missouri in Columbia, and one of the coeditors of the underground newsletter *PHRACK.* He was found in his room on the third floor of the Zeta Beta Tau fraternity house. Special Agent Tim Foley, who had been investigating the attacks on the telephone computer switches for seven months, and Reed Nolan, a security representative from Southwestern Bell Telephone, questioned Neidorf about an article in *PHRACK* on the electronic switching systems. They also brought up the E911 document. They knew that Neidorf had received a copy of the file from the Prophet, and had published it in *PHRACK* in February 1989. According to Foley, Neidorf admitted knowing that the E911 tutorial had been stolen from BellSouth.

The next day Foley returned with a search warrant and the

local police. The ESS article had been forgotten; Neidorf was instead charged with ten felony counts centering on the publication of the E911 file in *PHRACK.* If found guilty, he faced a sentence of up to sixty-five years in prison.

On January 24, 1990, the Secret Service operation moved to Queens, New York, to the homes of several known hackers. The first target was a twenty-year-old known among the underground as Acid Phreak. When the Secret Service arrived, they told him that he was suspected of causing the AT&T crash nine days earlier. One of the agents pointed to his answering machine. "What's that for?" he asked. "Answering the phone," Acid Phreak said. He wasn't arrested, but instead was asked to accompany the agents to their headquarters in the World Trade Center, where he was questioned until the early hours of the morning.

Phiber Optik, who also lives in Queens, was raided next. According to hacker lore, he was awakened in the middle of the night and confronted with nine loaded guns, which seems unlikely, as most other raids were conducted by one or two agents, usually accompanied by a telephone security man. Another New York hacker, the Scorpion, a friend of both Phiber Optik and Acid Phreak, was also raided on that day.

On March 1st the action moved to Texas, with an almost comically aggressive bust of a games publishing company.

The day started early, in Austin, with a dawn raid on the home of Loyd Blankenship. Loyd, known as the Mentor to colleagues in the Legion of Doom, was also sysop of an underground bulletin board, the Phoenix Project, and the author of a series of "hacker tutorials" in *PHRACK.* He and his wife were roused from their bed by a team of six Secret Service agents, a local cop, and a representative from Bellcore.

While his own computer and equipment were being seized, Loyd was driven to his office at Steve Jackson Games. The company specialized in publishing computer games, most of them involving role-playing of one sort or another. At the time it employed fifteen people and had a turnover of $500,000. Founded by Steve Jackson, the company also ran its own, completely legitimate bulletin board, which functioned as an information service for its customers. The only remarkable thing about the bulletin board was its name—Illuminati, after the secret, world-dominant sect that had so exercised the Soviet hacker gang. Computer enthusiasts the world over clearly read the same books.

Steve Jackson himself arrived at the office just as the Secret Service agents were attempting to kick down the door. The agents were offered a key instead. They spared the door but did prefer to force open a locker and to cut the locks off of the outside storage sheds, despite being offered the appropriate keys.

The agents seized all the computer equipment they could find. They also tore open cartons in the warehouse, looking for a handbook on computer crime that was in preparation: they intended to seize all copies before it could be distributed.

The "handbook on computer crime" later turned out to be an innocent game about computers called GURPS Cyberpunk, published by Steve Jackson Games.[5] The mere fact that Loyd had chosen the name Cyberpunk had led the authorities to conclude that the program was part of a conspiracy to spread hacking techniques nationwide. The Secret Service seized all copies of the game at the company's premises and made doubly certain that they collected the data for Loyd's manual as well.

Two months later Operation Sundevil struck again.[6] On May 8th coordinated raids on hackers in fourteen cities were carried out. Over 150 Secret Service agents were deployed, teamed with numerous local and state law enforcement agencies. The agents served twenty-seven search warrants in Chicago, Cincinnati, Detroit, Los Angeles, Miami, Newark, New York, Phoenix, Pittsburgh, Plano (Texas), Richmond, San Diego, San Jose, and Tucson. Forty computers and 23,000 diskettes were seized.

The official reason for the busts was telecommunications fraud. The raids were synchronized in order to completely surprise the hacker community and prevent important evidence from being destroyed.

But that nearly happened anyway. As reports of the Atlanta and New York raids circulated, a number of hacker boards carried warnings that another "major bust" was imminent. (Captain Zap, the Philadelphia hacker arrested years before for theft, takes credit for the messages.) One of those who took the warnings seriously was Erik Bloodaxe, the LoD member who was so keen on selling U.S. military secrets to the Soviets. All his equipment, as well as any documents that could incriminate him, was hidden away before the raids. When the Secret Service and local cops burst in on him, he was the picture of innocence. With little to choose from, the agents considered taking away his PacMan game—then decided to take his phone instead. It was the only piece of hacker equipment they could find.[7]

Others were less lucky. As the Secret Service raided homes of known hackers, carrying away boxes of diskettes and computer equipment, they were invariably asked, "When do I get my system back?" The authorities were well aware that confiscating equipment for use as evidence later—should there ever be a case—was punishment in itself.

During the raids half the members of the Legion of Doom were busted. MoD and DPAC were less affected than the Legion by the busts, but the aftershock would cause DPAC to split up, and MoD would come to grief the next year.

The spluttering, intermittent hacker wars had ended in default. The Secret Service had broken the hacker gangs and brought law and order to Cyberspace. Or so it seemed.

But support for hackers was building—unwittingly aided by the FBI, the Secret Service's rival in the bureaucratic battle for responsibility for computer crime. On May 1, 1990, an FBI agent named Richard Baxter, Jr., drove to Pinedale, Wyoming, for a meeting with John Perry Barlow. The two men came from different worlds. Barlow was a bundle of idiosyncrasies and contradictions, the sort of man who seems to survive only in the American West: aged forty-two, a former rancher, the lyricist for the Grateful Dead, and also the local Republican party county chairman, he believed in the frontier, both the real one around Pinedale and the electronic one accessible through his computer. Barlow wasn't a hacker, but he was part of something called WELL—the Whole Earth 'Lectronic Link, the embodiment of the sixties counterculture surviving in the 1990s on an electronic bulletin board based in Sausalito, California. His philosophy was a mix of sixties liberalism leavened by a rancher's rugged individualism; he was a Republican hippie with a computer.

Agent Baxter was a country boy who "didn't know a ROM chip from a vise grip," according to Barlow.[8] He wanted to talk to Barlow about high-tech crime, although hackers were not his usual beat.

Baxter was investigating the theft of the operating system source code for the Macintosh computer. According to Baxter, it had been stolen by a group that was threatening to destroy the American company by releasing the code to East Asian manufacturers of Apple clones.

Briefed at length by his San Francisco office, Agent Baxter told Barlow that the FBI wanted to interview John Draper, the legendary Captain Crunch. Draper, the FBI believed, was a known member of the Hackers' Conference, an underground association with likely ties to those responsible for the theft. The FBI also believed that Draper was the chief executive of Autodesk, a software company with many top-secret government Star Wars contracts.

Jurisdiction for this particular investigation had fallen to the FBI, not the Secret Service. It was one of the oddities of U.S. law enforcement that even when the responsibilities of the two agencies overlapped, their intelligence and resources were almost never pooled. And in this case, Barlow knew that the FBI agent's information was almost completely wrong.

Draper wasn't the chief executive of Autodesk, though he had worked there as a programmer at one time, and Autodesk was not a major Star Wars contractor, but a software developer. Also, the

Hackers' Conference was not an underground association, but an annual gathering of the nation's brightest and most respected computer experts. As for the group that had supposedly stolen the Macintosh source code, Barlow presumed that the agent was referring to the self-styled nuPrometheus League, which had been circulating filched copies of the Macintosh code to annoy Apple. Opinion in the computer underground was that the code was probably picked up by kids who'd been dumpster diving. (The ethos at Apple had changed since 1979. Then it was a small company with roots in the hacker community; now a major corporation, it called in the FBI to chase down kids for dumpster diving.)

The only thing that the FBI had gotten right, Barlow reckoned, was the address of Autodesk. So Barlow explained to Baxter what was really going on, spending most of the two-hour interview educating him about source codes. THINGS HAVE RATHER JUMPED THE GROOVE WHEN POTENTIAL SUSPECTS MUST EXPLAIN TO LAW ENFORCERS THE NATURE OF THEIR ALLEGED PERPETRATIONS, he said in his posting to the WELL about the incident.

Barlow's message produced an unexpected response. A number of other WELL-beings—the users' excruciatingly cute name for themselves—had also been interviewed by the FBI. They had all heard pretty much the same garbled story. Baxter had only been repeating the information contained in the agency's files. The entire Bureau seemed to be working on erroneous data. It was enough to tweak the ideological hackles of any Republican hippie, particularly one who believed in the new frontier of the computer village.

So, a week later, when news of the Secret Service crackdown broke, Barlow decided to investigate, to ensure that officialdom wasn't looking at the hacker threat through a haze of ignorance. Barlow had been inundated by messages, up to a hundred a day, after his posting to the WELL. Most had expressed indignation at the FBI's ignorance, and worries about the treatment of hackers who had been picked up in the dragnet. Barlow also met with

Mitch Kapor, another WELL-being and the coauthor of Lotus 1-2-3, a best-selling computer program. Kapor had been shrewd enough to sell his stake in Lotus at (or very near) the top. Among other things, his earnings enabled him to operate his own business jet, which he used to fly to Wyoming for the meeting.

Both Kapor and Barlow empathized with the raided hackers—though neither would ever condone criminal or malicious activity of any kind. Their concern was about whether the Feds knew what they were doing or were merely being pulled along by uninformed hysteria about hacking.

Together, Barlow and Kapor agreed to set up the Electronic Frontier Foundation. Its purpose was not necessarily to protect hackers, but to extend the protection of freedom of speech, freedom of the press, and freedom of expression to computer-based media: bulletin boards, electronic publishing, computer conferencing, and so on. The foundation dedicated itself to six aims, all related to influencing future legislation so that the civil liberties of computer users, whether they were hackers or not, would not be ignored. It attracted the support of a number of affluent technocrats in the computer industry—including $150,000 from Steve Wozniak, one of the Apple founders. (Woz had remained faithful to the original ideals of Apple. He resigned his position at the company in the early 1980s when it became too "corporate" and busied himself promoting music festivals and teaching, among other things.)

By the time the Foundation was established, the full force of the federal crackdown had already been felt. The New York hackers Acid Phreak, Phiber Optik, and the Scorpion had been raided; Craig Neidorf had been arrested; the Atlanta Three had been indicted; Loyd Blankenship (the Mentor) and Steve Jackson had been busted and their equipment confiscated; and the nationwide raids had rounded up LoD, MoD, and DPAC members, as well as an assortment of independent hackers.

The catalog of charges ranged from wire fraud to handling stolen property, from unauthorized possession of access devices to misappropriating source codes. There were also allegations of credit card fraud, bank fraud, and altering hospital computer records, and references to specific incidents: dropping computer bombs in telephone switches and stealing the E911 documents. It had all of the makings of a nationwide conspiracy.

The first case the Foundation took on was in Chicago. Assistant U.S. Attorney William Cook, who had earlier successfully prosecuted Kyrie—the "Fagin" of the stolen access code gang—and who had become something of an authority on computer crime, was now in charge of the case against *PHRACK* editor Craig Neidorf. Neidorf had been indicted for transporting the stolen E911 document across state lines. He finally came to trial in Chicago on July 23rd.

The prosecution's case was opened by Cook, who outlined the government claim of a conspiracy involving Neidorf and members of the Legion of Doom and asserted that the E911 file was "a highly proprietary and sensitive document" valued at $79,449.

Four days later the case collapsed.

The defense demonstrated that the same E911 information was available from local bookstores and in libraries. Furthermore, by dialing a free 1-800 number, two publications could be obtained from Bellcore for $34 which contained even more detailed information. Neidorf's lawyers also argued that, far from being the serious and imminent threat represented by Bellcore, the file had been published in *PHRACK* nearly a year before the telephone company bothered to do anything about it. Neidorf was cleared of all charges, but though he was helped by the foundation, he was still left with some $100,000 in legal costs.

The E911 file, however, was to come up once again.

On November 16, the Atlanta Three pleaded guilty to a number of charges variously described as computer fraud, wire fraud, access code fraud, and interstate transportation of stolen property—the latter referring to the E911 document.

Because the three agreed to guilty pleas the charges were reduced, but as a result no defense could be mounted. In the sen-

tencing memorandum, the prosecution said that Robert Riggs
(the Prophet) had stolen the E911 file "containing the program
for the emergency 911 dialling system," adding that "any damage
to that very sensitive system could result in a dangerous breakdown in police, fire and ambulance services." The file's value, the
prosecution added, was $24,639.05—the 5 cents presumably in-
cluded to indicate that the figure had been very accurately determined. The memo also stated that the three had gained free
telephone service and access to BellSouth computers.

The Electronic Frontier Foundation was enraged. Although
the plea bargaining precluded a formal defense, the Foundation
said the claims about the E911 file were "clearly false. Defense
witnesses . . . were prepared to testify that the E911 document was
not a [computer] program, that it could not be used to disrupt 911
service, and the same information could be ordered from Bell-
South at a cost of less than $20." The foundation also noted that
the prosecution had begun its memorandum by detailing the
planting of computer bombs. "Only after going to some length
describing these allegations does the prosecution state, in passing,
that *the defendants were not implicated in these crimes* [Founda-
tion italics]."

Despite the protests, Robert Riggs (the Prophet) was sentenced
to twenty-one months and his two colleagues—Adam Grant (the
Urvile) and Frank Dearden (the Leftist)—received fourteen
months each. They also had to make restitutional payments of
$233,000 for the value of the "access devices" found in their
possession. The access devices were the IDs and passwords that
they had collected from BellSouth during their various raids.

There was no question that the Atlanta Three were hackers
who had, without doubt, broken into BellSouth. But the valua-
tion of the "access devices"—computer codes, telephone card
numbers—was highly questionable. As the foundation asked,
how can a value be assessed when no loss can be demonstrated?

But in the new climate engendered by the crackdown, everything associated with hacking was suspect. Every self-proclaimed
hacker acquired a Secret Service dossier, irrespective of his activi-

ties; every hacker with a handle qualified for a bust; every busted hacker was suspected of belonging to the Legion of Doom; and the mere mention of the word *Cyberpunk* seemed enough to bring down the full force of the law.

Under the circumstances, Steve Jackson had drawn a full house. Not only did he employ a known hacker—Loyd Blankenship, who had a handle and was even a member of the LoD—he was also engaged in producing a "hacker handbook" called Cyberpunk.

During the raid on Steve Jackson Games, the Secret Service had confiscated much of the company's computer equipment, without which equipment the company could barely function. It took months, and the assistance of a foundation-supplied lawyer, before the Feds returned the equipment—some of it, according to Steve, damaged, with valuable data missing.

The Secret Service kept the equipment as potential evidence for a "crime" that was never committed. For, while GURPS Cyberpunk does contain information on dumpster diving and social engineering, it is ultimately a game. It is no more a "handbook on hacking" than, say, this book is. (The game was finally published later that year, without causing any noticeable increase in hacking crimes.)

Even though no charges were filed against Steve, his business suffered while the Secret Service held his computer systems. His turnover was down and half of his staff was laid off. He estimates his losses for the period at over $300,000. With the help of the foundation, he has since filed a civil suit against the Secret Service and two of its agents, Assistant U.S. Attorney William Cook, and a Bellcore security manager.

At the time of writing, Loyd Blankenship (the Mentor) has not been charged with anything either, although he still has not received his computer equipment back. Given his background in the LoD, it is not thought likely that he ever will. As a known hacker, he is not pressing the Secret Service too hard; instead, said a friend, he's "lying low."

▪ ▪ ▪

The Electronic Frontier Foundation couldn't help everyone. Phiber Optik was sentenced to a period of thirty-five hours of community service for a relatively minor hacking offense. Even worse, he suffered the shame of being thrown out of the Legion of Doom—though that had nothing to do with his arrest. His crime, in the LoD's eyes, was that he and Acid Phreak (a non-Legionnaire) had demonstrated their hacking skills for a magazine article published in *Esquire* in December 1990. Although both he and Acid Phreak had kept their identities secret—even using phony handles—the other Legionnaires felt that the young hacker was on "an ego trip," a charge confirmed for them when he appeared on a number of television shows. Phiber Optik, the other Legionnaires decided, had too high a profile for the Legion.

Not being in LoD didn't stop him from hacking. He joined the MoD instead—but then he was busted along with four other MoD members: Outlaw, Corrupt, Renegade Hacker, and the Wing. These arrests were devastating to the gang, principally because their equipment was confiscated. (The MoD accused the Legion of turning them in as a last reprisal in the hacker wars, but this seems unlikely.) In July 1992 a federal grand jury indicted Outlaw, Corrupt, Phiber Optik, Acid Phreak, and Scorpion for breaking into telco and credit agency computers, and for stealing data.

Given all the effort, this was a modest payoff—hardly justification for a massive crackdown. Even the Operation Sundevil busts of May 8th, which the foundation called a use of "force and terror which would have been more appropriate to the apprehension of urban guerrillas than barely postpubescent computer nerds," have yielded remarkably few indictments. Gail Thackeray, an attorney in Phoenix dealing with the aftermath of the Sundevil busts, notes that "80 percent of those arrested were adults [over eighteen years old]"—hardly postpubescents. She says that more indictments are still being prepared, and that the delay was caused by the sheer weight of evidence: more than twenty thousand diskettes have been examined, which has taken the authorities over twelve months.

But perhaps indictments were never the point. Sundevil was a search-and-seizure operation; the quarantined computers and diskettes will be held until the material can be analyzed. Only at that point will the indictments, if any, be handed down, and the authorities are in no rush. While the computers are in their possession, the Cyberpunks are out of action.

As for the Phoenix Project, it, too, was probably a false alarm. The vaunted rebirth of hacking, which convinced the Secret Service that there was a nationwide conspiracy, may not have been what it seemed. After all, the Project's organizers had only exhorted hackers to welcome the new age "with the use of every *legal* means available." A sympathetic interpretation of the Phoenix Project would suggest that older hackers were simply counseling others not to break the law. It was a timely warning: the Computer Fraud and Misuse Act had entered the statute books two years previously, and some jail sentences had already been handed out. Hacking was no longer being viewed tolerantly, and the Phoenix Project's organizers expected a crackdown by the authorities. They got that right at least.

However, there was yet another hacker swept up in the Secret Service busts, who, unlike the others, was unquestionably hacking for profit. In mid-June 1989 BellSouth had begun investigating two relatively minor incidents on one of its switches in Florida. In the first incident, on June 16th, an intruder had hacked into the switch and rerouted calls for the city offices of Miramar, Florida, to a long-distance information number. On the next day the same hacker (or so it was assumed) had also rerouted calls intended for the Delray Beach probation office. This time the hacker demonstrated an impish sense of humor: callers to the probation office instead found themselves connected to a Dial-a-Porn service in New York State.

As a result of the two incidents, BellSouth had stepped up the monitoring of its switches. On June 21st, security agents were told that the monitors had detected a hacker loose in one of its computers.

The carrier put a trace on the call, following it back through a series of loops around the country. The hacker had tried to disguise his entry point into the system by first dialing into his local exchange, jumping to a connected switch on another network, then skipping from there to yet another network, and so on. Each time a loop was made through a network, it had to be traced to the entry switch. But the precautions must have given the hacker a false sense of security, because he stayed in the system too long, allowing the trace to be followed all the way through, from network to network, right back to a phone number in Indiana.

BellSouth passed the number they had traced on to Bellcore, which began monitoring all outgoing and incoming calls. The telephone company agents had discovered a hard-core hacker: they watched as their target looped calls around the country, from system to system; they recorded him breaking into a credit agency computer in Delaware belonging to CSA; and they listened as he had money wired to Paducah, Kentucky, on a credit card number.

Their target, of course, was Fry Guy, the fifteen-year-old Indiana hacker who had spent months perfecting his credit card scam.

With evidence that the young hacker was committing fraud, the telco agents turned the details over to the Secret Service, which included him on the Atlanta Three's DNR request. The inclusion was mostly a matter of convenience, but the agents had noted a geographic coincidence that intrigued them: Fry Guy lived in Indiana, as did the recipient of the anonymous telephone call warning of the computer bombs in the switches; Fry Guy also knew his way around BellSouth, where one of the bombs had been planted—indeed, other hackers regarded it as his "sphere of influence."

In mid-July the Secret Service recorded Fry Guy charging $500 to a stolen credit card number. With that piece of evidence (previous telco monitors had not been court-approved and therefore could not be used as evidence), the Secret Service was also able to include Fry Guy in the Atlanta Three search warrant.

The house in Elmwood, Indiana, was raided the same day the three addresses in Atlanta were busted. Fry Guy awoke from his summer-long haze to find that he was suspected of the two Florida incidents, the anonymous telephone call to Indiana Bell's security manager, planting the computer bombs, and credit card fraud.

Hackers are often victims of their own hype. The LoD was the principal target of the crackdown because it promoted itself as the biggest and meanest gang in Cyberspace—and because the authorities believed them.

The computer underworld is a hall of mirrors. Reality becomes bent, the truth shrunken. The authorities who organized Operation Sundevil and its related investigations believed they were dealing with a nationwide conspiracy involving $50 million in telecommunications fraud alone. And that, they said, was only the tip of the iceberg.

What they got in the end, notwithstanding the Atlanta Three's guilty pleas, were some relatively minor convictions. After the barrage of criticism from John Perry Barlow's Electronic Frontier Foundation, the investigators began to pull back. The Phoenix officials, such as Gail Thackeray, are now keen to distance both themselves and Operation Sundevil from the other antihacker actions that year. The wilder suggestions—that the AT&T incident had been caused by Acid Phreak; that hackers were looting banks; that hospital records were being altered, and patients put at risk—have been dropped. The word *conspiracy* is used less and less, and the computer bombs, the specific catalyst for the whole crackdown, have been quietly forgotten. No one has been officially charged with planting the bombs, and it is unlikely that anyone ever will be. Everyone in the underworld's hall of mirrors claims to know who did it, but they all finger different people.

As for Fry Guy, he denies any responsibility for the bombs: "They're just pointless destruction. I can't understand why anyone would do it. I'm not malicious or destructive: I only do things for gain."

That was Fry Guy's downfall: he operated for gain. When he was raided, the Secret Service found more than a hundred "access devices" in his possession—credit card numbers and telephone calling cards. He could never be charged with planting the bombs, and no one was able to pin the Florida incidents on him, but he was caught red-handed on the credit card fraud. Following his arrest, it was estimated that his little scam had netted him $6,000 that year. He is now on probation, his equipment confiscated, but if you ask him why he hacked, he still sighs: "It's the greatest thing in the world."

New technology requires new approaches. The reactions of the authorities to the computer underworld show a dependence on old ideas. Hacking becomes "breaking and entering"; role-playing games become "conspiracies"; exploration becomes "espionage." The dated terms obliterate the difference between the "bad" hackers and the "good" hackers.

And there is a difference. Society might tolerate some activities of the computer underground. Hackers are mostly explorers exercising intellectual curiosity. Undoubtedly, they will break into computers, sometimes causing ancillary damage or taking up system time, and they probably will exploit the telecom systems to do so. But their intent, for the most part, is not malicious.

On the other hand, the black arts of virus writing or hacking to steal money are unjustifiable. Virus writers are electronic vandals; hackers who rob are high-tech thieves.

The difference between the good and the bad is often blurred. The distinction is one of motive: the malicious and the criminal should be viewed differently from the merely clever or curious.

Someday it may be possible to get a clearer picture of what the activities of the computer underground actually cost industry and telecom companies. Present estimates vary so widely as to be worthless. Figures seem to be plucked from the air: it is utterly impossible to verify whether the true cost in the United States is around $550 million each year (the *Computerworld* estimate), or whether total losses could actually amount to as much as $5 billion (as was estimated at a security conference in 1991). These exaggerations are compounded by the hackers themselves—who are only too willing to embellish their accomplishments. With both sides expounding fanciful stories and ever wilder claims, truth is lost in the telling.

What is ironic is that the activities of the hackers are leading to a situation they would decry. Security managers have a clear responsibility to protect their sites from electronic intrusion. As hackers become bolder, security is becoming tightened, threatening the very "freedom of information" that hacking, in its benign form, is said to promote.

Hackers are an engaging bunch, even the "bad" ones: bright, curious, technically gifted, passionate, prone to harmless boasting, and more than a little obsessed. They are usually creative, probing, and impatient with rules and restrictions. In character, they closely resemble the first-generation hackers.

Computing has always gained from the activities of those who look beyond what is there, to think of what there might be. The final irony for the computer industry is that the hackers who are being shut out today will be the programmers, managers, and even security experts of tomorrow.

9

■

THE FUTURE OF
CYBERSPACE

The main effect of the Secret Service crackdown on the computer underworld was to create a new climate of fear that anyone could get busted and be thrown in jail. The crackdown was called a witch-hunt, the innocence of its victims taken for granted—though with few exceptions, most of those raided were at least guilty of some hacking. The difference between the authorities' and the computer underworld's perceptions of the busts is ideological: it pits the government's right to control information against the hacker's belief in free access to all knowledge.

In the new atmosphere, hackers moved farther underground. Some left the United States altogether to get beyond the jurisdiction of the Secret Service.

In 1989 one such hacker, Bill Squire, packed his bags and left San Francisco for the friendlier climes of Amsterdam. It was becoming too restrictive in the States, he said; hacking and phreaking were becoming dangerous. "In Holland," Bill says, "hacking is still legal." Or rather, it's not expressly illegal.

Sometimes Bill regrets having had to move. He was one of the old-timers in the computer underground, and was twelve years old when he started phreaking. His mentor was the same man who showed Captain Crunch the way into a telephone's heart with a Hammond organ in 1969. He rubbed shoulders with the two Steves in the early days of Apple and, like many others, would marvel at the fortunes to be won in Silicon Valley. He witnessed how phreaking helped create personal computers, and how PCs begat hacking, which had all stretched the frontiers of computing. "But who's going to teach the young American hackers of tomorrow?" he asks. The U.S. computer industry, he says, will be poorer for not having young hackers; the country will lose its lead in software design, as it did in computer hardware manufacturing.

When the computer underworld was new, back in the 1960s, phreakers such as Bill who could work the systems were pretty much immune to busts by telco security agents or the Feds; the systems were much less secure and the methods of detecting intrusion were also much less sophisticated. At that time John Draper, as Captain Crunch, had thoroughly explored telephone switches before anyone else even knew what they were. He could line up tandems across the country and bounce his voice around the world and back again. He is the real father of the computer underworld, and even the new kids, the Cyberpunks, have heard of him. They may not realize he's still alive, but they know the legend.

Bill Squire keeps in touch with Captain Crunch and other friends in California courtesy of the PTT, the Dutch telephone company. A call to Draper in Alameda, California, involves him phreaking his way into Brazil, then up to Mexico, then by satellite into the United States. If he wants to call Great Britain, he goes in through Greece. He can set up three-way calls with California and the U.K. from his apartment in Bijlmeer, in southeast Amsterdam.

Bill complains that American hackers are now so paranoid that they don't call him. Instead he is forced to call them. Even Draper doesn't phreak anymore; he's so paranoid that he won't even joke about it. "Hey, John, I'm whistling this call!" makes him shout: "I don't wanna know!"

Draper is convinced that his line is being monitored. In fact, he believes that federal agents regularly listen in on telephone calls, looking for key words and taping suspicious conversations. He doesn't mean some calls, or those routed to a place like Libya or Iraq, but *all* calls, all half billion or so a day. "Otherwise why does the NSA need half the nation's Cray computers?" he asks darkly. (The Crays are the fastest and most powerful supercomputers in the world.)

He listens to the background noises during telephone conversations. "What's that?" he asks abruptly, in mid-conversation. "Did you hear a hum?"

"It's okay, John. I'm sitting beside my computer."

"It's not a computer hum. It's a monitoring hum."

Now aged forty-eight, Captain Crunch is still concerned that he is being watched. Afraid to phreak and out of work, the spiritual leader of the computer underworld is staring at a financial abyss: he has cut down on watching television and traded down the wattage in his light bulbs just to save electricity.

But he is mostly worried about finding the money to pay his phone bill; he is afraid that it might be disconnected. It would be unthinkable for Captain Crunch to be without a phone.

When one door shuts, another opens.

The computer underworld is still a growing force, despite the raids, despite the crackdown and the Secret Service. The heirs to Captain Crunch are continuing the tradition.

If one hacker board gets raided, another springs up. If one gang gets busted, another forms.

There is no organized structure in the computer underworld, no mysterious chairman of the board to keep it running. The underground is anarchic, a confederation of phreakers, hackers, and virus writers from all over the world whose common interests transcend culture or language. Most hackers have two or three handles and operate on a number of boards. They have learned to change IDs, aliases, sites, their methods, targets, and gang membership faster than the authorities can track them. Stamping out hacking is like trying to pin down mercury.

Captain Crunch once described hackers as the Silicon Brotherhood. Membership in the Brotherhood is fluid, informal, and subjective—you're a member when you know you are. At a guess there are now about two thousand members of the Brotherhood in the world—two thousand of the best, the really dedicated, experienced, computer freaks—and probably another ten thousand wannabes. Most of the Brotherhood keep in touch across Cyberspace. But the trend now is to work alone—it's safer that way—though some gangs still exist.

After the Operation Sundevil busts in 1990, the Legion of Doom rapidly re-formed for its fourth incarnation. But the LoD may have finally been overtaken by new American gangs, such as Rabid, NEUA (the National Elite Underground Association), or the Legion of Lucifers, which combine hacking with virus writing. They don't necessarily hack into sites and drop viruses, but fight their own hacker wars with computer bugs. The rival gangs now lob the viruses at each other's systems, trying to wipe out valuable data: one gang receives one from a rival group, and sends one back, and then the conflict escalates. The Global Village has degenerated into a Cyberpunk battleground.

Rabid is particularly keen on viruses. Zodiac, one of the gang's more prolific virus writers, is the creator of DataRape!—the name combining just the right notes of topicality and menace to suggest that Zodiac is a boy to watch. Since Rabid is locked in a particularly nasty battle with the Legion of Lucifers, to whom they refer as the Legion of Lamers, the Datarape! virus is targeted specifically at LoL files (those including an LoL "copyright" notice). As Zodiac explained to the Rabid crew,

> A feature that I know we were all looking forward to was finally implemented. Whenever any Legion of Lamer files are located, the FAT table destruction command is automatically issued. This is due to the spite Rabid holds towards one Michael T— who runs a bulletin board in the 213 area code called HMS Queen Mary's Revenge. He is believed to be fifteen years old and attends Le

Lycée, a private school in the Beverly Hills area. This information will be verified and released with the Militia Virus and the T—— Virus . . . , now under development. A word now to Rabid members. Keep up the good work, and make sure this spreads. We could totally ruin the image of a certain egotistical pirate group, featuring our good friend Ken S——.

Zodiac also explained his reasons for producing the virus:

I'm not a particularly malicious person, and I do not have a "vendetta" towards the computer community. I just enjoy programming viruses, as many others do. That, to me, is what Rabid is all about—a society of those who like to program viruses. To the antivirus people, I must say a few words. You should be paying us money and not trying to "bust" us. We're keeping you in your dirty business. Any of your efforts can be gotten around, because you, like the pigs, are too stupid to realize our higher intelligence/motives. So leave us alone; you'll get more money and we'll be happier.

Zodiac represents the future of the computer underworld, a future that will see the continued growth of information technology and the consequent expansion of opportunities for those who would subvert it. It is increasingly apparent that computers work best as stand-alone machines; when linked together difficulties multiply and their vulnerability increases. It is a problem of ever-increasing complexity compounded by expanded scale: a machine that works well at one level can become unreliable when just one seemingly innocent feature is added.

In that, computers mirror society. There is a feature of government known, colloquially, as the Law Of Unintended Consequence, that suggests that every change or reform or regulation, however benign, has an unintended and unforeseen consequence, sometimes beneficial, but often the opposite of what the framers of the change had in mind. Computing has become like that: the networks are now so vast and so complex that any change, however minor, has an unintended consequence.

The whole of the computer underground grew out of the innocent decision by Bell thirty years ago to computerize its system. One of the other unforeseen consequences of that decision, more or less, was the rapid creation of the PC. And that, ultimately, gave us the information age.

In a curious, unplanned way, society evolves. The information age is evolving now, and with it the computer underground. It's been said that modern technology is dehumanizing society; in that sense the underground is a reaction to that dehumanization.

There is a "clock" called the Doomsday Clock, that is featured in a magazine founded by Einstein called *The Bulletin of the Atomic Scientist.* It tells the time left to twelve midnight—the nuclear holocaust. Throughout the 1950s it hovered menacingly at two minutes before the apocalypse; in the 1970s it hovered between nine and twelve minutes to midnight. Then, in 1991, after the end of the Cold War, it was set back again: now we have a seventeen-minute margin.

The clock and the time are symbolic. We're not really just a few minutes from nuclear disaster. Not in real time. But because the technology and means to create a nuclear holocaust exist, we could be said to be advancing ever closer to midnight.

We're approaching zero in the same way. Zero is when a computer system is devoid of data, of memory, of function. "Zeroing out" a computer can be done by hacking into it and wiping the data, or by dropping in a virus that will trash the hard disk. We're approaching zero now the same way we're counting down to midnight—because the technology and means to wipe out computer systems exist.

In the next few years the number of viruses will become uncountable. There will be thousands of new strains, each capable of infecting an infinite number of carriers—diskettes, hard disks, and so on. At present there are said to be five million infected diskettes in the world. In the next few years the number could become astronomical.

New viruses are being spawned every day, in the most unlikely corners of the world. In Bangkok, for example, one programmer set up his computer to produce six hundred viruses an hour, each guaranteed undetectable by any of the scanning programs currently available. That single machine now produces viruses faster than they can be analyzed and catalogued—even if all the world's virus researchers dedicated themselves to disassembling them. To date, the Thai bugs aren't included in any virus count because they've yet to reach the West. But they may start seeping through to Europe and North America within the next year.

Viruses from Thailand have a ready-made means of traveling. In Bangkok, visitors from the industrialized countries often shop for computer programs at one of the two dozen or so specialist software shops in Panthip Plaza or the Marboonkroong Center. The latest Western programs are available for 500 baht (less than $20), often less than 10 percent of the price in the developed countries. The software comes complete with manuals, often photocopies or cheap reprints. There's no attempt to pass these off as the originals: the sellers aren't pirates, simply businessmen working on 5 percent margins.

Why pay more?

But buyers often carry home an unwanted extra. Some 80 percent of the programs also contain a virus. Exactly which virus is hard to say: there are so many in Thailand that everyone has lost track, including the virus writers.

There is also an increasing number of virus-exchange bulletin boards, with probably twenty or thirty in operation at the beginning of 1992. (Bangkok has one, called the Virus Museum.) These serve to carry viruses around the world and make them available to almost anyone. All the boards work the same way: the latest viruses, often sixty or more, guaranteed undetectable by any known scanner, are kept in a restricted area. And source codes for many viruses, which allow programmers to create customized variants by changing the activation date or altering the payload, are also available.

An Italian virus writer called Cracker Jack operates his own virus lab, modifying Bulgarian bugs, often producing two or three new knockoffs each week. He gives them names: Antichrist, Bad Taste, Damage, Delyrium, Demon, Diabolik, Enigma, Erasmus, Greemlin, HIV, Lucifer, Pest—all listed in alphabetical order. There are now twenty-five to thirty of them, showcased on a virus exchange board in Merano, in northern Italy. The system operator, Mauro, will provide details of the bugs: "Pest has coding for file deletion, Delyrium makes low-level formats, Enigma formats track number 20, Greemlin overwrites track 0, Lucifer's only effect is to display a message, but the program doesn't run correctly and sometimes corrupts files, Damage formats track 0: it is a stealth virus." Honest Mauro, the used-virus salesman.

In Germany virus writing has been completely automated. A group called the Verband Deutscher Virenliebhaber (Community of German Virus Lovers) has produced a virus construction set, designed for those "who want to give a virus to their worst enemy but have none at hand." The set allows novices to create their own unique viruses with personalized messages, and in the best hacker tradition, the Hamburg group supplies the construction set free, but users who like it are asked to donate about $15 to the Red Cross.

The virus the Dark Avenger had promised in his message on Fidonet duly appeared in May 1991. He called it the Mutating Engine, and it may well be able to disguise itself in four billion different ways.

A virus like this one, which can continually change its appearance, is potentially the most difficult to detect. It contains no constant characteristic, such as a text string, that could be used by virus scanners to register its presence. All that can be detected of the Mutating Engine is a mass of encrypted code—a code that changes every time it infects a file. It may be the most dangerous virus ever produced. Worse, it isn't only a virus: it was distributed as a routine which other writers could build into their own bugs, giving them the same ability to evade detection. A number of these have now been discovered, all of them mutating Engine clones, with names like Coffee Shop, Cryptlab, Fear, Groove, Little, Pogue . . .

But The Dark Avenger now has competition from the East. Russians are developing whole new families of clever and malicious bugs, so many that they may soon replace Bulgaria as the leading virus-producing country.

As the sources of viruses multiply—from pirate boards, construction sets, or manic Thai, Russian, and Bulgarian computer freaks—incidents of infection will become much more common. In the future anyone will be able to plant a virus on his "worst enemy": disgruntled employees, industrial saboteurs, blackmailers, or vandals. We may no longer be able to trust technology. A computer program could, without warning, become an uncontrollable force, triggered by a date, an event, or a timer.

One of the more malicious Russian viruses is called LoveChild. When it infects a computer, the virus initiates a countdown that begins at five thousand. As long as the virus remains undetected, the counter ticks down with each successive use of the computer. Nothing happens until the counter reaches zero.

Then it wipes out the hard disk.

No one knows how many LoveChild viruses are in existence. Or how many counters are now silently approaching zero.

NOTES

1 PHREAKING FOR FUN

1. There is no firm lexicon for boxes. What one phreaker might call a red box could be called a black box by another. There were, however, three principal designations in the early days: red, black, and blue. Present-day phreakers use devices that have been nicknamed beige boxes.

2. Because of the publicity generated by his arrest—and later, because of Rosenbaum's article—Engressia became widely known as a telecommunications wizard. Shortly after his conviction he was offered a job at a local phone company; he later went to work as a troubleshooter for Mountain Bell, where—at the time of this writing—he remains.

3. "Mark Bernay" eventually outgrew his fascination with phreaking and hacking. Today he is described as a "respectable and respected citizen of Oakland, California." He is still employed in the computer industry.

4. Within the computer industry the term *PC* is generally used to designate only the IBM PC. In this book, however, the term is used to denote any personal computer, regardless of the manufacturer.

2 BREAKING AND ENTERING

1. The GPO, which ran the phone system in the 1970s when the Captain was traveling in Great Britain, was a publicly owned service. Its successor was the privatized British Telecom.

2. It is unlikely that Prince Philip actually used his Prestel MBX, which was presented to him by British Telecom as part of a publicity campaign when the system was launched.

3. The supposed information about surveillance of the CND, the Labor party, and the Cabinet was certainly fantasy. Nick also denies even attempting to hack the MoD or MI5 computers.

4. The Witness Protection Program is a scheme, funded by the federal government, to provide protection for key witnesses in important criminal prosecutions, generally involving organized crime or drug smuggling. The witnesses and their families are provided with new identities and new lives in return for their testimony.

3 DATA CRIME

1. AT&T has estimated the losses due to blue boxes in the years prior to the mid-1970s as between twenty and thirty million dollars annually. Though the use of MF-ers has certainly declined, some canny phreakers are still said to be making use of blue boxes as well as their more complex successors, called beige boxes.

2. Copy protection was introduced by software manufacturers to prevent the unauthorized copying of their programs. It is often implemented by inserting special code into the programs which then prevents their transfer on diskette from computer to computer.

3. According to computer security consultants this is astoundingly easy to do. Until recently, credit agencies are said to have been notoriously lax about computer security.

4. The worm could work at night because the Palo Alto Research Center, like most labs, has always kept its computers on twenty-four hours a day, seven days a week.

5. The German title translates directly as "The Big Computer Virus Book." However, the English edition is entitled *Computer Viruses—A High-Tech Disease.*

6. Burger's book is now in its fourth German edition, having sold 24,000 copies; editions in English, French, and Italian have sold a further 20,000 copies. Unauthorized pirate editions are said to have been published in Saudi Arabia and Russia.

4 VIRUSES, TROJANS, WORMS, AND BOMBS

1. UNIX was originally designed by AT&T. It became popular at universities because it could be converted to run on a variety of different computers. There are now hundreds of versions of UNIX; the rogue program attacked some versions of what is known as 4 BSD UNIX, a variant developed at Berkeley.

2. Computer-speak for more than one VAX computer.

3. Subsequent to the incident, one university tried the virus's list of passwords against passwords that were in use on its own systems and achieved a 14 percent match.

4. To the layman and most of the press, all malicious programs are viruses. To computer specialists, however, malicious programs have different properties and are divided into categories: viruses, worms, trojans, and logic bombs. Though it was often called a virus, the ARPANET rogue program was actually a worm.

5. Despite initial comments on the "high quality" of Morris's code, other experts have been less impressed. Some have pointed to the supposed uneven quality of the program as evidence that part of it was borrowed from somewhere or someone else. The semiofficial Cornell Report on the incident, presumably the final word, suggested that the program could have been written by any reasonably competent computer science student.

6. *Wank* is English (as opposed to American) slang for masturbate. But the word has somehow crossed the Atlantic and is commonly used by U.S. hackers.

7. Inevitably, computer bombs have been subclassified as either "time bombs," which explode on a given date, or "logic bombs," which go off at a specific event.

5 THE BULGARIAN THREAT

1. Tippett limited his projection to two years, from 1990 to 1992. Had he extended it to five years, it would have shown that all the world's

computers would have become infected, suggesting that his mathematical model was somewhat flawed.

2. The supposed Chinese virus is called Bloody! and contains the message: "Bloody! Jun. 4, 1989"—the date of the Tiananmen Square massacre of students by the Chinese army in Beijing.

3. The authors have agreed not to reveal the identity of the publishing company; the financial-services company in the next section is also not identified. Few companies are willing to admit publicly to having been the victim of a computer virus.

4. Teodor abandoned Version 1, keeping neither a copy nor a record of its program code. Though he eventually produced fifty-one versions, only sixteen are known to have survived.

5. Viruses like "Find Me!" are known as companion viruses, in that they create a "companion" COM file to the EXE file.

6. Though the writers called their virus Creeping Death, it is known to researchers as DIR-2. It is quite common for viruses to have multiple names: researchers have been unable to agree on a naming convention, so even a virus as common as Jerusalem has alternatives, including Friday the 13th and Israeli.

7. The Murphy viruses were named by their authors, and each contained a text message. HELLO, I'M MURPHY. NICE TO MEET YOU, FRIEND. I WAS WRITTEN IN NOV/DEC. COPYRIGHT © 1989 BY LUBO & PAT, SOFIA, USM LABORATORY, was the message contained within Murphy 1. Murphy 2 carried the following text: IT'S ME, MURPHY. COPYRIGHT © 1990 BY LUBO & PAT, USM LABORATORY.

8. English, or a sort of English, is the lingua franca of the computer industry. These messages are reproduced as they were written.

6 HACKING FOR PROFIT

1. Some of the counters on the Install programs had glitches in them and attacked the hard disk after only nine start-ups.

2. The Computer Crime Unit also tried sending a check for $189, the minimum license fee, to the post office box in Panama City, but six weeks later their letter came back marked "Return to Sender."

3. Two other virus writers have been identified by the Computer Crime Unit but have not been prosecuted. In one case there was an apparent lack of criminal intent; in the other the author was "extremely young" and said to be "remorseful."

4. All were juveniles at the time, and can only be identified by their handles.

5. "Degaussing" means changing the magnetic polarity on disks or tapes to erase data. In general "degaussing" units are very powerful electromagnets that will wipe magnetic tapes—such as audio and video cassettes, as well as computer diskettes—in a matter of seconds. Hackers use the devices to destroy evidence during a raid.

6. Convictions were also obtained in the cases of other major members of her ring. All were juveniles at the time, and details of their convictions cannot be published.

7. The curse of the unverifiable hangs over computerized bank fraud even more heavily than it does over credit card fraud. According to bankers, there has never been a successful hacker raid on their funds; according to anecdotal evidence from hackers, banks are regularly being looted. The truth is probably that it has happened and will continue to happen, but is probably not as prevalent as hackers would like to think.

8. X.25 is an international standard for the transfer of data.

7 THE ILLUMINATI CONSPIRACY

1. Similar data and information systems were set up in the 1980s in the U.K. (Prestel), the Netherlands (Viditel), and France (Minitel). These systems all had the common aim of bringing computers into people's homes to provide them with on-line information and shopping services.

2. The students' real names are known to the authors, but they have requested anonymity.

3. Most computer programs contain errors or bugs of one sort or another. It is estimated that programmers are likely to inadvertently introduce about fifty errors in every thousand lines of code.

4. The "orange book" is the popular name for TCSEC, Trusted System Criteria, which specify security controls for information stored on computer.

5. Later, it would be established that although early versions of the VMS operating system had been fully tested, later ones hadn't. It was these newer versions that contained the back door. (Users update their computers with the latest versions of the operating systems almost as a matter of course, so nearly all VAXen became insecure for a time.)

6. Steffen Weihruch died in December 1991.

7. The Verfassungsschutz is one of three German secret service organizations and looks after constitutional matters. Foreign affairs are handled by the Bundesnachrichtendienst (BND), and military matters by the Militarische Abschirmdienst (known, delightfully, as MAD).

8. Steffen's friend did arrive in Paris, but after waiting several hours without any word from Wernery, he wisely caught the next train back to Hamburg. It is believed that details of the pair's trip to Paris were passed to the French authorities by Philips-France.

8 CRACKDOWN

1. The message transcripts have been edited for clarity.

2. Typically, users of Black ICE would call a number in the 607 area code, which had been rerouted to the bulletin board. The rerouting was accomplished by the time-honored method of hacking into a switch and reprogramming it.

3. The original LoD board was shut down when Lex Luthor retired from hacking to return to college. LoD members then began using reserved areas on a number of other pirate boards, including Black ICE.

4. "Looping" refers to the technique used by hackers to route their calls from one telephone exchange to another to evade detection. It is not

to be confused with an "endless loop," a method for disrupting a telephone switch.

5. GURPS was Steve Jackson Games's acronym for Generic Universal Role-Playing System.

6. Operation Sundevil is often used to describe the entire national hacker crackdown, though strictly speaking it was confined to the Secret Service operation in Phoenix, Arizona.

7. Erik Bloodaxe, one of the LoD founders, was never charged with anything. In June 1991 he and fellow Legionnaires Doc Holliday and the Malefactor formed a computer security company. The Malefactor has since left the company, but Erik and Doc plan to expand and bring other Legionnaires on board when they finish their full-time education.

8. For those who share Agent Baxter's confusion, a ROM chip is a Read Only Memory microchip—allowing users to read from memory, but not write to it. Random Access Memory (RAM) chips allow users to both read and write.

SELECT BIBLIOGRAPHY

BOOKS

Bowcott, Owen, and Sally Hamilton. *Beating the System.* London: Bloomsbury, 1990.

Burger, Ralf. *Computer Viruses—A High-Tech Disease.* Grand Rapids, MI: Abacus, 1988.

Cornwall, Hugo. *The Hackers' Handbook.* London: Century Communications, 1985.

Denning, Peter J., ed. *Computers Under Attack.* Addison Wesley, 1990.

Franklin, Patricia. *Profits of Deceit.* London: William Heinemann, 1990.

Hafner, Katie, and John Markoff. *Cyberpunk.* London: Fourth Estate, 1991.

Landreth, Bill. *Out of the Inner Circle.* Redmond, WA.: Tempus Books, 1985.

Larsen, Judith K., and Everett M. Rogers. *Silicon Valley Fever.* London: George Allen & Unwin, 1985.

Roberts, Ralph. *Computer Viruses.* Greensboro, NC: Compute! Books, 1988.

Stoll, Clifford. *The Cuckoo's Egg.* New York: Doubleday, 1989.

ARTICLES, PAPERS, BULLETINS

Barlow, John Perry. "Crime and Puzzlement." Posting to the WELL, June 1990.

Bates, Jim. "The Casino Virus—Gambling with Your Hard Disk" *Virus Bulletin*, March 1991: 15–17.

Bontchev, Vesselin. "The TP Viruses." Postings to Virus-L, 1990.

Bromberg, Craig. "In Defense of Hackers." *The New York Times Magazine*, April 21, 1991.

Clough, Bryan. "Bulgaria—The Dark Country." *Virus Bulletin*, December 1990: 9–11.

Cook, William J. "Voice Mail Computer Abuse Prosecution: United States *v.* Doucette a/k/a Kyrie." collected in the *Safe Computing Proceedings* of the Fourth Annual Computer Virus & Security Conference, 1991, Organized by National Computing Corporation.

Elmer-De Witt, Philip. "Invasion of the Data Snatchers!" *Time*, September 26, 1988: 63.

Gliss, Hans. "Data Exchange and How to Cope with This Problem: The Implications of the German KGB Computer Espionage Affair." Paper Presented at Securicom Italia, October 1989.

————. "The Implications of the SPANet Hack." *Computer Fraud & Security Bulletin*, Vol. 10, No. 2, 1987.

Highland, Harold J. "The Brain Virus: Fact and Fantasy" *Computers & Security*, August 1988: 367–370.

————. "Computer Viruses—A Post Mortem." *Computers & Security*, April 1988: 117–184.

Hitt, Jack, and Paul Tough. "Terminal Delinquents." *Esquire*, December 1990.

Meyer, Gordon R. "The Social Organization of the Computer Underground," M.A. Thesis Submitted to the Graduate School, August 1989.

Mungo, Paul. "Satanic Viruses." *GQ*, February 1991: 126–130.

Rosenbaum, Ron. "Secrets of the Little Blue Box." *Esquire*, October 1971, Collected in *Travels with Dr. Death*. New York: Viking Penguin, 1991.

Shoch, John F., and Jon A. Hupp. "The Worm Program—Early Experience with a Distributed Computation." *Communications of the ACM*, Vol. 25, No. 3, March 1982.

Skulason, Fridrik. "The Search for Den Zuk." *Virus Bulletin*, February 1991: 6–7.

Spafford, Eugene H., "Crisis and Aftermath." *Communications of the ACM*, Vol. 32, No. 6, June 1989.

Sterling, Bruce. "GURPS Labor Lost: The Cyberpunk Bust" *Effector,*
September 1991: 1.

Stoll, Clifford. "Stalking the Wily Hacker" *Communications of the ACM.*
Vol. 31, No. 5, May 1988.

Tippett, Peter S. "The Kinetics of Computer Virus Replication." *Foundation Ware,* March 1990.

van Neumann, John L. "The General and Logical Theory of Automata."
Hixon Symposium, September 1948.

ABOUT THE AUTHORS

BRYAN CLOUGH is a member of the National Computer Virus Strategy Group, which is coordinated by New Scotland Yard's Computer Crime Unit, and an accountant who specializes in international computer security. He lives in Sussex, England, with his wife and two daughters.

PAUL MUNGO is a contributing editor to British *GQ*, and a feature writer for various British newspapers, including the *London Evening Standard* and *Sunday Express*. He previously covered the European entertainment industry for the trade journals *The Hollywood Reporter* and *Variety*.

ABOUT THE TYPE

This book was set in Times Roman, designed by Stanley Morrison specifically for *The Times* of London. The typeface was introduced in the newspaper in 1932. Times Roman has had its greatest success in the United States as a book and commercial typeface, rather than one used in newspapers.